GOD'S REDEMPTIVE PLAN

For Young Adults and High School Students

GOD'S REDEMPTIVE PLAN

For Young Adults and High School Students

Tyrone E. Wilson

Copyright © 2015 by Tyrone E. Wilson

Second Printing 2017

10 9 8 7 6 5 4 3 2

ISBN: 978-0-9963830-3-5   Trade Paperback
       978-0-9963830-2-8   Hardcover

Library of Congress Control Number: 2015908632

All rights reserved. No part of this publication may be reproduced, stored in, or introduced into a retrieval system, or transmitted in any form, or by any means (electronic, mechanical, photocopying, recording, or otherwise) without the prior written permission of both the copyright owner and the publisher of this book.

GRP Publishing, LLC
www.GodsRedemptivePlan.com

Dedicated to my family...

- My wife, Sharon, who has been loving and supportive beyond belief.
- My daughters, who are the apples of my eye ... Trina, Devon & Jennifer.
- A special thanks to my sister, Carolyn, who has been a pillar of strength. To my brothers Robert, John, Darryl and Carson. I love you much.
- My Sons-in-Law, Mo and Dennis, who are great husbands to great women.
- My grandkids ... Derrick, Diante, Aniya, Malaya, Ryan, Chase, Ari, Matthew and Jonah. I wish I could spoil you more.
- My Sunday School Class at Largo Community Church, who made me study and prepare. Mrs. Maharaj, who encouraged me along the way.
- My father in the Lord, Rev. Lawrence Walker who loved me no matter how hard I made it for him ... and then chastised me.
- High school teachers, Drs. Barry and Ruth Slepian, who surprised me at my home in North Philadelphia ... then made me pick a college.
- Dr. H. Jack Morris, who preached a sermon on forgiveness which helped plant me back on the straight and narrow.
- My Uncle James, who was the strength of our family in my formative years.

And written in Memory of…

- My mother, who taught us to believe and trust in the Lord. I miss you, but you are never gone from me.
- My best friend in life, Matthew C. Worrell, who passed away in February 2009. I miss you too. My grandson is named in his memory.

Contents

Introduction	1
It's OK to Peek—It's Not Really Cheating	4
Spiritual Warfare	7
What is the Bible to You?	11
It's All About God	17
In the Beginning, Really?	21
The Angelic Conflict	25
The Creation and Fall of Man	33
Let the Battle Begin	47
Water, Water Everywhere	50
Down the Hatch	56
Can't We Do Anything Right?	57
The Chosen Ones	61
A Nation is Born	67
The Kings of Israel	82
The Divided Kingdom	88
Setting the Stage for Plan B	99
Lay-off of Israel	107
The Times of the Gentiles	109
The Seventy Weeks of Daniel	122
The Messiah	133
The Seed is Planted	134
Parting Gifts	144
By Now it Should be Obvious	149
The Rapture of the Church	153
We Have Lift-off!	154

The Antichrist	**163**
Laying Low—For Now	165
A Wolf in Sheep's Clothing	169
On the Prowl	172
The Tribulation Period	**181**
Jesus Said It, I Believe It	192
The Great Tribulation	199
Time to Pay the Bills	201
God is Still in the Saving Business—Part 1	210
It's Crunch Time	213
God is Still in the Saving Business—Part 2 (aka The Two Witnesses)	221
The Antichrist	225
The False Prophet	226
Head for the High Ground	231
Recap	239
The Judgment Seat of Christ	**243**
The Marriage of the Lamb	**253**
The Bigger They Are…	**257**
Flip a Coin	258
Gotta Go!	265
The Second Coming of Christ	**269**
The Opening Act	270
The Second Act	272
The Final Curtain	277
The First Resurrection	283
The Separation of the Sheep and the Goats	285
The Millennial Reign of Jesus Christ	**291**
The New Beginning	293
Unfinished Business	**299**
Satan's Last Stand	299
The Great White Throne Judgment	302
It's Not Too Late	309
Out with the Old, In with the New	**311**
The Grand Finale	315
Let There Be Light	**321**
References	**327**

Introduction

"Train up a child in the way he should go: and when he is old, he will not depart from it."

Proverbs 22:6

I wrote this book for Christian young adults and high school students, but I pray that it will appeal to non-Christians as well. My aim is to provide you with a biblical foundation and knowledge concerning God and His redemptive plan for mankind. On the simplest level, it is enough to know that Jesus saves, as long as He is Lord of your life. But why stop there? As a Sunday school teacher, I promise you there are many more fascinating things to learn. I think you'd be amazed at how your life would change, for the better, if you took the time to learn God's plan, and understand how to piece together all the stories that formulate God's plan. Hopefully, with a little humor added here and there, this book will help you better understand God's plan a bit more easily.

Proverbs 22:6 points out the obvious. Parents are to instruct their children in the ways of God so that this understanding becomes a part of their everyday life as they grow up and into adulthood. This is an instruction of old (Deuteronomy 11:18-19). When children are taught the ways of the Lord, those ways become foundational to their way of thinking and behaving. It will become as basic as the language they are taught to speak.

"...the Lamb slain from the foundation of the world"

Revelation 13:8

This excerpted verse from Revelation 13:8 tells us God has a plan for mankind ... a plan that was formed in the mind of God before the earth came to be. That's what "from the foundation of the world" means. Before earth's foundation was set, God had a plan. That plan included the sacrifice of His Son, Jesus Christ, as the Lamb of God who takes away the sin of the world (John 1:29). That alone should tell you how big a deal sin is to God. He had to send His Son to take care of it. Sin separates man from God. God desires fellowship with man, but sin has to be dealt with first! A lamb was used frequently in the Old Testament as a sacrifice offered to Almighty God to atone for sin. So Revelation 13:8 means that God planned to sacrifice His Son as part of His specific plan of redemption for mankind ... and that includes you. And His plans for you fit within the broader plan He has for the whole human race!

God wants to have the kind of fellowship with man that He had in the Garden of Eden, prior to man's fall from grace and into sin. In fact, as you read on, you'll see that God is consistent in His ardent desire for fellowship throughout the ages, even as we approach the end times. God created Adam, placed him in the Garden to tend to it, brought the animals and birds to him to see what he would name them, and walked with him in the Garden. It was an intimate relationship.

Genesis 1:28 reads:

> *"...God said unto them, Be fruitful, and multiply, and replenish the earth, and subdue it: and have dominion over the fish of the sea, and over the fowl of the air, and over every living thing that moveth upon the earth."*

This verse lets us know that God's will was for **man to rule on this earth**. Man was given dominion. When man disobeyed God and listened to Satan, however, he fell into sin. As a consequence, man's dominion ended because his fellowship with God was broken. But God did not just sit back and let this setback go unanswered. He wanted the fellowship to continue. So what did He do? In an act that demonstrated unqualified love, God implemented His plan to redeem mankind from his fall in the Garden, just to restore the fellowship. How does God do this? The Holy

Introduction

Bible tells the whole story. To understand the fullness of this plan takes a bit of study, but the Bible and this book will aid you in putting all the pieces together. I think you'll find that you're aware of many of these pieces already, and during your reading (or after your reading) you'll understand a bit more clearly and coherently. In fact, I suspect many people will be familiar with the contents of this book up until we begin covering the Angelic Conflict, but I encourage you to read through what is presented beforehand just the same.

We will cover and uncover God's plan of redemption as we travel through the Bible from point A (Genesis 1) to point Z (Revelation 22). We will not cover a lot of other very valuable material in the Bible because that's not the focus of this book. Even so, I don't want anyone to think the information in the Bible we do not cover is not important. That is very far from the truth!

We will discuss many topics relevant to understanding God's plan of redemption, including:

- God
- The Angelic Conflict
- The Fall of Satan
- The Creation and Fall of Man
- God's Prophecies and Promises of Redemption
- The Nation of Israel and Her Role in the Realization of God's Plan
- The Times of the Gentiles
- Prophecies of the Latter (Last) Days
- The Church
- The Rapture of the Church
- The Tribulation Period
- The Second Coming of Christ
- The Millennium Kingdom
- The Great White Throne Judgment
- Ushering in of Eternity

To be spiritually and intellectually honest, I must tell you there are some Christians, just as spiritually and intellectually honest, who interpret some of what follows differently. My hope is that through prayer and earnest study, you will gain a fuller understanding of the significant points related to redemption, and not be overly concerned about the various interpretations.

Also, let me apologize now for my sense of humor. I'm not a comedian, but I try to make this book a little lively by tossing in a few quips, some woeful attempts at slang, and a few comments in hopes of eliciting a periodic laugh, or at least a chuckle with some eye-rolling. I hope you'll enjoy or at least appreciate the humor. But, hey, I'm much older than the target audience so I might miss a beat or two ... or three.

It's OK to Peek—It's Not Really Cheating

As an adult, I've developed a love of reading. I can't say the same was true when I was a child or even a young adult. One of the temptations I've been successful in avoiding is jumping ahead and reading the end of a book to see how the story ends. It seemed a bit like cheating to me. Many times I was able to guess the ending, but sometimes I was surprised (sometimes pleasantly, sometimes not so pleasantly). And, in case you're wondering, to this day I have never read the back of a book or novel to see its conclusion prior to actually getting there in the normal course of reading.

When it comes to the Bible, however, it is good to peek at the back of the book to see how the "story" ends. It's not really a story in a conventional or conversational sense as much as it is an unrealized or yet-to-occur series of facts. God wants us to know how things end in the last days because those are the days that will realize all God intends for His people and His creation. The term we use to describe this is **prophecy**. God tells us in advance *what* will happen, sometimes *how* it's going to happen, *why* it will happen, and sometimes *when* it will happen.

God made declarations throughout the Bible about the end times. Sometimes He used others to do the same thing—to act as His mouthpiece. In the Old Testament, He used the prophets Isaiah, Jeremiah, Ezekiel, and Daniel, all of whom are recognized as the "major prophets". There are quite a few "minor prophets", however, who also revealed end-time prophecy, as well as reported some unique and compelling events. In the

Introduction

New Testament, Jesus provided much in the way of prophecy, and God used the Apostles to do the same.

Prophecy is not the story in and of itself. It is just a part of a much bigger story … the *real* story that is the message of the Bible. Prophecy is definitely interesting, and perhaps even more challenging to understand compared to all else the Bible reveals. But it is just part of the Bible.

The last book of the Bible is The Revelation of Saint John the Divine, but most people simply refer to it as Revelation. This prophetic book tells us how it all ends. It's a difficult read, which is why we will spend a lot of time covering it later in this book. But if you know and understand God, even just a little bit, you shouldn't be surprised that God's will and Word win out.

So, in this case, it's ok to skip ahead to the back of the book. As a Christian, it should give you comfort to know the end of the story. As you read more of what follows, your faith will increase as you learn and understand the unfolding of God's plan. And, you will know that our God reigns. The Bible culminates in and concludes how God ordains eternity to be. This ending, as we will see later, is what God wanted from the beginning.

Spiritual Warfare

Let's get something straight right now.

> *"For we wrestle not against flesh and blood, but against principalities, against powers, against the rulers of the darkness of this world, against spiritual wickedness in high places."*

These words from Ephesians 6:12 spell out for Christians everywhere the backdrop of our struggles in this present world ... all of the trials, struggles, and temptations we endure. While we tend to think of the struggles of the day, or of the moment, in a physical or emotional sense, many of them in fact reflect a spiritual war that the enemy, Satan and his legions, perpetrates against us. They are the principalities, the rulers of darkness of this world, the spiritual wickedness in high places referred to in the above verse. Their mission is to provoke, entice, lure, lead, or instigate us in some manner that causes us to act contrary to the will of God and break fellowship with Him, which of course can render us weak and ineffective Christians.

My guess is only some Christians, and even fewer non-Christians, truly understand that there is a spiritual war going on all around us. A lot of people, even Christians, get a little nervous when people start talking about Satan and his demons messing around with people. I don't blame them—especially after seeing some of the movies Hollywood puts out there. But relax; we're not talking about demon possession here. We're talking about the spiritual influences satanic activity, which includes demons, has on and in our lives directly or through others ... a cause and effect kind of thing, not possession.

Sometimes we, saved and unsaved alike, make it easy for Satan to trip us up. Why is that? It is because of *what we are*. We are sinners. Let me repeat that. We are sinners ... born in sin to sin. It is part of our DNA so to speak. It is our nature to sin. That means **we are not sinners because we sin; rather, we sin because we are sinners**. As such, when we sin, we open the door to allow Satan to come in and have his way. Acknowledging that, let's understand some spiritual basics.

Here are some concepts that you might as well get used to: **the spiritual always outweighs the physical**. Why? The physical is an outgrowth or result of the spiritual—not the other way around. God is a spirit (John 4:24), and He created the physical and all it contains, and it was good ... until we put our hands on it. Spiritual beings see us, but we cannot see them unless God opens our eyes to them. For example, read the story in 2 Kings 6 about the prophet Elisha who asked God to open the eyes of the servant. He got a real eyeful when he saw what was out there. There are many other accounts in the Bible of times when God allowed physical man to see spiritual beings and things. A few examples are when Abraham saw the three angels who were on their way to destroy Sodom and Gomorrah in Genesis 18; when the prophet Daniel saw the angel Gabriel in response to his prayer in Daniel 9; and Jacob's ladder in Genesis 28.

The physical cannot overcome the spiritual. The Bible is replete with instances when physical beings are dominated by, subjected to, or influenced by spiritual beings. In the Old Testament, two angels in Sodom blinded the men outside Lot's home and subsequently destroyed Sodom (Genesis chapter 19). Daniel was saved from the lions within the lion's den by an angel (Daniel chapter 6). In the New Testament, Jesus sets loose the woman who was bound by Satan for 18 years (Luke 13). Jesus also freed the man who was possessed by a legion of demons (Mark 5). There are many other such examples. What's the point? The point is that we cannot overcome the spiritual by physical means apart from prayer and fasting, which are physical acts leading to spiritual victories (Mark 9:14-29).

We cannot physically force our way into God's domain, will, or favor. The physical can only be used to serve the spiritual; it can never overcome it. We are, in fact, physically impotent when it comes to touching the spiritual realm, although the reverse is not the case. Job was touched by Satan during his testing and was powerless to do anything about it. In Acts 12, Herod put Peter in jail just to win a popularity contest, but an angel walked in, unchained him from between two guards and walked him out pass two gates ... and none of the guards were aware of what happened. And, as much as I would like to, I can't decide to just walk into heaven as I am, and I certainly don't want to walk into Hell to see what that's like.

The physical does not have priority over the spiritual. The created (speaking of the physical realm—be it man, the stars, the moon, or earth) does not have power over the *Creator*. The physical is evidence of God's power, glory, and creativity. It comes from the mind of God. It is a result of God's thoughts. So, unless you have some equivalent God-like spiritual power, and let me assure you, you don't, don't go out there challenging the spiritual world on your own. You'll just get yourself beat up and get your feelings hurt.

The physical is temporal and can be destroyed; the spiritual is eternal. Remember, God is a spirit. Spiritual beings (the angels) are also created eternal. Their final destination is either with God in eternity or separated from God in the Lake of Fire for eternity (Revelation 20:10). We'll discuss this a bit more later, but meanwhile let's get back to the spiritual warfare.

1 Peter 5:8 sums up this spiritual warfare succinctly:

> *"Be sober, be vigilant; because your adversary the devil, as a roaring lion, walketh about, seeking whom he may devour."*

The devil (Satan) is also an accuser of the brethren (saints), presenting us to God as unworthy and failures. In Revelation 12:10, immediately following the casting down of Satan (and his angels) to earth, we read these words:

> *"...for the accuser of our brethren is cast down, which accused them before our God day and night."*

A great account of this is written in Zechariah chapter 3 (one of those "minor prophets" I mentioned earlier). I encourage you to read this chapter. We sometimes forget about or completely ignore the Old Testament, but it contains many very valuable lessons about God and how He deals with man and his sin. In summary, Satan accuses a high priest, Joshua, before God, but the Angel of the Lord defends the priest, and the priest is restored. The Angel of the Lord is the pre-incarnate Christ; that is, the Son of God before He became a man.

Satan looks to accuse us before God every opportunity he gets when we fall into sin. But, no sin, no opportunity, right? Yea, if only! Sometimes we make it so easy for him, don't we? As Christians however, God looks through us to see His Son, Christ Jesus, who paid the price for those sins, and forgives us ... *when we ask* Him.

How, you may ask, does Satan try to trap us? Consider this. Just before Eve took the fruit from the forbidden tree, Genesis 3:6 records this occurrence:

> *"And when the woman saw that the tree was good for food, and that it was pleasant to the eyes, and a tree to be desired to make one wise, she took of the fruit thereof, and did eat...."*

In the New Testament, there is a parallel reading in 1 John 2:16:

> *"For all that is in the world, the lusts of the flesh, and the lust of the eyes, and the pride of life, is not of the Father, but is of the world."*

The trap is sprung when we are drawn away from God to our own lusts (James 1:14), whether it be for physical satisfaction (good for food = lust of the flesh), or something visual that stimulates us in a covetous manner (pleasant to the eyes = lust of the eyes), or pride (desired to make one wise = pride, or that which feeds the ego). Our sin problems are manifested in one of these three ways, and they have their beginnings in the fall of Satan and the fall of man.

Young adults, especially, tend to look only at the present circumstances of predicaments, trials, challenges, and irritations. In an effort to overcome these things, they will talk to friends, analyze the thing to death, seek sympathy, wish upon a star, flip a coin, or find some other approach to rid themselves of the problems and burdens of the day. When push comes to shove, fewer will pray or seek out godly or parental involvement.

But it is only when we understand what we are up against, what the fight or struggle is truly all about (spiritual warfare), that we can overcome the real problem ... the real cause ... the real enemy. How? Through Bible study, prayer, obedience, and faith in the living God. Then, and only then, can we enjoy the real kind of life that God has always wanted for us ... a life that is full and abundant. But first things first ...

What is the Bible to You?

The Bible is one of the greatest tools you can use against spiritual warfare. But to use it properly, you have to understand what it is, and why it is. The Bible is many things to many people, saved and unsaved alike. Ask random people to share their thoughts about the Bible with you, and chances are you'll get as many different answers as people you ask. All the responses may be right, or certainly understandable, regardless of whether the person is a Christian or not. The saved person will undoubtedly talk about the Bible being God's Word about Himself and His people. From one perspective, that answer is right. Another Christian may say the Bible is about Jesus Christ as the Son of God, or as the Savior of the world in reference to His sacrificial death, or as our Lord in reference to His standing in our life. Others may say the Bible is about love, salvation, and fellowship, or perhaps a few other concepts, verbs, or adjectives.

The unsaved may speak of the Bible as "The Good Book", an age old standby kind of description. I can't tell you how many inebriated people I've heard say that just before they started to cry and talk about how they need to "get right with the Good Lord" after realizing how messed up they've become from all that drinking. Other more sober opinions may describe it as a book that contains messages on how we ought to live, or say that it provides guidelines on how we ought to behave. Most, I assume, would not hold to our belief that the Bible is the inerrant Word of God.

What does the Bible say about itself? Well, there are dozens of verses that speak about the Bible, most of which, I believe, rests in the power of the Word, and attest to the sum meaning of John 1:1, John 1:14, and 2 Timothy 3:16-17. John 1:1 and 1:14 reads as follows:

> *"In the beginning was the Word, and the Word was with God, and the Word was God."*
>
> *"And the Word was made flesh, and dwelt among us..."*

These verses tell us all that can be expressed about God becoming flesh in the person of Jesus Christ, who was God, and with God from the beginning, and then came down from His heavenly home to live among us. These verses represent the Triune God acting together to walk among man in the person of Jesus Christ. The Bible is God in His Word, the centerpiece of which is Jesus Christ. Our problem, however, is that God is too awesome, glorious, and magnificent for words to capture all that He is. Perhaps that is one reason God loves those who believe, by faith, in who He is and what He is. There is no earthly comparison, in terms or word or imagination, in how we can understand His fullness.

The third reference, 2 Timothy 3:16, reads as follows:

> *"All scripture is given by inspiration of God, and is profitable for doctrine, for reproof, for correction, for instruction in righteousness."*

A lot can be said about this verse, but it points out:

1. *The Bible is by inspiration of God.* God chose a select group of 40 different authors to write down what He wants us to know. In form, the Bible is a collection of 66 books and letters written over a period of 1,600 years. It is filled with verses and passages on promises, blessings, warnings, deliverances, victories, and prophecies of the past and those yet to come. Many of these books were written by men of long ago which cross-reference other books written by other men of long, long ago. In other words, most of these men did not know one another, and lived in different times. So the Bible is a collection of books written

by men who lived centuries apart, but whose writings cross reference with amazing consistency.

It is inconceivable to me that even the greatest collusion could bring about the collection of books known as the Bible. Further, the belief that man could and would write down in error what Almighty God has ordained is to completely and utterly misunderstand and underestimate any knowledge of God's authority and power.

2. *It is good for doctrine.* Doctrine is a belief, or system of beliefs that is accepted as authority. Simply stated, that means man operates, acts, or is guided by what he believes. As it relates to the Bible, doctrine is the authoritative basis of our belief, and what we are taught. The Bible is one of the oldest books in man's history. It contains centuries of truths and knowledge. Imagine what truths we can learn from it. The lessons are still there, so get to it!

3. *It is good for reproof or correction.* When we sin or act in ways contrary to the character of Jesus Christ, the Bible is the basis for correction. The Bible is our objective standard! We use the Bible to learn and understand what is holy, what is right, and how we should behave. God knows we will sin and act out of Christ's character, so in His wisdom He provided the Bible to point out those acts and attitudes that are contrary to His will, and provides us with a way of correcting our missteps.

4. *It is good for instruction in righteousness.* This means that all Christians must use the lessons contained in the Bible as a guide to grow in our Christian walk. We are expected to grow in the knowledge of Christ and mature in Him ... to become like-minded with Him. The Bible provides guidance for us to do just that. After all, you don't want to be stuck in "spiritual first grade" year after year while your peers keep getting promoted, do you?

To what end? 2 Timothy 3:17 reads:

> ***"That the man of God may be perfect, thoroughly furnished unto all good works."***

We are to be prepared to walk perfectly (in completeness) and be capable of doing good works. By faith, we believe the Bible is the inerrant Word of God.

Okay. So let's say you believe all that. *Is that it? Do you think you can just put this book down now and go outside and play?* Well, no. There is still the "why" of the Bible. Don't you want to know *why* and *how* this whole story came to be? How did it get to the point that God *had to* come down in the flesh? If it was simply to pass along "good living" information, surely God could have written down what He wanted us to know on more tablets of stone as He did for Moses. Or, maybe He could have had Moses take dictation. Moses did a pretty good job writing the first five books of the Bible. Maybe he could have finished the job. Or God could have spoken to us audibly as He did to Adam and Eve way back when, and as He did with some of the prophets. Jesus didn't come down from His heavenly home just because He wanted to stop by for a visit and check us out. He could have just continued watching us make a mess of things from His heavenly throne. He's probably up there shaking His head at the things going on down here.

But God wants us to understand it all, which is why He gives us more information. In New Testament times, God sent His Son, Jesus Christ, to earth to be born of a woman *on purpose*. Christ had a mission to accomplish. The acts of Jesus' life on earth are written in the first four books of the New Testament. Here are just a few of the things Jesus said about His earthly mission.

Luke 19:10:

> **"For the Son of man is come to seek and save that which was lost."**

Jesus, in John 3:16-17, puts it another way:

> **"For God so loved the world, that he gave his only begotten Son, that whosoever believeth in him should not perish, but have everlasting life. For God sent not his Son into the world to condemn the world, but that the world through him might be saved."**

According to these verses, Jesus is clearly on a rescue mission. People are lost and about to die a spiritual death, which would keep them eternally separated from God. Jesus left His throne in heaven to come to earth to find the lost and save the dying—to save all mankind. That includes you and me! That "saving" from dying, or death, is what we call salvation; the saving of man or mankind from an eternity apart from the grace of God. Mankind is offered salvation through the sacrificial death of Christ. The unfortunate thing is many people don't know, or believe, that they are lost and about to die apart from God.

Let me expand on this explanation a bit. God created man and fellowshipped with him in the Garden of Eden. Everything was cool until man sinned, and broke fellowship. He got lost ... and he was dying. Mankind became a slave to sin, and God required a price be paid to free us from its spiritual consequences, which is eternal separation from God and death. Christ came down to pay that price, and free us so that we can be restored, or redeemed. We call that redemption. Without the work of Jesus, there is no redemption. We are "saved", but it is Christ who redeems.

To summarize, God offers all mankind salvation through the redemptive work of Jesus Christ. The Bible tells us how and why, and you should know both!

I humbly submit, then, that the principal purpose of the Bible is to reveal God's plan for man's redemption, through which comes our salvation and freedom from the bondage of sin. As important as it is to know and understand what the Word is, it is just as important to know and understand why God has given us the Word. The Bible also discloses what God would have us know about all the other things previously mentioned, but unless we are saved from the penalty of sin, redeemed from the curse of fallen man by the perfect man, Jesus Christ, then all the lessons in the Bible would be nothing more than great reading. This is why the Bible starts with Genesis and ends with Revelation—to tell the whole story—from the creation of the world and the beginning of man's fall into sin in the Garden of Eden to the realization of God's plan to redeem fallen man and restore His creation. Unfortunately, many, if not most teachings on the Bible do not fully explain how God goes about this plan. Sunday school lessons and sermons tend to stop at the death of Christ on the cross, preaching repentance.

Don't get me wrong. That is not a bad thing. In fact, it's the most central—the most critical part of the whole story. Of course, time limits what can be taught in the 30 minutes to an hour the minister has to address the congregation. Admit it, we have short attention spans. After 30-45 minutes we tend to lose focus, especially if we stayed up late on Saturday night. Christians who dedicate their lives to the Lord's service, however, will undoubtedly learn more about the things that help strengthen their walk in the Lord on their own through Bible study, fellowship with other believers, and other Bible-centered activities. Fewer still will take the time to understand the fullness of God's plan.

My hope is that this will spark your interest to read on. As you do, you will gain a fuller understanding of how God will fulfill His plan of redemption for mankind.

So let's get started!

It's All About God

God wants to have fellowship with all His creation, but that fellowship must be on *His* terms. Why? Because...

> *"And all the inhabitants of the earth are reputed as nothing: and he doeth according to his will in the army of heaven, and among the inhabitants of the earth: and none can stay his hand, or say unto him, What doest thou?"*

Nebuchadnezzar said that in Daniel 4:35 after being taught a lesson about his high mindedness.

> *"The earth is the Lord's, and the fulness thereof; the world, and they that dwell therein."*

David said that in Psalms 24:1 in praise to the Lord. David knew better than Nebuchadnezzar. He didn't need to be taught a lesson!

> *"...whatsoever is under the whole heaven is mine."*

God said that in Job 41:11 as a declaration of His sovereignty. Do you really want to take Him on?

Like it or not, we belong to God. It is He who made us, not we ourselves (Psalms 100:3). Don't cop an attitude about this and challenge God's authority to do as He pleases. That will not go over well with God, nor end up well for you! Lucifer tried that once. It didn't turn out too well for him either. We'll cover Lucifer's fall shortly.

If we expect to have a good relationship and fellowship with God, then we should understand what He wants and expects from us. You may not believe this, but good parents want to have good relationships with their children. That may seem incredulous to you, but it is true. The same is also true of God. Good parents teach and expect their children to learn "the rules of the house" so to speak, and not just do anything they want, anytime they want. In that regard, parents are not different from God.

Just as parents expect their children to learn and abide by their rules, so God expects His children to learn and abide by His rules. Since we were made in the image of God, we have similar desires when it comes to our children. If you accept this premise, then it follows that we must have a good understanding of what God wants and why He wants it. The events of the Bible tell us what is important to God. To understand God, as best we can in this mortal body, we must understand the Bible. After all, it was written for us to understand, and know, what God would have us know.

I will always remember the first line of the first lesson in Dr. Rick Warren's book, *The Purpose Driven Life*. It struck me as awesomely simplistic, but extremely powerful in its essence and meaning. This line, following the verse to remember, reads as follows:

"It's not about you."

In this "me first" world, it is counter-intuitive for non-Christians to think of God or anyone else ahead of themselves. For many, not all, the desire to "get mine" is woven into their thoughts from the time they become aware of what and who they are as physical beings. And it's no wonder many are led astray. Look at the influencers in the world today. What impact do you think they have on the lives of young people? Our young people look at world and industry leaders, and other notable people of our day, especially those of wealth and "power", and try to emulate them in the hope they can, will, or even exceed, those accomplishments. The young look at and admire the rich, the world's politicians, business leaders, sports figures, entertainers, and others who they think "got it going on", and want to have what they have. Sometimes it doesn't matter how or what these influencers do to accomplish their status. It doesn't matter if they attained that status and power through misdeeds, lying, cheating, bragging or boasting, stepping on people along the way, putting others down, or generally disregarding certain principles, social norms, or other standards. Such behaviors are even applauded sometimes, sad to say.

Here's an example of young people emulating what they see. One of the oddest of the current norms in our society has young men walking around with their pants halfway down their backside! Can you believe this? It is considered "cool" or hip to walk around like that! C'mon ... *really?* It is inconceivable to me that this is accepted by any standard. But, that's how some rap artists dress, so for many, that makes it acceptable. The point is that too many young lives are dedicated to the "me generation"... my rights, my will, my freedom, my possessions, or my whatever, without regard to anything or anyone else. They believe they have the right to do anything that is self-satisfying; a stance that is natural for non-Christians.

As Christians, we too have difficulties sometimes casting off such pernicious thoughts from our minds, and living a life dedicated to our Lord. The truth is, apart from living a life truly dedicated to serving the Lord, it is a hard thing to do. We still have the old nature within us, messing with us, and it is pre-disposed to satisfying itself. The Apostle Paul says in Romans 7:18-19:

> *"For I know that in me (that is, my flesh,) dwelleth no good thing: for to will is present with me; but how to perform that which is good I find not. For the good that I would I do not: but the evil which I would not, that I do."*

Here the Apostle Paul acknowledges that Christians struggle against the old nature, and sometimes desire to do those things that are self-satisfying. We have the Holy Spirit to aid us in doing those things that are pleasing to God, yet we still struggle. Why? Because we still think it's about us, when the truth is it is not! When we change our focus from *me first* to *God first*, we move toward actualizing what life is supposed to be about, and recognize the spiritual warfare going on all around us. But this is a war we can win ... when we put God first in all things.

Now, let's move forward by going back in time.

In the Beginning, Really?

The Holy Bible begins with the book of Genesis, which presents the creation account. It is commonly accepted that all we know starts here. If you ask the unsaved about what happens first in the Bible, they will probably tell you it's the creation story. Christians will probably say the same thing. After all, Genesis does mean "beginning, or origin".

But was it, really? Well, in a manner of speaking, yes it is ... from the perspective of the creation of man. But in fact something happened before that, on earth, that is not commonly understood. Any guess what that might have been? Ask your friends; see if they know. Most will start with Genesis 1:1. But here's a hint: God already existed, and so did the angels.

I'm holding off with the answer until we talk about God, who was around long before Genesis 1, and thus deserves to be in the forefront. Psalm 90:2 tells us:

> *"Before the mountains were brought forth, or ever thou hadst formed the earth and the world, even from everlasting to everlasting, thou art God."*

This is a psalm by Moses. (And no, David did not write all the Psalms. Hmm, maybe I was the only person who believed that, but I doubt it!) David was the author of many of the Psalms, but there are at least five other named authors of various psalms, including Moses, and many who are not named. At any rate, this particular Psalm was written by Moses to tell us God exists in eternity past (from everlasting) and will exist in eternity future (to everlasting). There was never a time, nor will there ever be a time, that God did not, nor will not, exist.

To those of us who believe in God the Father, it is a given that He is the creator of all things, beginning with the cosmos, universe, the planets, the stars, and everything pre-existing before the earth came to be.

Let me throw in another thought relative to God's existence. The concept of time means little to God. Time was created for man's benefit. 2 Peter 3:8 reads:

> *"But, beloved, be not ignorant of this one thing, that one day is with the Lord as a thousand years, and a thousand years as one day."*

This means that God sees in the present everything that was, and is, and will be. This is truly a mind-blowing thought. We should know and be strengthened by a few Bible verses that support this truth. Read Revelation 1:8. Also, in speaking about our redemption by Christ, relative to time, 1 Peter 1:19-20 states:

> *"But with the precious blood of Christ, as of a lamb without blemish and without spot; Who verily was foreordained before the foundation of the world..."*

Before the foundation of the world, before it was even created, God, somewhere in eternity past, provided for our redemption through the shed blood of His Son, Jesus Christ, our Savior.

This is a good place to talk about God's attributes, or natural qualities. These are some of the things that make God who He is. The Bible is replete with verses that reveal and extol God's attributes. We will quickly examine a few below that will enable us to get a better glimpse of the God we serve.

As mentioned earlier, God has always been around. Hence, one of God's attributes is being **eternal**. God has no beginning and no end. The Bible tells us in Habakkuk 1:12:

> *"Art thou not from everlasting, O Lord my God, mine Holy One?..."*

He is **omniscient**, meaning God knows everything. He is the only true Know-It-All! There is nothing known, or to be known, that God does not know. Psalm 147:4-5 says:

"He telleth the number of the stars; he calleth them all by their names. Great is our Lord, and of great power: his understanding is infinite."

Not only does God know how many stars are out there, He knows all their names. Man gets excited when he finds a new star that he can identify. Compared to that, God yawns. Been there, done that. God's knowledge is also perfect. Not only does He know all there is to know, He knows it all perfectly. He knows all things and He *understands* all things.

God is **omnipresent**, meaning He sees all and is present everywhere at all times. Plain and simple! God is in heaven and sits on His throne (Psalm 47:8; Isaiah 6:1; Daniel 7:9; Revelation 5:1), but His presence is everywhere. The psalmist David records a wonderful praise to Almighty God on His being omnipresent in Psalm 139:7-12. I encourage you to read it.

God is **omnipotent**, meaning He is all-powerful. God created the heavens and the earth, the universe, and the stars. All things natural and spiritual are a testament to His power. Job 42:2 tells us:

"I know that thou canst do every thing, and that no thought can be withholden from thee."

Even the heathen king Nebuchadnezzar recognized the power of Almighty God in Daniel 4:35:

"...and he doeth according to his will in the army of heaven, and among the inhabitants of the earth..."

So what's the conclusion? God's power cannot be overcome by anything in heaven or on earth!

God is **holy**. What is holiness? The best way I can define it is to say that it is God's absolute moral standard ... a standard of behavior and state of being. It's an objective moral standard against which we are measured. It is objective because it is not a standard set by man, but rather a standard set by God. When we operate, by deed or thought, against that standard, we are guilty of violating that standard, and God calls it sin. Thus sin is that which violates the moral standard God requires of us.

The Bible commands us to be holy. Psalm 99:9 states:

"Exalt the Lord our God, and worship at his holy hill; for the Lord our God is holy."

Probably the more well-known verse about holiness is found in 1 Peter 1:16:

"Because it is written, Be ye holy; for I am holy."

There is much, much more to holiness than what I have said here, but the point here is to understand that because God is holy, we ought to be holy. It is a commandment, not a request! The attribute of holiness is imputed to man through the acceptance of His Son, Christ Jesus.

God is *immutable*, that is, God does not change. Malachi 3:6 tells us:

"For I am the Lord. I change not..."

The God of the Old Testament is the same God we serve now, and He will be the same God we serve in the future. What God wanted and wants does not change.

In summary, here's what we have:

God is Eternal—God always was, is, and will be.

God is Omniscient—He knows all. He can't be out-smarted, and man will never know anything that God doesn't already know.

God is Omnipresent—you can't run and hide. Jonah did his best, but just provided amusement for God. There is no hide-n-seek from the presence of the Lord.

God is omnipotent—He is all-powerful! He created the heavens and the earth. Nothing or no one even comes close.

God is Holy—it is His absolute moral standard, against which we are measured.

God is immutable—He does not change. We serve and worship the same God as in the Old Testament. God doesn't have a bad day and acts differently.

Man cannot understand the fullness of God and we never will, at least on this side of heaven. In eternity, we'll understand a lot more, but that's a discussion for later.

So let's go back to the "beginning". Did the real creation account start in Genesis? Consider this...

The Angelic Conflict

The Angelic Conflict, summarized, is a doctrine discussed and debated among Biblical scholars which espouse the belief that man was created in response to a rebellion by some of the angels in heaven. While I don't subscribe to the totality of this doctrine, some of its elements are interesting and worth a look to see how this rebellion affected man, and led to the need for man's redemption.

Somewhere in eternity past, prior to the creation of man on this earth that we know, the Triune God (Father, Son, and Holy Spirit) reigned over the universe and was in fellowship with eternal beings known as angels, of which there are different kinds. Without going into detail, the major categories of angels include:

- The Angel of the Lord (the pre-incarnate Christ)
- Cherubims
- Seraphims
- Arch Angels
- Guardian Angels
- Messengers
- Ministering Angels (spirits)

Cherubim (plural; cherub, singular) are generally recognized as the most powerful or highest class of angels, apart from the Angel of the Lord. Some might say that the Seraphim are the highest class because they tend to the Throne of God, but we won't debate that here. However, among the cherubim was an angelic being named Lucifer, who was unique among all the angels.

Lucifer means "Morning Star", "son of the morning", or "shining one". These terms denote his brightness or brilliance. The term "star" in the Bible is sometimes used to describe angels. For example, Revelation 1:20 specifically interprets the stars to mean angels. Revelation 12:3-4 also discusses the dragon's (a description of Satan) tail drawing a third part of the "stars of heaven" and casting them to earth. These stars are angels.

So if the angels are characterized as stars, just think of what Lucifer was, being characterized as the Morning Star. He was the first of the order; the brightest of the stars of heaven. Ezekiel 28:12-19 gives a description of a being "full of beauty" and "perfect in wisdom". Further, the description in verse 13 uses every precious stone to describe the beauty of this being in the day he was created. It was like he had a different gem stone on each finger. He was "the anointed cherub" (angel), which indicated that he outranked all the other angels. Verse 14 tells us God Himself established this privilege. These verses refer to Lucifer. Before you read the verses that follow, it is important to understand the Bible sometimes uses earthly events to depict heavenly occurrences to aid our understanding. In these verses, the King of Tyre is sentenced for his sin, which is spelled out in verse 2 of the same chapter. As we read on, however, we begin to recognize that these specific verses could not be about the King of Tyre. How do we know this for sure? Well, this king certainly was not in the Garden of Eden (verse 13), nor was he the anointed cherub (verse 14). The cherub is clearly Lucifer (Satan). There are similarities between the king and Satan for sure. In fact, if you go back to the start of the chapter and read verses 1 through 4 you will see the similarities.

So Lucifer (Satan) was perfect in all his ways from the time of his creation ... until iniquity (sin) was found in him (verse 15). Because of his beauty and wisdom, his heart was lifted up in pride (verse 17). We should take note that Lucifer had no external source or stimulus to induce or cause him to sin. There was no sin in heaven. There was no external pressure, no temptation, no one whispering in his ear to do that which was displeasing to God. There were no x-rated movies or television shows, no rap music, no suggestive videos, no magazines with lewd pictures, no good-looking angels with wings that can't wait or legs that won't quit, or no billionaires tempting him with heavenly currency to sell out other angels. *His sin was his own.* He chose to sin because he became obsessed with himself. He was the angel in charge. He looked good and he was smart ... and he knew it. In human language, he was "the man". But he didn't stop there.

Enter Isaiah 14:13-14. Lucifer decided that since he was "all that", and first among the angels, he should be treated like God Almighty, the Creator. He decided that he should share God's throne and glory. Satan declared:

- I will ascend into heaven (usurp or share God's throne).
- I will exalt my throne above the stars of God. The angels already reported to him, but that wasn't enough. He wanted the angels to do his bidding, without any direction from Almighty God.
- I will sit also upon the mount of the congregation, in the sides of the north. "Mount" or "mountains" refer to kingdoms or rule, so Satan wanted to sit on the seat of the Triune God's government of heaven.
- I will ascend above the heights of the clouds. The clouds refer to God's glory. Satan was saying he wants God's glory for his own.
- I will be like the Most High. He wanted to be worshipped!

God cocked His head, looked at him sideways, and said:

- No, you won't!

The problem with Lucifer's stated goals were, and still are, that God does not share His glory with anyone—not even the brightest star in heaven. So Lucifer had to go, and take what was left of his pride with him. Imagine someone, like a friend, relative, or stranger coming into your home that you built with your own bare hands and trying to take over. Imagine further that this person tells your family members that they must worship and obey him over you! I don't think you'd take too kindly to such an attempt. Well, neither did God! In Isaiah 48, God states it plainly in His decree against the nation of Israel. I strongly encourage you to read Isaiah 48:1-11 in its entirety, which concludes with God stating:

"...*I will not give my glory unto another.*"

While this charge is against the house of Israel, it is God's firm position on His sovereignty and His deity. Ever hear of the Ten Commandments? What is the first commandment? Exodus 20:3:

"Thou shalt have no other gods before me."

Although God was speaking to the nation of Israel at the time, God's will in heaven and earth are one and the same. Satan clearly stepped over the line in this matter. Satan's declaration was an act of sin that resulted in his expulsion from heaven.

Some well-respected biblical scholars believe a trial was held in heaven, and as Lucifer (now renamed Satan) tried to defend his position, some of the angels sided with him. This gave rise to Lucifer's name change to Satan (the Adversary, which defines his nature and character). So when Lucifer was expelled from heaven, the one-third of the angels who sided with him was expelled right along with him. These angels underwent a categorical name change too. They are now referred to as demons. These name changes introduce the concept of names reflecting character. Lucifer was once the Morning Star, but after his fall he was known as Satan, the Adversary.

Just for the record, Christ was around to witness this event, as it happened, when He exclaimed in Luke 10:18:

"...I beheld Satan as lightning fall from heaven."

So after his rebellion, Satan was booted out of heaven ... and quickly too. This meant that Satan could no longer call heaven his home, and he lost his station as first among the angels. But while Satan could no longer call heaven his home, he still has limited access to God (see Job 1:6 and Zechariah 3:1). But that too will change.

That is how Satan came to be on earth before the creation account in Genesis 1. How do we know that Satan was booted to earth after his rebellion? Isaiah 14:12 tells us:

"How art thou fallen from heaven, O Lucifer, son of the morning! how art thou cut down to the ground, which didst weaken the nations!"

In the Beginning, Really?

This demonstrates Satan's fall to earth ("the ground"); meaning that when God cleaned up this earth in advance of the creation of man, Satan was already here along with the angels who chose to follow him. There is no indication how long he preceded man before the creation account, but he was there. There's more to this story, which we will pick up in the next chapter.

Here's a valuable lesson for all of us. God is the one who blesses us with the gifts we have. Some of us are gifted with intelligence; some are mathematical whizzes; others are gifted in the field of medicine or other fields of science, and whose discoveries are revolutionary or abilities to diagnose and heal are breathtaking. Still others are physically gifted athletes who are superior in any sport they play. They are bigger, quicker, and faster than anyone else. They can shoot a basketball better, hit a baseball farther, throw a football 80 yards on a dime and hit a receiver in stride. Then there are the artists among us of all kinds—painters, sculptors, songwriters, poets, singers, and others whose works are so dazzling they bring tears to our eyes. There are charismatic orators, who possess such presence and power of persuasion they can convince the masses to do just about anything they want done, like some grand Jedi mind trick. These orators reside in the halls of government, run zillion-dollar companies, and yes, even preach from the pulpit.

The one thing all these prodigies have in common is their gifts come from God. They did not endow themselves with these gifts, no matter what they think, no matter what they say, or how often they say it. Thus, to act "God-like" and pretend their gifts were self-bestowed, or demand to be worshipped, adored, idolized, or recognized as God, or act like God, is absolute foolishness. That is where Satan went wrong!

So whenever you hear people boast about themselves—be it how smart they are, how good-looking they are, how much money they have, or what talents they possess—recognize where this attitude comes from. You should recognize it was Satan who started that self-destructive trend. It was his failure to recognize that he was created and gifted. He was privileged by God to be first among the angels. Likewise, it would be a failure on our part not to recognize that we are created. It would be a failure not to recognize God as the gift-giver and take on a God-like attitude. Don't be like that. Don't emulate Satan.

So here's the question of the day: *Why did God create man on this earth knowing it was occupied by Satan and his fallen angels? Why did God create man on earth, knowing that man would fall into sin?* Ok, let's look at the question. The fact that man was created on earth, in the presence of the fallen angels, does suggest some things. It was clearly not by accident because God doesn't say "oops"... *ever!* As stated at the beginning of this section, some people believe that God created man in response to the angelic rebellion, aka the Angelic Conflict. These Bible scholars and students suggest that God used the lesser (man) to defeat the greater (Satan), to demonstrate God's greater glory. This is certainly consistent with how God operates, as we will see going forward. In point of fact, God did use man to defeat Satan. But did God create man to defeat Satan? We may never know the answer to that question with absolute certainty. God does keep some things to Himself (Deuteronomy 29:29), and the Bible doesn't specifically state He did it for that specific purpose. So while I neither endorse nor dismiss this theory, I do understand how that conclusion was reached.

But here's another point of view. The Bible repeats the fact that "the earth is the Lord's and the fullness thereof" (Psalm 24:1, Exodus 19:5, and 1 Corinthians 10:26). It belongs to God to do as He pleases. And it pleased God to create man. Revelation 4:11 and Colossians 1:16 attests to the simple biblical fact that God created man for His pleasure and His purpose, in recognition of His sovereign right to do as He pleases, and for His own glory.

This is not a totally one-sided deal though, so don't start thinking that it is. In exercising His sovereign right, we, as God's creation, benefit if we are in fellowship with Him. In doing God's good will, we are blessed, and we fill the earth with His glory. Of course God knew Satan would mess things up by enticing man to sin. So what would God do? God turned that whole thing around. He would use man, the lesser being who Satan defeated, to defeat Satan, the greater being. The man God would use to do this is Jesus Christ, His son, born of a woman, born a lesser being, and born a little lower than the angels (Psalms 8:5). And guess what? He did it! Christ defeated Satan at the cross (1 John 3:8, Hebrews 2:14). Only God could pull that off! Can you say Amen! So my belief is God created man for His pleasure and for His glory. I do, however, recognize that the "end game" so to speak, takes care of Satan. But at this time, my belief in the creation of man is more rooted in God's pleasure, not the rebellion.

It's a mouthful, I know, but we will see how this all plays out as we go forward.

Let's find out how this happens.

The Creation and Fall of Man

In the previous sections, we learned that Satan and his demons were expelled from heaven to earth, which would be their new home.

But what do you really know about their new home? Many people think Satan and his gang of demons inherited the earth as it is described in Genesis 1:2. Would you be surprised to find out they didn't? This is what the Bible has to say about the formation of the earth as found in Isaiah 45:18:

> *"For thus saith the Lord that created the heavens;*
> *God himself that formed the earth and made it;*
> *he hath established it, he created it not in vain, he*
> *formed it to be inhabited: I am the Lord; and there*
> *is none else."*

I can hear you saying, "So what? What does this mean?" Well, what it means is when the earth was created, it was created to be inhabited. In fact, what it means in a deeper sense is when the earth was created, it was created perfectly, like all things God creates. If you do any research on the word "created", as found in the original text, you'll find that it is from the word "bara", which implies more than creating something out of nothing. It means the creation of something perfectly. However, Genesis 1:2 states:

> *"And the earth was without form, and void; and*
> *darkness was upon the face of the deep..."*

This verse says the earth was without form; it was void and covered by darkness. That doesn't sound perfect. In fact, it is far from perfect. Also, darkness is symbolic of judgment, so something is terribly wrong here. Recognizing these biblical facts, we then know that sometime between the original creation, which was perfect, and Genesis 1:2, something occurred to make it imperfect. Something happened to make it formless, void, and dark. In the original Hebrew language, this formless void is "tohu wabohu", which can literally be interpreted ruin (tohu) and desolation (wabohu). Also, the word "was" in Genesis 1:2 is translated from "hayah", which can be interpreted "had become". So what we have is God creating the earth perfect for habitation, only to have it become a dark, ruinous, desolate place. The combination of these words can also be interpreted as a wasteland. What in the world happened to make it this way?

The answer is the expulsion of Satan, and his angels, from heaven to earth. Look at the description of earth prior to the fall of Satan, according to Isaiah 45:18, and then look at its condition after his fall. God created something perfectly. However, when Satan and his demons were expelled from heaven, they were cast to earth (Isaiah 14:12), which then became this dark, ruinous, formless void, or wasteland. If you think about it, even for a second, it should come as no surprise to you that the abode or dwelling place of demons is unholy, dark and unclean. The conditions reflected the nature of those who were resident there. These descriptions were also signs of judgment. In Revelation 18:2, the fallen Babylon becomes a wasteland because evil spirits dwell there. Such conditions are a natural consequence of the unholy nature and characteristics of the residents involved. Would you want to live in a place like that? Of course not! The lesson here is that such conditions or places are not where any Christian (especially) or any sane person would want to go, hang out, or should hang out! Christians are to be the light of the world (Matthew 5:14) in contrast to the dark ... no matter if we're operating like a 100 watt bulb or 15 watt bulb. Accordingly, we must exercise care where we go, or where we hang out. If we find ourselves in an unholy or dark place, keep your light on and find the exit! It took the supernatural intervention of Almighty God to clean up the earth, so unless you can do what God did (and you can't!) it is wise not to dwell in any such place.

Here is when God steps in and introduces the beginning of man's history, or time, as we come to know it. God begins His renovation of earth between Genesis 1:2 and Genesis 1:3:

> *"...And the Spirit of God moved upon the face of the waters. And God said. Let there be light..."*

We know the rest of the creation story. God created ("bara") the world, its inhabitants, and man in six days, and then rested on the seventh day.

This goes back to the earlier question: Why did God do this? Why did God create me? The two verses I mentioned earlier help answer these questions.

The first is found in Revelation chapter 4:11:

> *"Thou art worthy, O Lord, to receive glory and honor and power: for thou hast created all things, and for thy pleasure they are and were created."*

God's creation is for His pleasure and for His glory. Is that so hard to believe? Think about that for a minute. When God and His creation (mankind in this case) are in fellowship, as they were in the Garden of Eden, both are happy! But, if the created (man) isn't in fellowship, then the Creator (God) can't be happy with him. You know what else? We're pretty much the same in that regard. As students and young adults, think about what you create. Think about your works and achievements. How did you feel when you got that "A" grade in high school (please tell me you got at least one!), or that 4.0 grade in college? Pretty good, didn't you? The hours you spent studying was work ... and your work paid off. Did you ever create, build, or construct something of value that worked out the way you wanted? If you did, then I'll bet you felt pretty good about it when all was said and done. I used to put together model cars when I was a kid. When I was finished, and I knew all the parts were used and in the right place, I was sooo happy! I paraded that thing around, and then placed it on the mantelpiece so everyone could see it. You couldn't tell me anything! Now, look at the reverse. How did you feel when things didn't work right? Pretty frustrated I'm sure, particularly if you put in a lot of time, money or effort to make it work right. Well, guess what? God gets pleasure when His works (man) work right (in fellowship), and He gets frustrated when we don't work right (sin).

Those of us who are parents feel the same way about our children and their works or accomplishments—from the first time the baby says "mommy" or "daddy", or lifts up that big head on their own, to the first step, to the first potty, learning to count to ten, reciting the alphabet, and on and on. As children get older and do well, parents are even more proud of what they've accomplished. I'm sure you've seen or heard examples of that. We (parents) want to say "that's my son" or "that's my daughter", as an expression of pride, as opposed to what a parent might say after picking up a child at the police station. I image that doesn't go over too well, and you don't have to tell me how parents might express themselves on that occasion. I do have an imagination, so let's leave it at that. But aside from that, parents like to celebrate their children's successes. Have you heard parents say "My son or daughter, the doctor, or lawyer, or other big-time, big name something or other!", or perhaps heard them brag about the child who graduated with honors? We stick our chests out just a little bit, smile a little brighter, or maybe even brag more than we ought to. We do this kind of thing all the time. As parents, we like it even more when our children recognize our contributions in helping them experience success or positive achievement. We love it when they recognize the parental guidance that helped them succeed. Well, here, God is the parent and we are the child. And God likes compliments too ... only we call it praise and worship!

While these may be imperfect comparisons, it is nevertheless true that God enjoys His creation, but only when it is in fellowship with and in obedience to Him. Said another way: God *gets glory* from His creation when it is in fellowship and obedience with Him.

Psalm 19:1-2 says:

> *"The heavens declare the glory of God; and the firmament sheweth his handiwork. Day unto day uttereth speech, and night unto night sheweth knowledge."*

Alternatively, man and creation *gives glory* to God when they are in fellowship with Him. God is glorified when we, His creation, walk in the light of His Word and His will, especially when we praise Him, knowing that all good things come from Him.

The second verse is found in Colossians 1:16, which tells us:

> *"For by him were all things created, that are in heaven, and that are in earth, visible and invisible, whether*

> *they be thrones, or dominions, or principalities, or powers; all things were created by him, and for him."*

This verse tells us Christ created EVERYTHING! Regardless of where it was created, whether seen or unseen, regardless of its substance, what it represents, its authority or its power, Jesus created it all ... for Himself! We are created for Christ to be used for HIS purpose. The issue thus becomes: *Will you allow yourself to be used for His purpose?* God does have a specific will for you, but you must understand His will for you fits within His plan for mankind. It doesn't make sense for anyone to believe that God's will for him, or her, would be outside of His broader will for all mankind.

Here on earth, in the midst of the fallen angels who are watching all that occurs, God is getting the glory He deserves from these lesser creatures, especially when these lesser creatures strive with God to accomplish His will.

Psalm 139:14 says:

> *"...I am fearfully and wonderfully made: marvelous are thy works; and that my soul knoweth right well."*

It is a two-way street of sorts—God *revealing* His glory through His creation and God *getting* His glory from His creation. If you acknowledge the gifts of God, then praise and thank Him for them. God gets the glory, and you get the blessings.

So God, in His infinite wisdom, decided to create and place man in the presence of Satan and his demons. He cleaned up the earth in six days, created man to rule over it, despite the presence of Satan, and placed him a perfect place, known as the Garden of Eden. Man (Adam) was to manage Eden and keep it. Genesis 1:27-28 states:

> **"So God created man in his own image, in the image of God created he him; male and female created he them. And God blessed them, and God said unto them, Be fruitful and multiply, and replenish the**

earth, and subdue it: and have dominion over the fish of the sea, and over the fowl of the air, and over every living thing that moveth upon the earth."

In what has come to be known as the **Adamic Covenant**, God gave man dominion over the earth. In brief, a *covenant* is an agreement or a promise between two parties. As used in the Bible, a covenant is an agreement between God and man. God tells man what He will do, and what He expects man to do in obedience to Him. While there may be some disagreement among biblical scholars over some of this, some points are not in dispute. With regard to the Adamic Covenant, these points include:

1. Man was commanded to "be fruitful and multiply". God wanted man to reproduce and fill the earth.

2. Man was to subdue or have dominion over all the earth; the fish of the sea, the beasts of the earth, and every fowl of the air. (This means that pit bulls are supposed to be afraid of you ... not the other way around.)

3. Man, beast, and fowl were provided with food from the herbs or fruit yielding trees (man was vegetarian, so there were no cheesesteaks ... *the horror!*).

4. A command not to eat of the tree of the knowledge of good and evil. The punishment for violating God's command not to eat of this tree was death. This was the one thing God commanded man strongly not to do. It wasn't an option although man has free will. If he ate, he would die. So man had a choice ... even though he was under the command not to do this. He could live life under the grace of God who gave man all the good things in life, or he could eat of the tree. He could continue to have fellowship with God, enjoy His provision of food, companionship, and dominance over all life that God created, or he could die. Does man choose to be obedient, or does he choose death?

The above covenant points are found in Genesis 1:28-30 and Genesis 2:16-17.

So, all forms of life, even the beasts of the field, were in obedience to Adam. God completed His creation in six days, and on the seventh day He rested from His labor, and sanctified that day as a day of rest unto Himself. This day of rest, which will become known as the Sabbath, is an observance that will become important.

What do you think Satan was doing all this time? Well, he sat around watching and listening. I don't think he was happy with what he was seeing. We'll get to that in a minute.

In Genesis 2:18-25, God created Eve from the rib of Adam as a companion and helper. It was a simple job—just help Adam run stuff. Nothing complicated. Provide companionship, help tend to the Garden of Eden, manage the animals, and perhaps a few other little things. But by inference, we know Adam told Eve of God's command not to eat from the forbidden tree. How do we know this? Because Eve, when confronted by Satan in the Garden, recites the commands God told Adam—well, sort of. But, let's not jump the gun here. The point is we know that Eve knew what God said about eating from that tree. Now, the trouble starts.

Enter Satan. I have a minister friend who believes Satan's approach to get to Eve was subtle, just as Genesis 3:1 tells us. He believes Satan would, just occasionally, whisper something like "look at that tree" (of knowledge of good and evil) in Eve's ear and then go on about his business. Every now and then, he would come back and do it again. He might have added more enticing words about the fruit on the tree—maybe he pointed out how luscious and delectable it was—but he kept at it. Now, the Bible doesn't say Satan did this, but I tend to believe that's exactly what he did. I can see that happening.

When we are tempted to sin, it usually comes after the thing desired, or lust, churns in our hearts and minds (James 1:15), and I think that's what happened here with Eve. She thought on it and thought on it, and finally, after all this churning, she was confronted directly by Satan, who provided that extra push over the edge. He tempted her to eat of the tree with multiple lies (Genesis 3:1, 4 and 5), which would put her in direct violation of God's expressed command. By the way, Satan's lies also demonstrated that he, too, was in the Garden of Eden when God gave the commands to

Adam. But anyway, how would Eve respond? Not well! Now, here's why I said "sort of" a moment ago. In her response to Satan, Eve watered down what God said. God's command to not eat of the tree was unambiguous ... don't do it! And, God was equally clear about the consequence when He said "thou shalt surely die" (Genesis 2:17). In Eve's recitation to Satan however, she said "lest ye die" (Genesis 3:3), as if there was a possibility that death may not occur, rather than stating the fact that it would certainly occur. Hmm ... sounds like someone wasn't really paying attention. Satan then replied to Eve with the lie that she would not die (Genesis 3:4). His lie and rationale, as if that made sense, was that if she were to eat of the tree, then she would be as gods, knowing good and evil (Genesis 3:5). That really must have gotten Eve to thinking about it even more. Sometimes we rationalize our way into sin—to do what it is we really want to do. Deep down, we know it's wrong, but it's what we really want. Be honest ... you ever do that? We know its sin, but we sort of talk our way into it through some back door and backward mental process. Here's the comparison. That's like eating chocolate cake for breakfast all the time because the ingredients include eggs and milk, which are supposed to be good for you. That's just crazy ... and unhealthful! So it is when we rationalize sin.

At this critical point, a few things occur. First, Eve forgets about God. Her eyes and her attention were focused on the wrong thing ... the fruit of the tree. That's all she thought about. Thoughts of God and Adam were waaayyy in the background, if at all. Instead of backing away from what she knew was forbidden, she stood her ground. She just kept on eye-balling that tree. Anytime and every time we focus on sin, it's easier to sin. What are we supposed to do to combat this? I recommend you step back (to physically create distance between you and the temptation, if possible), think God first, say a prayer, take a deep breath, and walk away.

Second, she was drawn in by her own lust. The thought of being "as gods" (pride), must have resonated with Eve. Pride and lust, both for food and its appeal, worked against her because at the end of the day Satan got Eve to do his bidding. Listening to Satan will make that an easy thing to do. Going back to Isaiah 14, this is just what Satan wanted—to be as God and be recognized as a god, meaning he would be obeyed.

Third, she ignored God's command to not eat of the tree. Eve made the decision to eat from the tree apart from the consequences. They did not factor into her thinking. It was a decision based on emotion, not truth! She had already compromised what God said about the consequences, so she was on what we call a "slippery slope". Once you head down that path, all you do is pick up the speed you need to do it again.

Eve reasoned that having the fruit from this tree would:

1. Satisfy her physical appetite. I can't imagine Eve was so hungry she couldn't wait to eat from another tree, and had to eat from this tree. But that's what temptation and sin does. It makes the perceived need immediate.

2. Bring pleasure to her. It was pleasing to the eye. How many of us have said "Man! That food looks good", even when we weren't hungry? I know what that's like. Put a freshly roasted Thanksgiving turkey, or hot apple pie and ice cream in front of me and I'm drooling ... hungry or not.

3. Make her wise, meaning it appealed to her pride, which was Satan's angle. The thought of being "as gods", knowing good and evil might have a lot of appeal to a lot of people.

Eve listened to Satan and followed his lead.

Here is another lesson for us all. Whereas God merits obedience based on His goodness and mercy, Satan gets obedience from deception and seduction. What else can this mean? Satan is attuned to what God wants us to do, and he will seize every opportunity to try to get us to do something different—however slight that difference might be. You must know by now that partial obedience is not obedience. It is disobedience. When we take our focus off God and what He wants, and are drawn by our own lusts for the things we desire (flesh, eye, pride), we lose!

So Eve ate the fruit from the forbidden tree, and then gave it to Adam who also ate it! The fact that Adam ate the fruit is even more confounding to me, and perhaps many others as well, than what Eve did. Why? Because Adam was not tempted to eat from the tree as Eve was (1 Timothy 2:14).

She gave him the fruit, and he ate it. Why? I don't know! I haven't a clue. Did he do it to keep the peace, or to get excused from his "honey do" list? You know ... like when she says "honey, do this", or "honey, do that". Get it? (Is this where that all began? Hmm, I wonder...)

Before we jump all over Adam and Eve and claim that we would not have violated God's direct command, let's pause for a moment. Gather your thoughts about you and your sin. Think about all the temptations and occasions to sin that you have faced in your own life, and reflect on how you avoided committing *every single one* of them. Does that change your perspective? Thinking twice about that now, huh? I know what your come-back will be. Is it something like, "in the Garden, God told them directly, and if God spoke directly to you, you would have obeyed"? And, "they didn't have the sinful nature that we do"? And, "if it wasn't for them, I wouldn't have this sinful nature"! Ok ... you did get your sinful nature from them. True, God did speak to them directly. But you know what is also true? Unlike Adam and Eve, we have much, much more of God's Word ... we have The Bible to tell us the whole story ... to tell us what God wants! AND, we have His Holy Spirit to guide us. We have much more light. Yet despite all of that, we still sin. Anybody still want to protest? It's all right. Don't feel embarrassed. You're not alone. Let me remind you what the Bible says in Romans 3:23:

"For all have sinned, and come short of the glory of God."

Adam and Eve's transgression plunged mankind into sin, which was passed down to you, me, and all of mankind to this day. The punishment for this sin brought about several very important consequences and promises, set forth in Genesis 3:14-19:

1. Satan (the serpent) was cursed above every beast of the field. It shall eat of the dust all the days of its life as a testimony to the fall of mankind and his participation in that fall. This is a perpetual curse.

2. Still speaking to the serpent, God says, in **His initial landmark prophetic statement**, that He will create enmity, or conflict,

between the serpent and the woman that will be manifested through the seed of the serpent and the seed of the woman (not the man!). The seed of the woman would crush the head of the seed of the serpent, who in turn would bruise the heel of the seed of the woman. This is the first prophecy of Christ. The seeds will be in conflict; they will engage in battle from this point forward, and continue to do so until the fulfillment of God's plan. Jesus Christ is the realization of the seed of the woman, being born by virgin birth through Mary (without the involvement of a man). God's promise to crush the head of the serpent was realized through Jesus' death on the cross, and resurrection (to which we should all say *Praise the Lord!*).

This prophecy cannot be overemphasized because it is upon this prophecy that God established what it is He would do with regard to man's redemption going forward ... all the way through until the end time. At the time of Adam, this was obviously a future event because no seeds or offspring had been born yet, and the verse tells us the battle would be between the seeds. It is also obvious that it is spiritual warfare between the serpent, who represents Satan (a spiritual being), and man through the woman. It is upon this prophecy that God would reveal more of his redemptive plan, and how it would be achieved as history unfolds. The Bible explains it all!

3. To the woman, God promised pain in childbirth. I think all mothers can attest to the truth of this promise. Yep, ladies, this is what happens when you don't listen. Also, her relationship with her husband was and is affected perpetually. God gave him, the man, rule over her. Now, ladies, don't get mad at me. *God* said this in Genesis 3:16, not me! And brothers, don't stick out your chests because God ... not you ... made this happen.

4. Up to this point, it was summertime and the living was easy for good ol' Adam. God told him that since you listened to your wife instead of Me, no more easy life! Before the disobedience, man ate the fruit of the ground that was freely yielded. God told

Adam that henceforth he would work hard—by the sweat of his brow (toil!) for food all the days of his life. No longer would the ground easily yield its fruit for his consumption.

5. Mankind suffered physical death. God said that man would return to the earth from which he was taken.

Looking forward, God laid the groundwork for how He would deal with disobedience and sin. Disobedience would be punished—just as the parties involved in the fall of man were punished. Sin would be judged and require payment. That payment would involve a sacrifice and the shedding of blood. In the case of Adam and Eve, an animal was sacrificed and blood was shed to provide clothing made from its hide to cover the nakedness of Adam and Eve. This would become the basis of the sacrificial system going forward. In an act of mercy, God expelled Adam and Eve from the Garden to prevent them from eating of the Tree of Life and remaining in a sinful state forever. To fortify this command, God placed armed angels (cherubim) to protect the way to the Tree of Life (Genesis 3:24) so Adam and Eve couldn't sneak back in and eat from that tree too. I guess they couldn't be trusted. Just kidding about that ... but God did place armed cherubim to protect the Tree of Life.

So, it's clear. In God's landmark prophetic statement, He implemented a course of action, or plan, to permanently defeat Satan through the conflict between the seed of the woman and the seed of the serpent, and deal with the payment of sin through a sacrifice—a life for a life.

One of the interesting things about the Bible is how God reveals, or unfolds, His plans as time goes on. Bible scholars refer to this as the *process of revelation*. As we read through the Bible, we come to understand, in more and more detail, how God plans to accomplish His will. In prophesizing the conflict of the seeds, for example, there was no mention of Christ, Israel, the Gentiles, or any other factors that would become a part of God's plan to redeem man, and ultimately defeat Satan. As we read more, however, we don't just stumble upon these things. God reveals more of His plan. This process of revelation continued through the New Testament in the writings of Paul and some of the other apostles.

The good news is that God promises a way of salvation to those who wish to follow Him on His terms. God does not change. ***"I am the Lord, I change not"*** (Malachi 3:6). He works His will as He always has. The fall of man gives rise to a principle that you may as well get used to: *Obedience promises fellowship; disobedience promises punishment.* Just as Satan rebelled in heaven and was punished, so man was disobedient on earth, and was punished. Both suffered as a consequence of their disobedience. Satan, however, sinned on his own accord, for there was no temptation in heaven. There was no one to save him from his sin. Man, on the other hand, was lured and tempted to sin by the rebellious Satan. Before the fall, man lived in innocence. But through God's grace, man was given another chance through the seed of the woman, who became Jesus Christ. And God still gets the glory!

Let the Battle Begin

Let's recap. In the previous sections, we learned that Satan was expelled from heaven, and took a third of the angels (now demons) with Him to earth. Because of their presence, earth became a wasteland ... it was dark and void. But God cleaned it up, turned on the lights, created the beasts of the field, the fowl of the air, the fish of the seas, and then He created man (and woman). God gave man dominion over everything He created ... with one proviso. Don't eat of the Tree of the Knowledge of Good and Evil. If you eat from it, you die. Satan's temptation led to man's violation of God's command not to eat from the tree, and thus sin and death entered the world. Sin and death meant eternal separation from God. What's even worse, the punishment for the sin of Adam and Eve wasn't limited to them. It has been passed on through the ages. All of mankind, through all generations, are sinners (see Romans 5, with emphasis in verse 12). However, God graciously implemented His plan for the redemption of mankind from his sinful state—a plan that will be manifested through conflict (enmity) between the seeds. In one corner, we have the seed of the serpent (Satan), and in the opposite corner, we have the seed of the woman. The seeds will duel it out throughout mankind's future. The action started almost immediately.

Satan tried to thwart God's plan by controlling the seeds. His first act was enticing Cain to kill his brother Abel (see Genesis 4:8). How do we know this about Cain? 1 John 3:12 tells us:

> "...Cain, who was of that wicked one, and slew his brother. And wherefore slew he him? Because his own works were evil, and his brother's righteous."

"That wicked one" is a reference to Satan. So Cain was clearly under his influence when he murdered Abel, who was described as righteous. With this move, Satan took the first step in his campaign to eliminate the seed of the woman and secure an advantage in this conflict. That would not be his last attempt.

In John 8:44, Christ says:

> "*...he was a murderer from the beginning, and abode not in the truth...*"

Christ, in responding to the Jewish leaders, called Satan a murderer from way back, referring to Cain's slaying of his brother, Abel. This verse is just a portion of a larger conversation between Christ and the Jews when Christ called Satan their father, an obvious spiritual reference connecting Cain to the Jewish leaders of His day.

Satan, and those under his control, would make other attempts to destroy the seed of the woman, including:

- The spread of wickedness among men through defilement of "the daughters of men" (Genesis 6:2), which we will explore fully in the next section.
- The attempts of Pharaoh of Egypt to exterminate all newborn male Hebrew children in Exodus 1.
- King Herod's murder of all male children two years of age and under in Bethlehem in an attempt to kill the promised Messiah (Matthew 2:16).
- In the last days, Satan will try again as found in Revelation 12. Satan will come against Israel after he is confined to earth.

In the latter half of Genesis 4 through Genesis 5, an interesting dichotomy is revealed. After Cain murders Abel, God declares him a vagabond and fugitive. Cain, along with his wife (Adam and Eve had daughters as well—see Genesis 5:4), in another act of defiance against the Lord, established a home in a place called Enoch, a city named after his first-born son. Adam and Eve, meanwhile, continued to have children, including Seth. God provided Seth as a replacement for the righteous Abel, as Eve proclaimed in Genesis 4:25. The offspring of these seeds take very different paths with respect to acknowledging God. The genealogy of each seed reveals this:

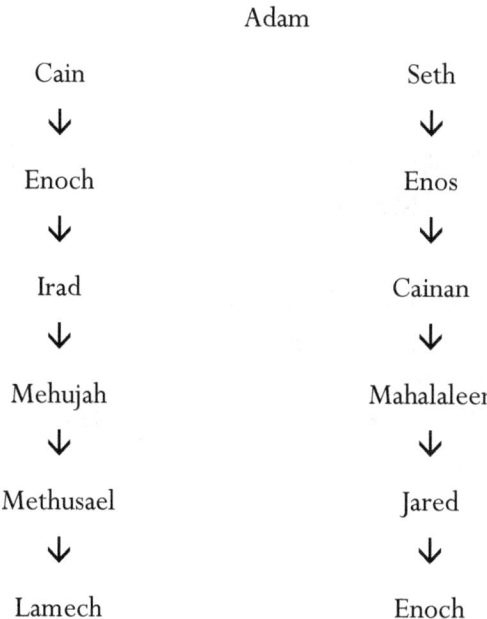

The interesting thing about these seeds is how they chose to live their lives. Lamech, the sixth seed in the line of Cain, had two wives, breaking from God's commandment in Genesis 2:24:

> *"Therefore shall a man leave his father and mother, and shall cleave unto his wife: and they shall be one flesh."*

Lamech, like his great-great-great-grandfather Cain, also slays one of his brethren, declaring in Genesis 4: 23-24:

> *"...Hear my voice; ye wives of Lamech, harken unto my speech: for I have slain a man to my wounding, and a young man to my hurt. If Cain shall be avenged sevenfold, truly Lamech seventy and seven fold."*

They say "like father, like son". Although a few generations removed, Lamech followed after his great, great, great grandfather, Cain. The seed of Satan clearly dominated Cain and his descendants.

Meanwhile, Seth and his descendants clearly followed the voice of God. While Cain's descendant Lamech was slaying his brethren, the sixth seed in the line of Seth was Enoch, who walked so closely with God that God translated (or took) him for a yet undisclosed purpose. In the days of Enos, one of Seth's seeds, men began to call upon the name of the Lord (Genesis 4:26).

The Bible does not provide more information about Cain's descendants following Lamech, but does provide more information about Seth's descendants. Further down the line, Seth's descendants include another man named Lamech, but this Lamech was the father of a man named Noah, who happened to find favor in God's eyes and built a pretty big boat called the ark. Between the seed of the serpent and seed of the woman, it's pretty clear whose seed he followed.

Water, Water Everywhere

Though there are several interpretations of what happened next, the result is not subject to debate. But first, let's review what happened in the passages covering Genesis 6:1-5.

Genesis 6:1-2: tells us:

> *"And it came to pass, when men began to multiply on the face of the earth, and daughters were born unto them, That the sons of God saw the daughters of men that they were fair; and they took them wives of all which they chose."*

What the Bible means when it says these women ("daughters of men") were fair is this, to put it succinctly—there were a lot of good-looking women back in those days! They were beautiful! They were drop-dead gorgeous! They didn't have to get up early in the morning, pull the rollers out of their hair, and rush to put on make-up before anybody saw them ... if you know what I mean. They were "hot" in current day terminology.

How hot were they? They were soooo hot that ... oh, wait. Excuse me. Ok ... I am exaggerating the case a little bit. Ladies, please don't be offended. Smile, please! But apparently there were a lot of good-looking women out there. So much so that these "sons of God" wanted as many as they could get their hands on. But here's the rub. Guess who these "sons of God" were?

The "sons of God" are interpreted as angels. The book of Job uses this term in reference to the angels who presented themselves to God as found in Job 1:6 and 2:1. There are some scholars who do not believe that the "sons of God" were angels, but rather ordinary men. The justification for that belief can be quite detailed, so we will not discuss it here. Likewise, many, if not most, do believe these "sons of God" were angels based on the reference in the book of Job.

There are a couple of reasons, the Job reference notwithstanding, I believe that the "sons of God" are angels. First, the wording "sons of God" and "daughters of men" is compelling to me. It seems to me that the Bible is making a distinction between the progenitors of the two different offspring. The sons are of God, the daughters are of men. It is not unreasonable to believe, then, that the sons are angels. Also, this goes back to the conflict between the seeds. Satan's fallen angels infiltrated or possessed men who impregnated women, who then gave birth to offspring dominated by the fallen angels. Hence, Satan tried to control the seeds through birth. The evil that follows is a natural consequence.

The second reason for this interpretation is found in two separate, but related, passages in the Bible. These passages cite instances of angels (demons) who are bound, delivered, and cast into Hell until the final judgment. Just so you know, not all demons are bound, so there must exist particular reasons why these demons were bound. The first indication is found in 2 Peter 2. This chapter gives three examples of those who were condemned for their wickedness.

1. Those angels who are bound (verse 4), which is our focus here.
2. The world in the days of Noah (verse 5).
3. Sodom and Gomorrah (verse 6).

Many Bible scholars and students, including me, believe these reference points, written by Peter, are taken from Genesis. Clearly points 2 and 3 are from Genesis. Point 1, it is argued, is from Genesis 6, and begins to offer at least some common support for the argument that the "sons of God" were angels. Granted, Peter is stating simple facts: the condemned angels were bound; the world in the days of Noah was judged through the flood; and Sodom and Gomorrah was judged and went up in smoke. Condemnation is the commonality among the three instances. Each subject was condemned for an atrocity; a sin so heinous God would not let it go unpunished in an immediate sense. But Jude, in the New Testament, will add something to this interpretation. Peter and Jude provide a common frame of reference from an historical perspective. But let's move on to the reason *why*.

The second related instance is found in Jude 6, which gives the reason these fallen angels were bound and reserved for judgment. The reason given is these fallen angels left their first estate, which has been interpreted to mean they engaged in sexual immorality with women. This fits the context of those stories in Genesis. How so? Jude makes the comparison for us. Jude 7 mentions Sodom and Gomorrah (just like Peter did), and then specifically cites "fornication" and "strange flesh" as their downfall. Strange flesh is intended to covey the idea of a different kind of flesh; something that is unlike yourself. For example, God condemns sex with animals in Exodus 22:19 and Leviticus 20:15-16. These verses condemn those who commit such acts to death ... even the abused animal. So this type of perversion required an immediate sentence of death. Jude uses the comparative words "even as" and "in like manner" in verse 7 to explain the similarity of acts these fallen angels committed to those acts in Sodom and Gomorrah. So "even as" Sodom and Gomorrah committed such heinous acts, "in like manner" so too did these angels commit acts of fornication with strange flesh. Any man or woman who committed bestiality was sentenced to death. Likewise, angels who committed like offenses were sentenced and bound in everlasting chains under darkness. They don't get to run around unpunished. Thus, the common ground and consistency of both 2 Peter and Jude would seem to support the interpretation that these demons engaged in forbidden sexual relations with women in the days of Noah, and are the "sons of God" referred to in Genesis 6:2.

The Bible supports the concept that Satan and his fallen angels can be in control of, or at least certainly influence, man. Luke 22:3 and John 13:27 tell us Satan entered Judas, which led to his betrayal of Christ. In Matthew 8:16, the Bible records that many who were possessed by demons were brought to Jesus, who cast out the spirits with His Word. There are many other accounts of demons being cast out of individuals, so the possession of men in order to commit such acts is plausible.

Further, the idea that demons can control the affairs of men, in a corporate sense, is also not unique. Daniel 10:13 discusses the control of *a kingdom* by an angel (the prince of the kingdom of Persia). At the time, Daniel was still in Babylon and distressed about the nation Israel. In response to his prayer, God sent an angel to Daniel to inform him of the future of Israel. This angel (presumably Gabriel), however, was hindered from delivering God's message by the prince of the kingdom of Persia. This prince of Persia was a demon. God then sent Michael, whom the Bible describes as one of the chief princes, to the rescue. This allowed the messenger to get through and deliver the message to Daniel. So the idea that Satan and his demons are involved in man's actions and the affairs of men is certain.

Returning to Genesis 6, the point of the passage (Genesis 6:1-5) is really not whether the seeds are controlled through demonic possession or not. The point, as stated in Genesis 6:5, is to tell us that mankind's wickedness was great:

> *"And God saw that the wickedness of man was great in the earth, and that every imagination of the thoughts of his heart was only evil continually."*

Wickedness and thoughts of evil ran rampant. All of man's thoughts were evil. This is a direct result of the "sons of God" and the "daughters of men". So this verse is quite an indictment against man. As a consequence, God passed judgment, as stated in Genesis 6:7, which reads:

> *"...I will destroy man whom I have created from the face of the earth; both man, and beast, and the creeping thing, and the fowls of the air..."*

God told Noah to build an ark (Genesis 6:14) and gave him the specific dimensions. The ark was to carry Noah's family and two of every kind of living creature, male and female, and food for all. In Genesis 7:4, God told Noah that He would cause it to rain forty days and forty nights. Prior to this time, it had never rained upon the earth. The earth was watered from the mist of the ground (Genesis 2:6). Further, God said He would establish His covenant with Noah (more on that later). Noah then built the ark, God shut them in, and then executed His judgment through the flood.

Before we go on, there are a few lessons here for us all, three of which I want to mention here. First, it took Noah 120 years to build this ark. There is no mention of God speaking to Noah during that time. What's the point? The point is, when God tells us to do something we need to accomplish it; do what He told us to do. When, as an act of faith, we do what we are told to do, only then we can expect to hear from God ... not before! You might want to ask Jonah about that when you see him in heaven. When he was finished building the ark, Noah heard from God (Genesis 7:1):

> *"And the Lord said unto Noah, Come thou and all thy house into the ark; for thee have I seen righteous before me in this generation."*

Second, because Noah obeyed, demonstrating his faith, God credited him as righteous. This is more than a mere compliment. This is a state of "rightness" before the Lord. It is by this "rightness" (or righteousness) that we are pleasing to and worthy of fellowship with God. Faith in God compels us to obey His commands. Without faith, we fail to act and thus fail to please God. Noah had no such failing. He believed and acted because God commanded ... and thus he was deemed righteous.

Third, God did not destroy the righteous with the wicked. Noah was a great example of this. Also read Ezekiel 9. This chapter details God's protection of the righteous when the wicked are about to be slain. This is a recurring theme throughout the Bible. This will be evident as we continue reading.

So, to continue, God executed His judgment. It rained, and rained, and rained! The earth was flooded, and every living creature upon the face of the earth at that time died. Only Noah, his family, and the creatures living aboard the ark survived. It finally stopped raining, the waters subsided, and the ark came to rest upon the mountains of Ararat (Genesis 8:4).

After disembarking from the ark, Noah built an altar to sacrifice to the Lord, and the Lord was so pleased with the sacrifice that He vowed never to curse the ground again for man's sake, and acknowledged that man was evil from his youth (Genesis 8:21). Even so, God promised never again to destroy every living thing as He had done. God also promised that the seasons would continue (Genesis 8:22).

Let's discuss the covenant mentioned earlier. In what introduced the **Noahic Covenant**, God reissued to Noah and his sons an old command (Genesis 9:1):

> *"And God blessed Noah and his sons, and said unto them, Be fruitful and multiply, and replenish the earth."*

This is what God said to Adam in Genesis 1:28, remember? God also instituted new commands. In Genesis 9:3, God told man that all living things were now food for him, including meat, which was not a part of man's diet prior to the Flood.

> *"Every moving thing that liveth shall be meat for you…"*

God also instituted a system of capital punishment that required the life of a man who took the life of another man (verse 6).

> *"Whoso sheddeth man's blood, by man shall his blood be shed; for in the image of God made he man."*

God was sanctifying the life of man in this commandment because man was made in the image of God! It was not meant to be a deterrent as some would say. It was intended as a punishment. It may deter some people to know that if you take a life, then your life would be taken. But its purpose was to let us know *God says* life is sacred, and is not to be taken away just because we feel like it. To keep this simple, the idea is that no one should commit murder. This is different from taking life in a war, for example, or defending your life or the life of your family members.

To visually and perpetually demonstrate His commitment to this new covenant, God said in Genesis 9:12-13:

> "...This is the token of the covenant which I make between me and you and every living creature that is with you, for perpetual generations: I do set my bow in the cloud, and it shall be for a token of a covenant between me and the earth."

Whenever we see a rainbow, we are reminded about God's promise never to destroy the earth by flood again.

Down the Hatch

Something kinda significant happened after the flood that must be mentioned here because it included a prophetic statement made by Noah in Genesis 9.

After the flood, Noah planted a vineyard ... you know ... the kind that grows grapes used to make wine. Over the course of time, Noah made wine, imbibed a bit too much, got drunk and fell asleep naked and uncovered (Genesis 9:21). Noah's youngest son, Ham, saw his father naked, which was a big no-no. He then told Japheth and Shem, his two older brothers, what he saw (Genesis 9:22). Japheth and Shem walked backward into their father's tent with a blanket, and covered Noah's nakedness (Genesis 9:23).

The significance of this is that Noah, who knew what Ham had done, pronounced a curse on Ham's descendants, who would become the Canaanites. They would become servants to their brothers, as found in Genesis 9:25-26:

> "And he said, Cursed be Canaan; a servant of servants shall he be unto his brethren. And he said, Blessed be the Lord God of Shem; and Canaan shall be his servant."

Here's the deal. Prophetically, Ham's descendants, the Canaanites would dwell in what we now know was the Promise Land. Shem's descendants would include a fairly prominently known guy by the name of Abraham. We will discuss him in much greater detail in a moment. The descendants of Japheth and Shem will dwell securely with one another, but Ham's descendants, the Canaanites, shall serve them both.

It is also worth mentioning that Ham's descendants included a guy who was a bit notorious. That guy was named Nimrod, who descended from Ham's son Cush. Nimrod established a kingdom in a place called Babel (Genesis 10:10). You ask why is that noteworthy? Check out what's next.

Can't We Do Anything Right?

> *"And the whole earth was of one language, and of one speech."*

This verse is found in Genesis 11:1 and told us all of mankind spoke the same language at one time. This makes sense since all of mankind after the flood descended from Noah, his sons, and their wives. Have you ever wondered how people came to speak different languages? Well, it was the result of a judgment, and here it is!

God's plan continued to unfold at the Tower of Babel. In defiance of God's command to replenish the earth, mankind sought to control his own destiny, without God, and built a tower to reach heaven (Genesis 11:4). Why did man do this? The same verse gives us the answer:

> *"...let us make us a name, lest we be scattered abroad upon the face of the whole earth."*

I find this verse particularly interesting for no other reason than it demonstrated that man knew of God's command to spread out. But apparently man liked where he was just fine. They didn't want to be scattered abroad. That's what they said in the verse. However, God said replenish the earth. When God speaks, His will is accomplished, no matter our preferences, how we might feel at the moment, what rights we think we have, what we're doing at the time, where we may or may not be, whether it's too hot or too cold, what's on TV, the dog ate my homework, or whatever. No excuse will work. God's will wins out.

God responded to this act of hubris on the part of man.

Genesis 11:6-9:

> *"And the Lord said, Behold, the people is one, and they have all one language; and this they begin to do: and now nothing will be restrained from them, which they have imagined to do. Go to, let us go down, and there confound their language, that they may not understand one another's speech. So the Lord scattered them abroad from thence upon the face of all the earth: and they left off to build the city. Therefore is the name of it called Babel; because the Lord did there confound the language of all the earth: and from thence did the Lord scatter them abroad upon the face of all the earth."*

The Trinity acted in unison as evidenced by the use of the words "let us" in the verse, which is similar to the language used in Genesis 1:26 when God created man. Here, God intervened, scattered mankind throughout the earth, and introduced new languages because of man's disobedience. Man unified and worked together in defiance of God, but instead incurred judgment, expressed when God confounded their languages and scattered man across the earth. Prophetically, the time for a one world government was not to occur back then, but much later in the latter days.

As was mentioned before, it's not about you; it's not about me. It's about God! It was about His program and what He wanted. What they didn't understand was God wanted good for us, even if they didn't see it. As His program unfurled and was revealed, we saw (or will see shortly if you don't know already) it was good for us! This is why faith is important. We are to act on faith, just as Noah had done. When God tells us to do something, we must act on what God said, even if we don't see the "end game" so to speak.

Personally, I think the story of the Tower of Babel is kinda funny. Have you ever tried to picture yourself observing one of these situations? Imagine the conversation. *God said, "Spread out and fill the earth." Man said, "No, we don't want to leave." God said, "I said move ... there's a plan." Man said, "No, we like it here just fine. We don't want to be scattered." God said, "For the last time, get moving and have babies!" Man said, "No, we even started building stuff. Can't you see this big ol' tower? We can make a lot of money off that thing!" God said, "Ok, I'll fix that."* Not only did God spread them out, but He changed their languages so they couldn't conspire to get back together. They probably didn't like that, but hey, what could they do about it? Not much! We just don't listen, do we? I hope you realize this is just my sense of humor kicking into overdrive. This last bit of conversation between God and man didn't actually happen.

But God's act of scattering the people and creating languages accomplished another purpose. It introduced *nationalism*, or the birth of nations. People of common languages and geographies would form local communities, cities, kingdoms, and nations. What this would lead to is a system of government by man. God ordained man to rule the earth, and in the course of his rule God gave man the authority to govern his affairs with the knowledge that God sanctified life (Genesis 9:6). Through this edict, nations were born. True to form, man messed that up too, but that topic is for another time.

The Chosen Ones

God has an interesting way of manifesting His plans. Sometimes He simply tells us what He's going to do, and sometimes He doesn't. Here is a case where His plans were not readily apparent. While the various nations of people in their various geographic locations around the world did their thing, God implemented the next step of His plan for man's redemption.

There was a man by the name of Abram who lived in a place known as Ur of the Chaldees. When Abram was 75 years of age, God called him to go out from his country, his home, and his father's house unto a *land* that God would show him. Abram obeyed, by faith, and removed himself from Ur as instructed. God made certain promises to Abram in Genesis 12:1-3 and 12:6-7, specifically:

Genesis 12:1-3:

> *"Now the Lord had said unto Abram, Get thee out of thy country, and from thy kindred, and from thy father's house, unto a land that I will shew thee. And I will make of thee a great nation, and I will bless thee, and make thy name great; and thou shalt be a blessing: And I will bless them that bless thee, and curse him that curseth thee: and in thee shall all families of the earth be blessed."*

Genesis 12: 6-7:

> *"And Abram passed through the land unto the place of Sichem, unto the plain of Moreh. And the Canaanite was then in the land. And the Lord*

appeared unto Abram, and said, Unto thy seed will I give this land..."

These promises of God are known as the **Abrahamic Covenant**. Simply stated, under this covenant, God promised Abram:

1. A great name and blessing (wealth)
2. The promise of a great nation coming from him (Abram's seed)
3. A promise to bless those who blessed him, and to curse those who cursed him
4. Through him all nations would be blessed
5. The promise of land to his seed

Upon these promises, God continued His plan for the redemption and blessing of all mankind to this day and beyond. Abram was to experience individual blessings ... a great name, wealth, and be the father of a great nation. And because of him, the world was to experience a corporate blessing.

These passages are very important because they bring into focus two important prophetic elements:

1. The yet to be named *people of Israel*. God would fulfill His promise to make a great nation, which became Israel. A little later in this book, we will explore the birth of this nation. Few would argue that Abram was blessed because he became very wealthy in his time. Throughout the Bible, Abraham, as his name would become, is revered as a father of faith to Christians everywhere, not to mention his standing within the Jewish community as the Father, or Patriarch, of the Hebrew people. However, of greater importance is the latter promise concerning the blessing of all the families of the earth. That promise was accomplished through the birth, death, and resurrection of Jesus Christ, who was descended from Abraham's lineage.

2. The Land of Promise.

    As Abram entered into the land of Canaan, God then added this promise to him in addition to the promises previously made in verse 7:

"...unto thy seed will I give this land."

God promised Abram the land of Canaan, which you may recall is where Ham's seed is located. These promises were repeated to Abram or Abraham in Genesis 13:14-17, 15:18, and 17:8. These repetitions make it sound as though God was pretty serious about this thing—and He was. But there was a problem. Abram wasn't married to Fertile Myrtle, who could have a bunch of kids. He was married to Sarai, who could not have a child (Genesis 11:30). Sarai was barren. This had become an issue of some importance to Abram, especially since God told him his seed will inherit the land, and their numbers would be too large to count (Genesis 13:16).

But, in Genesis 15 an interesting thing happened. God appeared to Abram in a vision (verse 1), and Abram once again mentioned being childless. God repeated His promise and told Abram that he would have so many descendants no man could number them. He used the stars in the sky as a reference for how many offspring Abram would have. Abram believed, and because he believed, the Lord imputed righteousness to him.

God then commanded Abram to prepare a sacrifice (verse 9). The manner and meaning behind the sacrifice represented a pivotal point related to the redemption of man, so pay attention. This particular Old Testament sacrifice required splitting the sacrificial animals (not the birds) in two, and laying each half opposite of one another. Normally, the two people entering into this covenant would walk between the two halves, thus binding them to the agreement. Also, because it was a blood sacrifice, it could not be broken. The dividing of the animal sacrifice symbolized what would happen to either party if they broke the agreement, so there existed an inherent motivation not to break the agreement. In other words, this wasn't the type of agreement one entered into unless you were deadly serious.

Following the preparation of the sacrifice, we are told in verse 12 that a deep sleep fell upon Abram, and he dreamt a horror regarding his yet to be born descendants. The dream revealed that his people were to be captives in a land that was not theirs, which of course was realized when the Israelites were made slaves in Egypt.

Of greater significance is what we read in Genesis 15: 17-18:

> *"And it came to pass, that, when the sun went down, and it was dark, behold a smoking furnace, and a burning lamp that passed between the two pieces. In the same day the Lord made a covenant with Abram, saying, Unto thy seed have I given this land..."*

The smoking furnace and burning lamp represented the presence of God or, more correctly, the glory or visible presence of God, called the "Shekinah Glory", passing through the animal sacrifice. What is unique about this is God passed through the halves of the sacrifice alone. He did not walk through with Abram. Abram was still in a deep sleep. **This means the covenant was God's to uphold, and was not dependent on Abram's participation or involvement. God was saying, in effect, no matter what your seed does, or does not do, I am going to make this happen.** What do I mean by "this"? The fulfillment of the promises God made to Abram for a seed, a nation, a blessing to all nations of the earth, and the giving of the land. God would make all that happen on His own! Again, it was a blood covenant, which meant it was unconditional.

Moving on, we see that Abram and Sarai were still having problems conceiving a child. You can't be the father of a great nation without first having a child, can you? At the time of God's first promise to Abram, he was 75 years old and Sarai was 65. Abram was now 85 or 86 years old and not getting any younger. Here we are ten years or so later, and no offspring, much less a son. Like most people, Abram and Sarai got tired of waiting, and wanted to take matters into their own hands—and they did so with dreadful results. In their impatience and wanting to "help God out", Abram was given Hagar, Sarai's Egyptian handmaid, and a son, Ishmael, was born out of this union, as reported in Genesis 16. Abram was now 86 years old (Genesis 16:16). Abram and Sarai foolishly thought this was the way to fulfill God's plan for Abram to have his seed. Well, it wasn't, as you'll see in a moment.

When Abram reached the age of 99, God spoke to him again in Genesis 17:5:

> *"Neither shall thy name any more be called Abram, but thy name shall be Abraham; for a father of many nations have I made thee."*

We are witnessing three things here:

1. God affirming His promise to Abram concerning his seed.

2. God's view from an eternity standpoint. Earlier we said time is relevant to man, but God sees all from a different perspective. What we call past, present, and future is before the all-knowing (omniscient) God at all times. God said a father of many nations have I *made* (past tense) thee. Therefore, in God's eyes, this was already done.

3. Abram (meaning "exalted father") undergoes a name change to Abraham, which means "Father of many nations or multitudes". Indeed, as the father of both Ishmael and Isaac, and the nations that would descend from both, Abraham is just that.

In verses 7-8, God repeated the covenant promise, but He added a little wrinkle in verses 10-11, as follows:

> *"This is my covenant, which ye shall keep, between me and you and thy seed after thee; Every man child among you shall be circumcised. And ye shall circumcise the flesh of your foreskin; and it shall be a token of the covenant betwixt me and you."*

This time, beginning in verse 10, God required Abraham, and all the males of his household, to be circumcised to demonstrate their commitment to the covenant. But let's be clear about this. This requirement was not between God and Abraham concerning the repeated promises made in Genesis 12, 15, and 17. God had already committed to fulfill those promises on His own. The act of circumcision is prospective on the part of Abraham and all the males of his household to demonstrate their commitment to the covenant. Any male could opt out of the covenant if he wanted to by simply not being circumcised (verse 14). Those who opted out would not, naturally, enjoy the benefits of the blessings under the covenant. Hence, the physical act of circumcision became an outward showing of a commitment to obey God, and distinguished them from all other males outside of the covenant.

God also told Abraham that his covenant would continue through the seed of his union with his wife, Sarah, as reported in Genesis 17:19:

> *"And God said, Sarah thy wife shall bear thee a son indeed; and thou shalt call his name Isaac: and I will establish my covenant with him for an everlasting covenant, and with his seed after him."*

In Genesis 17:20-21, to ease Abrahams's mind, God told him Ishmael, too, would be blessed, but the covenant would go through Isaac.

Jumping ahead a little bit, we find out Ishmael and Isaac had problems getting along, as recorded in Genesis 21. As a consequence, Hagar and Ishmael leave ... and their descendants haven't gotten along since. This bad blood between the two brothers sets in motion a struggle between the Arab nations, which arose out of Ishmael, and the Jewish nation, which arose out of Isaac. That struggle continues to this day. Need proof? Just pick up any newspaper and you'll find the Arab-Israeli conflict dominates the news coverage on a seemingly regular basis. The Arab nations' objective is the complete removal, some would say destruction, of Israel from the land both ethnic groups claim belongs to them. The news reports are replete with incident after incident, conflict after conflict, between these two nations. What's the lesson to be learned? *Don't try to "help God out".* The thought of "helping God out" should make you laugh. Do you really think there's something you can do that God can't make happen? Just be obedient and patient because God will perfect *His* plan in *His* time.

Returning to Genesis 17, we find God reiterated His promise to Abraham that he and Sarah would have a son. But first, God had to take care of this little problem called Sodom and Gomorrah. After that, Sarah got pregnant and Isaac was born (Genesis 21:1-3).

We should note Sarah's death is recorded in Genesis 23:2 and Abraham remarried in Genesis 25, and had six more children. These children, however, are not those through whom The Promise was fulfilled.

From Genesis 26:3-5, we know The Promise was affirmed through Isaac, not Ishmael, nor Abraham's children born to him in Genesis 25.

A Nation is Born

God's covenant continued with Isaac, as shown in Genesis 26:3-5. Prior to this chapter, Isaac married Rebekah (Genesis 25), and fathered twin sons, Esau and Jacob. These two boys also had trouble from jump street, which means *from the beginning* to those of you who are slightly slang-challenged. Specifically, in this case, it means *from the womb*. Rebekah noticed the struggle within her womb, and asked the Lord about it in Genesis 25:22. God responded in the next verse:

> *"And the Lord said unto her, Two nations are in thy womb, and two manner of people shall be separated from thy bowels; and the one people shall be stronger than the other people; and the elder shall serve the younger."*

Without going into a lot of detail, Esau was the firstborn (the elder) of the twins, and Jacob, the younger. Here's how their relationship played out.

- Esau sold his birth-right for food (Genesis 25:29-34). While both sons undoubtedly had knowledge of the blessing God promised to Abraham, and that it would pass through to his descendants, Esau didn't value it and traded it for a bowl of pottage (stew). That was like trading the number one draft pick in any professional sport for the worst player on an elementary school intra-mural team. Actually, it's much worse than that! Esau valued satisfying his physical hunger over the spiritual blessing from God. Jacob, on the other hand, valued this blessing, and sought to take it from his brother by withholding food.

- Jacob didn't stop there. With the help of his mother, Rebekah, Jacob tricked his father into bestowing the blessing of the first-born on him, although by birthright it was Esau's, as the oldest son (Genesis 27:1-4). This blessing entitled Jacob to the bulk of his father's wealth. As you might imagine, this did not go over well with Esau. After Esau discovered what Jacob and his mother had done to deprive him of his father blessings, Jacob's life was in danger (Genesis 27:41), and Rebekah knew it. To preserve his life from Esau, Jacob was sent to the land of Abraham (Haran) and while there find a wife. Isaac did not want Jacob to find a wife from among the people of the land where they presently dwelt, but rather from the people of his homeland. As a side note, Esau's descendants became the Edomites, who would become bitter enemies of Israel (who descended from Jacob). At the end of the day, the Edomites were judged by God, as recorded in the book of Obadiah. It's only one chapter, so I recommend you read it. I also recommend that you read Hebrews 12:15-17, which does not have very nice things to say about Esau.

On his way to Haran, Jacob experienced some pretty cool stuff from the Lord. In Genesis 28:10-15, Jacob had a dream. In this dream, he saw a ladder that extended from heaven to earth, from which angels ascended and descended. Above the ladder, God spoke to Jacob and blessed him with The Promise of Abraham and Isaac. This had a profound effect on Jacob, who memorialized his acknowledgement of God's promises and purpose in his life when he uttered these immortal words, found in Genesis 28:16:

"...Surely the Lord is in this place..."

Jacob anointed that place, built a memorial to the Lord God on it, made a vow to the Lord, and promised to tithe. This was a pivotal event in the life of Jacob. He abandoned the ways of his former life, and consecrated his life to the Lord God. He abandoned all of his scheming ways to provide for himself, like when he deceived his brother and his father, and thereafter relied on God to provide the protection and blessing he would need in the years to come.

Continuing on his way, Jacob traveled back to his grandfather Abraham's homeland and met his uncle, Laban, his mother's brother. While there, Jacob met and fell in love with Rachel, Laban's youngest daughter. Laban and Jacob agreed that he would work for Laban for seven years to marry Rachel (Genesis 29:18). Through some of Laban's own trickery, however, Jacob ended up marrying Leah, Laban's oldest daughter, with whom he had consummated the marriage vow thinking it was Rachel!

As you can imagine, Jacob was none too happy about being deceived in this way. We might conclude Jacob got what was coming to him. After all, he led a life of deception up to this point. Although he had since submitted to the Lord, he still received the just punishment of his past life. In Laban, Jacob met an older version of his old self. Jacob, who had deceived his father with the aid of his mother, was now deceived by his mother's brother. Jacob robbed his older brother of his father's blessing. Now the father of the one he loved, Rachel, deceived him by substituting the older sister in the stead of the younger sister. Hmm ... sounds like somebody got a payback, doesn't it?

When Jacob protested, Laban agreed to give him Rachel after the seven-day wedding period, on the condition that Jacob would agree to work for him for yet another seven years (Genesis 29:27-30). Jacob agreed, and after the seven days, Rachel was given to him as his wife. Through these marriages, and the servants given to both Leah and Rachel, Jacob had twelve sons and one daughter. The sons were the progenitors of the 12 Tribes of Israel, as follows:

Leah => Rueben, Simeon, Levi, Judah, Issachar, Zebulun, Dinah (daughter)

Zilpah (Leah's handmaid) => Gad, Asher

Rachel => Joseph, Benjamin

Bilhah (Rachel's handmaid) => Dan, Naphtali

Here's a point to remember. God has demonstrated a predictable way of achieving His will that centers on the things that are considered lesser in the eyes of man. In fact, the Bible tells us in 1 Corinthians 1:27-28:

> *"But God hath chosen the foolish things of the world to confound the wise; and God hath chosen the weak things of the world to confound the things which are mighty; And the base things of the world, and the things which are despised, hath God*

> *chosen, yea, and the things which are not, to bring to nought things that are:"*

What this means is all the "mighty" things man values, such as riches, stature, status, prominence, beauty, power, intelligence, wisdom and the like are countered by God's use of the opposite to accomplish His will. The case of Jacob's marriage fiasco is an example of that. Jacob clearly wanted Rachel (the greater thing). Why did he want Rachel? Simple ... the Bible describes her as "beautiful and well favored" (Genesis 29:17). In today's language, Rachel was hot! Leah (the lesser thing) was not. Leah was described as "tender eyed" ... whatever that means. I don't think that was intended to be a compliment, but whatever the intent behind Leah's "tender eyed" description, there was a clear contrast between the two sisters. Rachel was the more physically attractive of the two.

You know what that means, right? Honestly, you know how the brothers are when it comes to good-looking women. To borrow a phrase from the Olympics, we *go for the gold,* for the one that's "got it going on". If we don't get the gold, then we go for the silver; if not the silver, the bronze. The point is, the gold is going to get our attention first, and then (grudgingly) we work our way down. It is natural for both men and women (not all, but *most*), especially the young brothers and sisters, to go for what's attractive first, or we'll certainly look real hard! In time, though, after we grow up and mature a little bit, we'll focus on the quality of the person. Until that time, however, we're pretty basic and predictable.

Clearly, and thankfully, God doesn't work that way. Although Rachel was the more attractive, the blessing of The Promise would go through Leah, who was unwanted. God saw this (Genesis 29:31) and blessed her to have children first. Leah had hoped that having a child would result in Jacob falling in love with her (Genesis 29:32). Didn't happen! Then after having two more children, she hoped that he would at least become attached to her (Genesis 29:34). Still didn't happen! When she had her fourth child, she said:

Genesis 29:35

> *"...and she said, Now will I praise the Lord..."*

Leah gave birth to Judah, which means "let Him be praised". When we praise the Lord, good things happen. And something great will come out of Judah, as you'll see shortly. The world will be blessed because God used the lesser. Praise the Lord!

Left to their own (de)vices, mankind has, and will continue to select the greater, be it in the form of the beautiful, the strong, the rich, or anything related to that way of thinking in order to satisfy a need or solve a problem. Even today, man looks for answers to the world's problems from that perspective, and from that way of thinking. That approach will never provide a long-term solution, particularly to a spiritual problem. God gives us the reason why.

1 Corinthians 1:29 tells us:

"That no flesh should glory in his presence."

Said another way, man's approach to solving problems is self-reliant. It leaves out the Lord. If the world's problems could be solved by man's way of thinking, and I'm convinced they can't, man would certainly take all the credit and glory for himself. A great example of the way this is supposed to work is the story of Gideon, found in Judges 7. Gideon started out with an army of 33,000 men to fight the Midianites, but ended up victorious with only 300 men ... *because he obeyed the Lord*. And because Gideon obeyed, Israel defeated an enemy that forced them to hide and live in caves and dens for seven years. It is clear this victory came from the Lord. God was glorified, not man. It's a fascinating story, and I encourage you to read it.

Two things related to all of this come to mind. First, always remember that it was God who took a vow in Genesis 15. He would make this thing (The Promise of the Covenant) work by Himself, so that no one could boast. No one can achieve or earn redemption apart from the blessings of the Lord God. Man is completely reliant on Almighty God for redemption. We must look to Him first, and should do so in all things. We should *not* be driven by looks, works, money, status, or the appearance of external things. They mean nothing to God.

Second, God's will is accomplished by the use of the lesser things (as man would call them) in life, in this case Leah, to accomplish His purpose and receive the greater glory. This is a consistent theme throughout the Bible, so get used to that too! Examples include Joseph, a slave in Egypt; David, a young sheep herder; Daniel a captive in Babylon; Jesus born in a stable ... all these make clear God's pattern of using the lesser to accomplish His purposes.

Unless the above points are understood, man will always point to his use of the "greater things" as the reason for his good fortune, which is something God will not allow without punishment. You'll see an example of this when we read about king Nebuchadnezzar in the book of Daniel. If allowed to think that way, man is foolish enough to believe that he could work out his own redemption through his works, which we know cannot save us (Ephesians 2:8-9).

Let's go back to the story. So now Jacob was married to Leah and Rachel, and had children with both of them and with their bond-servants. (Don't try this at home, folks!) In Genesis 31, we read that Jacob and his family eventually headed back to his home. While on the way, God changed his name from Jacob (*heel-catcher*) to Israel (*strives with God*, or *God fights*; Genesis 32:28). As we discussed earlier, a name change denotes a change in character, and Jacob, now Israel, certainly changed in character from the man who left his father's home to the man he had now become.

Skipping ahead, Jacob eventually returned to the land that God promised would be his. You should know that on his way, Jacob made up with his brother, Esau (Genesis 33), even though Esau was misled concerning Jacob's destination. I guess old habits truly do die hard.

Jacob proceeded in life with his sons, daughter, bond-servants, and his entire household. Jacob, however, played favorites among his children. He favored Joseph more than his other sons (Genesis 37:3), and naturally his brothers didn't like that (Genesis 37:4). Joseph made it worse by telling his brothers of a dream he had in which the brothers bowed in obeisance to him. Not knowing when to shut up, Joseph then told them of another dream in which the sun, moon, and 11 stars made obeisance to him as well. At some point, jealousy ruled over Joseph's brothers, who, when the opportunity presented itself, sold Joseph into slavery (Genesis 37:28), to the Ishmaelites no less, and he ultimately ended up in Egypt.

To shorten the story, God blessed Joseph during his period of slavery. Joseph was given the gift to interpret the meaning of dreams. One dream he interpreted was Pharaoh's (Genesis 41). Pharaoh dreamt of seven big fat cows, and then seven skinny cows. But, the seven skinny cows ate up the big fat cows. Pharaoh woke up scratching his head, wondering what that was all about, but then went back to sleep. Then Pharaoh dreamt about seven healthy ears of corn from one corn stalk, followed by seven thin ears of corn, which ate up the seven healthy ears. You have to admit, cows eating cows was strange, but corn eating corn? That was really strange. Well, Pharaoh thought so too. He woke up troubled, and summoned the magicians to interpret the dream. Of course, they couldn't interpret the dream because the dream was from God. However, one of the beneficiaries of Joseph's gift remembered Joseph, and he was mentioned to Pharaoh. Pharaoh called Joseph and told him of the dream.

Joseph credits God first, so that everybody knew that it wasn't him. It is God who gave the dream, and God who gave the meaning of the dream. Joseph told Pharaoh that there would be seven years of abundance, followed by seven years of famine, and what Pharaoh must do to survive the famine. Because of this experience, Joseph was made second in command of Egypt.

When the famine hit the land, Joseph's brothers went to Egypt for corn and there they encountered Joseph, who eventually reconciled with his brothers after messing with them for a little while. Subsequently, Jacob and his entire household moved to Egypt.

Another important prophecy was revealed by Jacob after he took his family to Egypt, as we read in Genesis 49:10:

> *"The scepter shall not depart from Judah, nor a lawgiver from between his feet, until Shiloh come; and unto him shall the gathering of the people be."*

The scepter is emblematic of kingship. So the kingdom, as it relates to God's promise, is to come out of the line of Judah. Shiloh was a title of the Messiah to come. The general intent behind the meaning of Shiloh is *peace*, as in Prince of Peace (Isaiah 9:6). In short, what this verse means is the promise of the Messiah, who was to be King of Israel, would come through the seed of Judah. Jacob praised Judah in the verses that precede Genesis 49:10. Remember, Judah was born of Leah, the "lesser thing", the one who was unwanted!

We can now "connect the dots" to show that the prophecy in Genesis 3:15 (the seed of the woman) passed through to Noah, who descended from the line of Seth. Add to that the covenantal blessings mentioned to Abram in Genesis 12:3 (all families of the earth shall be blessed), passed to his son, Isaac (Genesis 17:19), and his grandson, Jacob (Genesis 28:13-14). Jacob would be renamed Israel, and his twelve sons would be the progenitors of the twelve tribes of Israel. Out of these tribes, the promise would be fulfilled through the line of Judah (Genesis 49:10). So the focus of determining how God's redemptive program and covenantal blessings would be realized is narrowed to the line of Judah.

Jacob (Israel) and his family remained as free people in Egypt until a new pharaoh, who did not know Joseph, rose to power in the land (Exodus 1:8-11). The house of Israel grew rapidly, and the new pharaoh became a little concerned about their growth rate. Out of fear, he decided to place them in bondage. This is the fulfillment of the prophecy revealed as the horror in Abram's dream (Genesis 15:13).

Many events occurred between the time Israel was held captive in Egypt and the next covenantal event took place. Without going into all the details, the nation of Israel was held captive in Egypt. God used Moses, miracles, and the death of the Egyptian firstborn males (Exodus 4-12) to redeem the children of Israel from Egyptian slavery (see Exodus 12:51). Once freed, God wanted to establish the nation of Israel as His chosen people for a special service—that being His representatives before the nations. *Two pivotal issues* would form the basis of the relationship between God and Israel. These two issues center on (1) a new covenantal agreement between God and people of Israel, and (2) the Promised Land.

The formation of the new covenantal agreement is found in Exodus 19:4-8:

> **"Ye have seen what I did unto the Egyptians, and how I bare you on eagles wings, and brought you**

> unto myself. Now therefore, if ye will obey my voice indeed, and keep my covenant, then ye shall be a peculiar treasure unto me above all people: for all the earth is mine: And ye shall be unto me a kingdom of priests, and an holy nation. These are the words which thou shalt speak unto the children of Israel. And Moses came and called for the elders of the people, and laid before their faces all these words which the Lord commanded him. And all the people answered together, and said, All that the Lord has spoken we will do. And Moses returned the words of the people unto the Lord."

The first thing we should note is God reminded the people of Israel what He did for them, that is, how He miraculously brought them out of slavery from Egypt. Then God set the scope of the new covenantal agreement; that is, what God wanted from Israel, and what God would provide. Israel was to obey the Lord in all that He said, and keep the covenant. For their obedience, Israel would be a peculiar treasure above all people. They would be a kingdom, a nation of priests. Of course, Israel would be insane not to agree to this after crying to God for deliverance (Exodus 3:7), and then witnessing the power of His deliverance.

The objective of this covenant was for Israel to be a peculiar people ... a nation of priests unto God. They were to be God's representatives before the Gentile nations of the world. Israel agreed, and was now beholden to keep this new covenant. This was far more than a simple handshake. It carried major blessings and major curses for the people of Israel. This new agreement came to be known as the *Mosaic Covenant*, and was the beginning of the Law, which was issued in Exodus 20-24. Further, this covenant was sealed by blood (Exodus 24:8), which meant it could not be canceled or voided. It does not void the Abrahamic Covenant, but rather was an addition to that covenant.

Notice the "if" and "then" in the above verses. That means the Mosaic Covenant was a conditional covenant—but not in the sense that it could be voided if either party failed to uphold their end of the agreement. What it did mean was if both parties kept up their end of the agreement, then there would be lots of benefits. But, if either party did not uphold its end of the agreement, then a "penalty clause", the curses, kicked in. Since we know God cannot break His Word, this meant it was up to Israel to uphold her end of the agreement. If the nation of Israel obeyed God, then His blessing of provisions and protection continued. If, however, Israel did not follow His commandments, then they would suffer the curses for their disobedience. A list of these blessings and curses can be found in Leviticus chapter 26, some of which we will mention.

The second issue was related to the Promised Land, the beginning of which is found in Leviticus 25:1-4:

> *"And the Lord spake unto Moses in mount Sinai, saying, Speak unto the children of Israel, and say unto them, When ye come into the land which I give you, then shall the land keep a sabbath unto the Lord. Six years thou shalt sow thy field, and six years thou shalt prune thy vineyard, and gather the fruit thereof; But in the seventh year shall be a sabbath of rest unto the land, a sabbath for the Lord; thou shalt neither sow thy field, nor prune thy vineyard."*

When the children of Israel entered the Promised Land, they were to observe a Sabbath of the land. They could cultivate the land and prune it for six years. They would enjoy the fruit of their labors for the six years, but in the seventh year they were to let the land rest as a Sabbath to the Lord. No pruning, no reaping, no harvesting, no anything. They could eat from whatever fell from the crops, but they could not cultivate the land in any way, or in any manner intended to produce more crops. Obedience demonstrated their faith that God would provide for their needs in the seventh year. As a part of the Mosaic Covenant, Israel had already vowed to keep the Sabbath day (see Exodus 31:12–17), so perhaps a Sabbath of the land would not have been a surprising concept to them.

Israel would be the beneficiary of many blessings, but only if they obeyed God in all that He told them to do. In Leviticus 26:1-12, God outlined the following blessings (excerpts) to the people of Israel *if* they followed Him and heeded His Word:

- Verse 4:

    "...I will give you rain in due season; the land shall yield her increase; the trees of the field shall yield her fruit."

- Verse 5:

    "...ye shall eat your bread to the full, and dwell in your land safely."

- Verse 6:

    "...I will give you peace; none shall make you afraid; I will rid evil beast out of the land."

- Verse 7:

    "...ye shall chase your enemies, and they shall fall before you by the sword."

- Verse 9:

    "...make you fruitful, and multiply you, and establish my covenant with you."

- Verse 11:

    "...I will set my tabernacle among you..."

- Verse 12:

    "...I will walk among you, and be your God, and ye shall be my people."

Not a bad life, huh? In fact, it was a pretty sweet deal. Indeed, the people of Israel were promised a full life if they heeded the Word of the Lord, and obeyed the covenant. They would get food in abundance, fertile land and trees. They would not have to worry about wild beasts that could kill their people and cattle, or about enemies who sought to harm them. They would enjoy a life filled with peace and safety.

On the other hand, if they did not listen to the Lord God, then they would suffer His punishments, as found in these excerpts from Leviticus 26:

- Verse 16:

    "...I will even appoint over you terror..."

- Verse 17:

  "...I will set my face against you, and ye shall be slain before your enemies..."

- Verse 18:

  "And if ye will not yet for all this hearken unto me, then I will punish you seven times more for your sins."

Yikes! Clearly, God intended the punishments to draw Israel back to Him. If they failed to listen, however, then the punishments would increase *seven* times.

- Verse 19:

  "...I will break the pride of your power..."

- Verse 20:

  "...your strength shall be spent in vain; your land shall not yield her increase; neither shall the trees of the land yield her fruits."

- Verse 21:

  "...I will bring seven times more plagues upon you according to your sins..."

Yikes! Yikes!

- Verse 22:

  "I will also send wild beast among you..."

- Verse 23-24:

  "And if ye will not be reformed by me by these things, but walk contrary unto me; Then I will walk contrary unto you, and will punish you yet seven times for your sins."

Yikes! Yikes! Yikes!

- Verse 25:

  "...I will bring a sword unto you; I will send the pestilence among you; ye shall be delivered unto the hands of the enemies..."

There's much more. I urge you to read the entire chapter (Leviticus 26) to understand how God planned to deal with Israel if they chose not to heed His Word. Every blessing would be taken away! So, going forward, the people of Israel knew and understood exactly what was required of them. There would be no surprises.

The lesson should be clear. God took His covenantal relationship with Israel very, very seriously. And God takes His relationship with us very seriously as well. Makes you think twice about fooling around with God's Word, doesn't it? If it doesn't, it should! Nowadays, we don't hear too much, if anything, about God's wrath or His punishments. Most people want to come to church and hear the good stuff about God's blessings, and the nice things he's done for the church, and fellow worshippers. We hear about those things all the time. Brother so-and-so finally got that promotion he deserved after working for that evil boss of his; Sister so-and-so was healed from whatever ailed her for oh so very long; we finally raised enough money to build that addition to the church, or to the house; the Cubs finally won the World Series, or the Eagles finally won the Super Bowl. These are all good things to praise and thank God for. But don't forget the spankings which serve to remind us that God will not tolerate our foolishness, pride, or waywardness forever.

As if the curses associated with violation of the Mosaic Covenant weren't enough of a deterrent, God stated that if Israel continued in her sins, and also violated the Sabbath of the land, the punishment included not only displacement from the Promised Land, but also put Israel into the hands of their enemies. In Leviticus 26:32–35, God pronounced the following:

> *"And I will bring the land into desolation: and your enemies which shall dwell therein shall be astonished at it. And I will scatter you among the heathen, and will draw out a sword after you: and your land shall be desolate, and your cities waste. Then shall the land enjoy her sabbaths, as long as it lieth desolate, and ye be in your enemies land; even then shall the land rest, and enjoy her sabbath. As long as it lieth desolate it shall rest; because it did*

not rest in your sabbaths, when ye dwelt upon it."

To put it plainly: God said if you keep messing up, and don't abide by the Sabbaths I require, I'm going to kick you out of the Promised Land. Even worse, God would let Israel fall under the hands of their enemies. And while they were captive in a foreign land, the Promised Land would get the rest God required. So instead of being on the receiving end of God's blessings, continued sin and disobedience would put them on the receiving end of God's curses; the ultimate curse was being evicted from the land. Definitely not the way to go! So what happens next? Can't you guess?

Perhaps not surprisingly, Israel turned its back on God, even after witnessing firsthand the miracles He performed to secure their freedom. Can you imagine doubting God after witnessing the plagues in Egypt, and the parting of the Red Sea? Well, that is exactly what they did. In what has to be considered a major brain freeze, Israel balked at God's command to take the Promised Land. If you don't know the story, the book of Numbers chapters 13 and 14 details the events. God told Moses to send 12 representatives, one ruler from each of the 12 tribes, to go and search out the land (of Canaan). After 40 days of searching out the land, ten of the men came back and delivered a false report (i.e., they lied!). Those fibbers told the people giants lived in the land, and it couldn't be taken. Only two of the 12 spies, Joshua and Caleb, trusted the Lord and believed that Israel would be victorious. Based on the false reports and their unbelief, the people murmured (protested) against Moses and Aaron (Numbers 14:1-2). As you might imagine, that made God really angry, and He initially threatened to destroy them all, but Moses pleaded mercy on their behalf. Though God spared them, He declared in Numbers 14:21:

"But as truly as I live, all the earth shall be filled with the glory of the Lord."

God declared that His will on earth would be realized no matter what Israel did, does, or will not do! God obviously had big plans for mankind, and Israel was to be a part of those plans. God was thinking of the big picture, but here Israel was demonstrating a lack of faith in the God who freed them from the Egyptians.

Although God did not wipe them out, He sentenced all of Israel to wander in the desert for forty years, one year for each day they spent spying out the land (Numbers 14:34). During this forty-year period, all those who were twenty years and older would die in the wilderness (Numbers 14:29), and the ten spies who "riled up the congregation" and caused them to murmur against God's plan would die from the plague before the Lord (Numbers 14:36-37).

In an act of utmost futility, Israel, after hearing God's punishment, decided to enter the land of Canaan to try to take it. They were soundly defeated (Numbers 14:45). There are many lessons to learn from this experience, but the most obvious is the most basic: *Do what God tells you to do when He tells you to do it.* Further, their failure to take the land when first instructed demonstrated an egregious lack of faith in God, particularly since it came on the heels of God's deliverance from Egypt.

Later, Moses disobeyed God and, as a consequence, was not allowed to enter the Promised Land (Numbers 20:7-12). However, God did allow him to see it, as recorded in Deuteronomy 34, which also records Moses' death.

Before Israel entered the Promised Land, Moses wrote most of Deuteronomy, which was a second ("deutero") writing of the Law, and a rehash of Israel's history. In it, Moses recorded what is now referred to as the **Palestinian Covenant**, also known as the Land Covenant (recorded in Deuteronomy 29-30), in which God renewed the promises concerning Israel's possession of the land to the new generation. Deuteronomy 29:12-13 states:

> *"That thou shouldest enter into covenant with the Lord thy God, and into his oath, which the Lord thy God maketh with thee this day: That he may establish thee to day for a people unto himself, and that he may be unto thee a God, as he hath said unto thee, and as he hath sworn unto thy fathers, to Abraham, to Isaac, and to Jacob."*

Remember, the people who were about to enter the land were under twenty years of age when the wandering began. God was reminding them of the promises He made to their fathers, and of His faithfulness in fulfilling those promises. In Deuteronomy 30 particularly, God promised to return Israel to the land if they repented, turned to the Lord, and obeyed His voice. The Palestinian Covenant contained provisions and consequences that were similar to the Mosaic Covenant. Israel would be blessed generously for their obedience, but be removed from the land and cursed for their gross transgression of God's commandments. They would be returned to the land of promise only if they confessed their sin (also found in Leviticus 26:40-46).

The principle behind this is *repentance must occur before God restores His blessings*. God will not bestow His blessings if we continue to act contrary to His will. Looking far ahead, Israel was displaced from the land, repented, and was returned to the land of promise. Daniel 9:1-2 introduces the pending return of the Jews to their land, after a period of captivity, as well as provides critical prophecy concerning Israel.

The Kings of Israel

After Moses died, Joshua became the leader of Israel, and led the people into the Promised Land following the forty years of wandering in the desert. The rite of circumcision was performed on all the male children born during the last forty years (Joshua 5:2-7) to reaffirm their commitment to the Mosaic Covenant. Beginning with the battle of Jericho, Israel took the Promised Land and dwelt there. Joshua led the people, and all Israel followed the Lord God during His leadership. He did have some help from the elders who witnessed the Lord's delivery of Israel from the Egyptians. Together, they kept Israel on the straight and narrow. Joshua and the elders proved to be an effective team. The leadership of godly men is something we should take note of in these present days. It served Israel well during the times of Joshua and the elders. The mentorship of godly leaders is something I strongly recommend young people seek out and hold fast to. This applies to all areas of our lives; whether in church, Sunday school, Bible class, secular school, work, or at home. In a testament to Joshua and the elders, and in recognition their godly leadership, Judges 2:7 states:

> *"And the people served the Lord all the days of Joshua, and all the days of the elders that outlived*

> *Joshua, who had seen all the great works of the Lord, that he did for Israel."*

The period following Joshua and the elders is known as the period of the Judges, and is recorded in the Book of Judges. As often happens, absent good leadership, people tend to wander aimlessly and will inevitably run into trouble. So it is here. Judges 2:10-12 describes it:

> *"...and there arose another generation after them, which knew not the Lord, nor yet the works which he had done for Israel. And the children of Israel did evil in the sight of the Lord, and served Baalim: And they forsook the Lord God of their fathers, which brought them out of the land of Egypt, and followed other gods, of the gods of the people that were round about them, and bowed themselves unto them, and provoked the Lord to anger."*

After Joshua and the elders died, there came a generation in Israel who did not know the Lord. This generation is probably the one following all those who entered the land after the 40 years of wandering. Prior to Joshua's death in Joshua 24, he called all of Israel to come before him, and he rehearsed the history of Israel. Joshua also issued warnings about what would happen if the people turned from the Lord and worshipped other gods. The people consented with Joshua and pledged to follow the Lord in acknowledgement and recognition of what the Lord did for them. However, after his generation died, the next generation failed to continue following the Lord, as their parents did. This generation did not experience, first hand, the Lord's deliverance from Egypt. I'm sure they knew the story, but perhaps because they didn't see it, they didn't believe it. What follows should be no surprise.

The children of Israel fell into the hands of their enemies repeatedly, but God delivered them repeatedly by raising up judges who brought them back to the Lord. Perhaps the verse that best reflects the attitude of Israel during these times is found in the last verse of Judges (21:25):

> *"In those days there was no king in Israel: every man did that which was right in his own eyes."*

Israel had no king, but it did have spiritual leaders in Joshua and the elders. However, no spiritual leaders emerged after their deaths. The book of Judges presents clear evidence of what man can and will do in the absence of divine guidance and godly leadership. Man did what was right in his own eyes ... until he got in trouble. And that is what we do apart from God. We get in trouble. And then we're "sooo sooorry" and plead, "Help me, Lord". True to His word, God raised up judges to deliver Israel from their enemies, but *only* when they repented. The book of Judges repeats the cycle of relapse into sin, repentance, and God's deliverance through the judges.

Moving forward, in 1 Samuel 8 the Bible chronicles the history of Israel which led to their decision to have an earthly king, just like the other nations. However, Israel was to be a theocracy, ruled by God under the Mosaic Covenant. In fact, God's statutes for the people of Israel were to keep them from emulating the practices of the surrounding nations, as God made clear in Leviticus 20:22-24:

> *"Ye shall therefore keep all my statutes, and all my judgments, and do them: that the land, whither I bring you to dwell therein, spue you not out. And ye shall not walk in the manners of the nation, which I cast out before you: for they committed all these things, and therefore I abhorred them. But I have said unto you, Ye shall inherit their land, and I will give it unto you to possess it, a land that floweth with milk and honey: I am the Lord your God, which have separated you from other people."*

In the course of time, however, after entering the Promised Land and after the death of Joshua and the elders, Israel wanted a king to judge them ... just like the other nations. God didn't like that idea. When the people came to Samuel the prophet to petition for a king, God said this in 1 Samuel 8:7:

> *"...Hearken unto the voice of the people in all that they say unto thee: for they have not rejected thee, but they have rejected me, that I should not reign over them."*

How did they get to this point? During these days, Israel's spiritual leadership came from the prophets, or seers, as they were called in those times. Samuel was the spiritual leader over all of Israel in his day. Traveling from city to city, he would act as God's mouthpiece, and communicate God's will, judgment, and instruction to the people. However, it was a troublesome time for Israel. They were in constant battle against the Philistines, no doubt a consequence of Israel's worship of other gods (1 Samuel 2:12; 1 Samuel 7:3-4). Samuel, however, was getting up there in age, and this seemed to concern Israel (1 Samuel 8:5). The fact that Samuel's sons, who also were judges in Israel, were corrupt didn't help matters either. Instead of seeking guidance from the Lord on this matter, they requested a king to judge them and fight their battles, just like the other nations (1 Samuel 8:5). Despite Samuel's warnings to them about the misery a king would bring upon them, warnings that came from God by the way, they stood fast in their request (1 Samuel 8:19-20). God acknowledged their rejection of Him, gave them what they wanted, and Saul was anointed as the first king of Israel. Saul came out of the tribe of Benjamin, so if you remember Jacob's prophecy about Judah, then you know Saul's reign as king would not be an everlasting one.

To shorten the story, let's jump ahead a little. During his reign as king of Israel, Saul messed up. He disobeyed God in 1 Samuel 13, and God pronounced judgment in verses 13-14:

> *"...Thou hast done foolishly: thou hast not kept the commandment of the Lord thy God, which he commanded thee: for now would the Lord have established thy kingdom upon Israel forever. But now thy kingdom shall not continue: the Lord hath sought him a man after his own heart, and the Lord hath commanded him to be captain over his people, because thou hast not kept that which the Lord commanded thee."*

Saul's sin was he offered a sacrifice in violation of Samuel's instruction to wait for his arrival, which was expected in seven days (1 Samuel 10:8). At that time *Samuel* would offer a burnt offering. Further, although not specifically stated in the passages, only the priest could offer a sacrifice, not the king. Saul was neither a priest nor a Levite. This command came from God through Samuel (1 Samuel 13:13), thus the sacrifice was not only an act of disobedience, but unlawful as well. As a consequence of his disobedience, Saul's kingdom was ordained to end. His sons would not inherit the mantle of the throne!

Guess what happened next? Saul messed up yet again! The final straw occurred when God commanded Saul to utterly destroy the Amalekites and not to spare anything that lived (1 Samuel 15:1-3). Saul disobeyed God again, and spared the best of the livestock and "all that was good", ostensibly to sacrifice unto the "Lord thy God" (1 Samuel 15:15). Maybe you're asking yourself "so what was the problem with that plan?" It seems like Saul had good intentions, right? He wanted to sacrifice the best animals to the Lord God for delivering the Amalekites into his hands. What's wrong with that?

Well, what's wrong is God told Saul to destroy EVERYTHING! When God said everything, He meant everything, not just the bad stuff. Further, Saul's intention to "sacrifice everything that was good" wasn't a sacrifice to God anyway. In order for a true sacrifice to be meaningful, it must be deeply personal and intrinsically valuable. You can't sacrifice something that belongs to someone else. Those things belonged to the Amalekites, whom God had already told Saul to destroy. That stuff was supposed to go up in smoke anyway. As a consequence for his disobedience, God rejected Saul as king as we read in 1 Samuel 15: 22-23:

> *"And Samuel said, Hath the Lord as great delight in burnt offerings and sacrifices, as in obeying the voice of the Lord? Behold, to obey is better than sacrifice, and to hearken than the fat of rams. For rebellion is as the sin of witchcraft, and stubbornness is as iniquity and idolatry. Because thou hast rejected the word of the Lord, he hath also rejected thee from being king."*

This was Samuel's message to Saul, but it applies to us as well. It is not enough for us to make or offer sacrifices, or tithes, to appease God when we are in direct violation of His commands. God requires obedience; anything less is not sufficient. Partial obedience is not obedience, as we have said before. Saul, for all of his or his people's intent to offer sacrifices from the livestock they took from the Amalekites, disobeyed God's direct command, and God's judgment was to remove Saul as king of Israel.

So God then looked for a man after His own heart to replace Saul, and found him in the house of Jesse, who was the father of David. In 1 Samuel 16:13, David, who was in the line of Judah, was anointed to be king of Israel, but he would not occupy the throne until after Saul's death (1 Samuel 31). David assumed the throne in 2 Samuel 2:4.

God spoke to the prophet Nathan concerning David in 2 Samuel 7, including promises regarding His kingdom in verses 12-16:

> *"...I will set up thy seed after thee, which shall proceed out of thy bowels, and I will establish his kingdom. He shall build an house for my name, and I will stablish the throne of his kingdom for ever. I will be his father, and he shall be my son. If he commit iniquity, I will chasten him with the rod of men, and with the strips of the children of men: But my mercy shall not depart away from him, as I took it from Saul, whom I put away before thee. And thine house and thy kingdom shall be established for ever before thee: thy throne shall be established for ever."*

The above promises have come to be known as the **Davidic Covenant**. In addition to 2 Samuel 7:10, which promised Israel the land first spoken of by God to Abram in Genesis 12:7, the above verses promised a kingdom and a throne that will be established forever. Prophetically, the fulfillment of the David's seed occurred with the birth of Solomon, as did the building of the house (the temple). More importantly, the promise of the everlasting kingdom continued through David, and David's seed, Solomon.

The exploits of David are too numerous to mention here. You are probably familiar with the main events—David and Goliath, David and Bathsheba, David and Absalom. But if not, read about them in 1 and 2 Samuel, 1 Kings, and 1 Chronicles. Though David did sin, and grievously so, his love for God never waned. He loved God with all his heart. In fact, David so loved God that God honored him when He administered judgment against Israel and Solomon. We will read 1 Kings 11:11–13 in just a bit to get the complete accounting of that judgment.

The Divided Kingdom

The death of David is recorded in 1 Kings 2, and Solomon, the son of David and Bathsheba, inherited the throne.

Most of us know the story of Solomon, who when God asked him what he wanted (1 Kings 3), requested an understanding heart so that he could judge the kingdom. God was so impressed with the request He gave Solomon not only wisdom beyond what any man possessed, but also riches and honor. God also promised to continue the covenantal blessings He had given to David. This promise is found in 1 Kings 9:4-5:

> *"And if thou wilt walk before me, as David thy father walked, in integrity of heart, and in uprightness, to do according to all that I commanded thee, and wilt keep my statutes and my judgments: Then I will establish the throne of thy kingdom upon Israel for ever, as I promised to David, thy father…"*

God also gave Solomon warnings if he disobeyed (1 Kings 9:6-7):

> *"But if ye shall at all turn from following me, ye or your children, and will not keep my commandments and my statutes which I have set before you, but go and serve other gods, and worship them: Then I will cut off Israel out of the land which I have given them; and this house which I have hallowed for my name, will I cast out of my sight; and Israel shall be a proverb and a byword among all people."*

This blessing and curse followed the building of the first Temple and the king's palace, both feats of great accomplishment. If Israel followed after the Lord, then God would continue the throne through Solomon's line (his children) forever. If Solomon or his children turned from the

Lord, however, then Israel would be cut off and removed from the land, the Temple would be destroyed, and Israel would be a by-word, meaning whispered about (in a not so nice way) and ridiculed by the other nations and people.

At the conclusion of the construction of these great structures, Solomon prayed for the Lord's blessings on the Temple. God heard him and hallowed (blessed) it with His name. And everything seemed to be going along reasonably well until...

1 Kings 11:1-2:

> *"But King Solomon loved many strange women, together with the daughter of Pharaoh, women of Moabites, Ammonites, Edomites, Zidonians, and Hittites; Of the nations concerning which the Lord said unto the children of Israel, Ye shall not go in to them, neither shall they come in unto you: for surely they will turn away your heart after their gods: Solomon clave unto these in love."*

How many strange women? Let's see. Verse 3 tells us Solomon had 700 wives and princesses. Seven hundred! As if that wasn't enough, he also had 300 concubines, or what we call mistresses in today's language! Wow! Can you imagine that? Remember Genesis 2:24:

> *"Therefore shall a man leave his father and his mother, and shall cleave unto his wife: and they shall be one flesh."*

It's kinda hard to cleave to 1,000 wives and concubines and be one flesh ... even in those days! While it may be permissible to have many wives in some countries around the world, it is clear that God is opposed to the idea (Deuteronomy 17:17).

I know many of you must be wondering what happened to all that wisdom. This is yet another great example of what happens when we turn away from what we know the Lord requires of us. At the end of all this sin and foolishness, Solomon neglected divine instruction, which led to further darkness and more sin.

And what happened as a result of this? His wives turned his heart away from the Lord and His commandments, just as Deuteronomy 17:17 warned. The wives were from nations that worshipped other gods, not the Lord God. Their influence on Solomon caused him to recognize and worship those gods. Remember the Mosaic Covenant? Israel was to be a nation of priests ... a holy people unto the Lord. They were not to be like the other nations. If they obeyed, God promised divine protection, provisions, and land. If they disobeyed, the curses would follow. Solomon knew all of this. God reminded Solomon of this back in 1 Kings 9, and told him what would happen if he disobeyed. While Solomon did not abandon the Lord altogether, he did worship these other gods, and even built places of worship for them (1 Kings 11: 7-8). For his idolatry, God became angry with Solomon (verse 9), and pronounced judgment in 1 Kings 11:11-13:

> *"Wherefore the Lord said unto Solomon, Forasmuch as this is done of thee, and thou hast not kept my covenant and my statutes, which I have commanded thee, I will surely rend the kingdom from thee, and will give it to thy servant. Notwithstanding in thy days I will not do it for David thy father's sake: but I will rend it out of the hand of thy son."*

So the dividing of the nation of Israel into two kingdoms began with Solomon. He was the catalyst that caused God to separate the nation. God would fulfil His promise to rend (or tear away) the kingdom from Solomon, but not right away. Because David honored the Lord all the days of his life, the kingdom would not be removed during Solomon's lifetime, but during the reign of his son, Rehoboam. God ordained one tribe, Judah, to remain in David's line (1 Kings 11:13). Why Judah? Don't forget about the prophecy of Judah back in Genesis 49:10. The kingdom would come through the tribe of Judah, so God protected them. Here's something else I want all young people to recognize. God's deferment of judgment on Solomon's sin is because of David. I believe this demonstrates that parents can be a source of blessings for children. David clearly was one for Solomon!

The events leading up to this split are found in 1 Kings 11:26-40, which introduces Jeroboam, who would become the king of Israel (ten tribes, aka the Northern Kingdom). God told Jeroboam, through the prophet Ahijah, that the kingdom would be torn out of the hand of Solomon, and he would be given ten tribes (1 Kings 11:29-31) to reign over, but not forever (1 Kings 11:39).

In 1 Kings 11:38-39, God told Jeroboam before he became king of the 10 tribes:

> *"And it shall be, if thou wilt hearken unto all that I command thee, and wilt walk in my ways, and do that is right in my sight, to keep my statutes and my commandments, as David my servant did; that I will be with thee, and build thee a sure house, as I built for David, and I will give Israel unto thee. And I will for this afflict the seed of David, but not forever."*

So God promised Jeroboam a kingdom if he heeded God's Word and did what was right before the Lord. Notice that Jeroboam's kingdom would not be forever because the promise of the covenant still went through the line of Judah and David.

Strangely enough, Solomon tried to kill Jeroboam, whom he once held in high regard, but failed (1 Kings 11:40). No reason for the attempt on Jeroboam's life was given, but it compares to what David must have gone through with Saul once he knew the Lord had rejected him. Perhaps it was because both Saul and Solomon knew their sons would not inherit the throne, but that is speculation on my part. Whatever the reason, Solomon must have really gone off the deep end when he learned that the Lord had taken the kingdom from him as well.

Rehoboam, the son of David, became the king over all of Israel in 1 Kings 12. The split of the kingdom had not yet happened. But here's how it began. Sometime after becoming king, Rehoboam heard complaints from the people about the tax burdens placed on them by his father, Solomon. Yes, taxes were an issue ... even in those days. They wanted the tax burden lightened. Rehoboam decided to ignore the counsel of the old men who advised his father. His father's advisors suggested that he lighten the tax burden if he wanted to serve the people. Well, apparently Rehoboam wasn't real interested in that. Instead, he listened to his boys; those he grew up with (1 Kings 12: 3-11). He listened to his "homies" who wanted him to lay down the hammer. So in response to the complaints, Rehoboam threatened even heavier burdens. Ten of the tribes reacted (1 Kings 12:16) to this by "seceding from the union". They packed up their tents, departed the cities of Judah, and made Jeroboam their king (1 Kings 12: 16-20). The tribe of Judah, of course, remained. This fulfilled God's prophecy of rending the kingdom of Israel from one nation, under Solomon, into two nations. The second tribe that remained with Rehoboam was Benjamin.

Now we have the Northern Kingdom, which would consist of ten tribes, referred to as "Israel", or by some others as the "lost tribes of Israel". The Southern Kingdom would consist of two tribes, Judah and Benjamin, under Rehoboam. The Southern Kingdom was sometimes referred to as "The Kingdom of Judah" or simply "Judah". Rehoboam was now king of Judah, and Jeroboam was king of Israel. Both of them messed up and fell away from serving God.

The root cause of Jeroboam's fall is found in 1 Kings 12:26-28, where we find he built Shechem, which became the capital city of the Northern Kingdom. He built two golden idols (calves), placed one in Bethel and the other in Dan, then told a big fat lie. He told the people that it was the idols of gold that had brought them out of the land of Egypt. So not only did he lie about God's deliverance, he committed idolatry and led the people to commit the same sin. Jeroboam did this for purely selfish reasons. He was concerned the people would go back to Jerusalem, and back to the temple to sacrifice. Jeroboam did not want the risk associated with the people's return to Jerusalem, which could, potentially, lead them to stay and recognize Rehoboam as their king. He simply wanted everybody to stay put within his kingdom. Jeroboam also thought he could be killed as a consequence, and he clearly wanted no part of that potential scenario.

Jeroboam's acts set Israel on a path of evil and idolatry, and they never recovered. This is a clear demonstration of what happens when leaders put themselves ahead of God and everyone else. This is also why we must know the Word of the Lord, and not blindly rely on another to lead us.

The kingdom of Israel continued in Shechem, under Jeroboam. The history of the twenty kings of Israel is much too lengthy to rehearse. Most of these kings came from their fathers before them, but not all. More important is the testimony of their history, as mentioned throughout 1 and 2 Kings, and it's not pretty. King after king after king of Israel did evil in the sight of the Lord. Many consider Ahab, who married to the wicked Jezebel, the worst of the kings, but let's not digress. The point is that Israel, the Northern Kingdom, continued the practices started by Jeroboam. These practices included idolatry, witchcraft, sorcery, the worship of Baal, human sacrifice, and other things as mentioned in 2 Kings 17... and because they did, God passed judgment.

God's judgment on the Northern Kingdom for her failures was they were conquered by the Assyrians (2 Kings 17:23) and deported. 2 Kings 17:18 provides a chilling summary of God's judgment:

"Therefore the Lord was very angry with Israel, and removed them out of his sight: there was none left but the tribe of Judah only."

The Lord was very angry. This is very meaningful. I only found two occasions in the Bible where God got very angry, and the other is found in Deuteronomy 9:20. In that instance, Moses related the account of when God was about to "take out" Aaron (and not on a date either, if you catch my drift) because he made the golden calf, but Moses prayed for him, and God spared Aaron. The point is God is prepared to act immediately when He reached the point where He is "very angry". Sometimes it takes a while before God reaches that point, but when He does, He acts. After many warnings through the prophets (2 Kings 17:13), God had had enough, and acted! Israel was kicked out of the land, and taken captive by the Assyrians.

But don't misinterpret this. Don't think you have the leeway to act up and not be punished immediately. When David slept with Bathsheba and murdered Uriah, God was displeased (2 Samuel 11:27) ... and He acted. Also, God doesn't always act out of anger. The flood is a perfect example of that. God was grieved. He was extremely sorrowful because of man's wickedness. His justice demanded action, but God wasn't angry.

The final testimony of the ten tribes (Northern Kingdom) is found in 2 Kings 17:21-22:

> *"...and Jeroboam drave Israel from following the Lord, and made them sin a great sin. For the children of Israel walked in all the sins of Jeroboam which he did; they departed not from them."*

How's that for a legacy? Jeroboam's name will go down in history as the king who set Israel's path on the road to sin, and they never recovered. In the here and now, most people only think about the here and now. Many give no thought to the legacy they leave behind. However, if you gave any thought to tomorrow, would you want it to be like Jeroboam and have your name disgraced and recorded as such in the Bible, or any permanent document forever? I think not! When you think about Judas in the New Testament, what's the first thing you think about? Probably that he betrayed Christ. That's how his name is associated in the New Testament in many verses. Get my point? Think about what you do, and how history and heaven will memorialize what it is you do! But let's move on to the Southern Kingdom.

The road to Rehoboam's fall as king was more fully described in 2 Chronicles 12 and 1 Kings 14:22-26. Both chapters pretty much describe the same event, but 2 Chronicles 12 has Rehoboam as its focus, and 1 Kings 14 has Judah as the focal point. It's not good news for either. Rehoboam and Judah transgressed the law of the Lord (1 Kings 14:22), and as punishment God sent the king of Egypt to overtake the city. But because they humbled themselves, God did not destroy them. You would think Rehoboam would take note of this and straighten up. However, here is how the Bible describes Rehoboam after God spared him:

2 Chronicles 12:14

> **"And he did evil, because he prepared not his heart to seek the Lord."**

He clearly didn't learn his lesson. Rehoboam regained much of what he lost following the skirmish with Egypt, but his reign remained evil because there was no change of heart. Consequently, Judah would fall just as the Northern Kingdom fell.

The kingdom of Judah continued in Jerusalem. They had about twenty kings, and did have a couple of kings that did right in the eyes of the Lord, unlike the Northern Kingdom. Hezekiah and Josiah are recognized as the best, but Manasseh, the son of Hezekiah, was considered the worst. Their history almost parallels that of the Northern Kingdom, but not quite as bad. Trust me, that is not a compliment to Judah. After all, they were taken into captivity. As a whole, their sins were pretty egregious as well. Judah committed many of the same sins as the Northern Kingdom ... and God passed judgment on them too, as reported in 2 Kings 23:27:

> *"And the Lord said, I will remove Judah also out of my sight, as I have removed Israel, and will cast off this city Jerusalem which I have chosen, and the house of which I said, My name shall be there."*

In the end, Judah suffered the same judgement as Israel. They were kicked out of the land, and made captive in Babylon. That makes sense since, as a whole, they did the same things Israel had done.

Knowing that the prophecy of redemption goes through the line of David, we must follow this captivity closely. The captivity of Judah is reported beginning in 2 Kings 25, and also in 2 Chronicles 36:14-21. The reference in 2 Chronicles is particularly relevant because it provides useful information concerning Bible prophecy and Judah. It also highlights the importance of the land of promise in God's plan.

While the story of Judah's fall is also lengthy, the short version is, as a result of God's judgment on their sins, king Nebuchadnezzar of Babylon came to town and took over. I found it interesting that God would use a person like Nebuchadnezzar, who had a pretty high opinion of himself. But, Nebuchadnezzar is described as God's servant in multiple references found in the book of Jeremiah (25:9; 27:6, 43:10), and it's not because of his devotion to God. He is called a servant because he was empowered by God, to be used by God, as His instrument to discipline the nation (Judah). So what did Nebuchadnezzar do? He came in to Jerusalem and started taking people and valuable stuff back to Babylon.

Actually, there were three deportations. Strangely enough, the first is mentioned in Daniel 1:1. Here it mentioned the first occurred during the third year of the reign of king Jehoiakim, another king who did evil in the sight of the Lord (2 Kings 23:37). It was at this time that Nebuchadnezzar came and conquered. He allowed Jehoiakim to remain as king, but took some of the treasures from the temple, the princes, the nobles, and the smartest and the brightest of Judah captive, including Daniel, Hananiah (Shadrach), Mishael (Meshach), and Azariah (Abednego).

During the second deportment, Jehoiachin, the son of Jehoiakim, was king. He was another evil-doer (2 Kings 24:9). Nebuchadnezzar came back and carried away king Jehoiachin, his momma, his wives, officers, the mighty men, craftsmen, Ezekiel the prophet, all others of significance, and the treasures of Judah back to Babylon. He cleaned the place out! Anything deemed of value was taken out of Judah. All Nebuchadnezzar left behind was the poorest of the land (2 Kings 24:14). In Jehoaichin's stead, he made Zedekiah king as a fealty, answerable to Nebuchadnezzar.

The third deportment occurred after Zedekiah "ruled" in Judah for eleven years, so now we have a dual situation going on here. Jehoiachin et al were in Babylon, while Zedekiah was forced to rule the leftovers. Zedekiah subsequently messed up too, and Nebuchadnezzar was forced to come back to deal with him. Captured trying to escape, Zedekiah was forced to watch as his sons were slain, and then he was blinded (Jeremiah 39). It was at this time the temple was destroyed by Babylon (Jeremiah 52).

Let this be another lesson. The short version is this. Don't mess up and keep messing up. Repent! Backsliders beware! You don't want a "Nebuchadnezzar" showing up on your doorstep! God will use evil to punish evil and wickedness. God will employ this approach again during the Tribulation Period.

The prophecy related to the length of Judah's punishment is found in two places:

2 Chronicles 36:20-21

> *"And them that had escaped from the sword carried he away to Babylon; where they were servants to him and his sons until the reign of the kingdom of Persia. To fulfil the word of the Lord by the mouth of*

> *Jeremiah, until the land had enjoyed her sabbaths: for as long as she lay desolate she kept sabbath, to fulfil threescore and ten years."*

Jeremiah 29:10

> *"For thus saith the Lord, That after seventy years be accomplished at Babylon I will visit you, and perform my good word toward you, in causing you to return to this place."*

We see that Judah will be in captivity for seventy years for their disobedience, so off to Babylon we go.

Setting the Stage for Plan B

Let's lay out the landscape here so there's no confusion.

Going forward, the Northern Kingdom (10 tribes) is out of the picture. They are captives in Assyria, and not to be heard from again, for all intents and purposes. The earliest deportment of the Northern Kingdom began some 135 years or so (depending on the source) before that of the Southern Kingdom. But that's ok because we know God's prophecy is through the line of Judah, according to Genesis 49:8-10. That prophecy was realized from Judah to David to Solomon to Rehoboam, and then the Southern Kingdom. So, all we need do is follow where it went from there. So where are they? The best and brightest of Judah (or "Israel"; both terms are used synonymously going forward) was now in captivity, in Babylon, for a bunch of reasons. Her sins were just as egregious as that of the Northern Kingdom, and included idolatry, worship of other gods, sacrifices (human and animal) to other gods, failure to honor God's Sabbath, failure to do as God commanded through the prophets, and a few other things. But, the poorest of the people remained in Jerusalem, with Zedekiah running the show under the control of Nebuchadnezzar. So let's look at what else happened in Jerusalem for a minute.

You might think those who remained in Jerusalem would have straightened up and repented once they witnessed Jehoiachin and the rich and famous taken captive and deported. You would think Israel would recognize her sin and disobedience as the cause of the captivity in Babylon, and change their ways. After all, the warnings contained in the writings of Leviticus 26 didn't just go away. Further, the prophet Jeremiah tried to warn them about what was going to happen again and again and again.

Once they witnessed the deportment into captivity, did those left behind in Jerusalem straighten up and fly right? Nope!

In chapter 8, the prophet Ezekiel is shown a vision of what's going on in Jerusalem. In this vision, the pre-incarnate Christ showed him the detestable practices still going on in the temple in Jerusalem ... while Jehoiachin and his crew were in captivity. Turns out it wasn't just the "high and mighty" of Judah being disobedient and misbehaving. It was the common class as well. In the temple, Ezekiel is shown:

1. Idols of creeping things and abominable beasts being worshipped and prayed to (verse 10).
2. 70 elders, standing in the dark, offering incense (verse 11), each to his own idol under the delusion that God can't see them, and had abandoned them (verse 12).
3. Women weeping for Tammuz (verse 14), a pagan god of fertility.
4. In the inner court of the temple, 25 men, with their backs toward the temple of God, worshipping the sun (verse 16).

Jerusalem clearly hadn't learned its lesson. If you read Ezekiel 9, you'll find that God executed judgment (death) against the priest of the temple first (verse 6), and then against all others who practiced such abominations. The righteous, however, were marked and spared. Because the temple had been defiled, God's presence (His Shekinah glory) departed the temple (Ezekiel 10-11), which then was destroyed when Nebuchadnezzar went back to take care of Zedekiah, some eleven years after being appointed king. Ezekiel 43 tells us that God's presence will not return to Israel until the Millennial Temple is built.

Simply put, Israel failed across the board. God, after forgiving them again and again and again, is about to move in another direction to fulfill His will. Of course, since God knows all, He knew Israel would fail and merely moved to the next step in His plan. How do we know God is about to move in another direction? Well, first let's look at the status report:

The "nation" of Israel is now really two nations, precipitated by the gross idolatry of Solomon, and consummated when Rehoboam listened to his home boys. To worsen the situation, these kingdoms would, periodically, engage in war against one another.

The Northern Kingdom (ten tribes) had been captive in Assyria for some time now because Jeroboam, for purely selfish reason, led them down the path to idolatry, and they never recovered.

The Southern Kingdom (Judah and Benjamin) is captive in Babylon for doing much of the same things the Northern Kingdom had done. The redeeming aspect of this kingdom is that the prophecy continues through Judah, otherwise they might've gotten lost too.

After the deportment of the rich and famous from Jerusalem to Babylon, those who remained in Jerusalem worshipped idols and committed acts of sacrilege in the temple. As a result, the presence of God departed the temple. Remember, God will not share His glory or His house with anyone.

The temple was destroyed by Nebuchadnezzar.

That's the status, and it effectively began what is known as The Times of the Gentiles. Up to this time, the kingdoms of Israel were independent nations. They were autonomous. They didn't really need help from the Gentile nations because God protected them when they acted right. Not anymore! They are now being ruled by the Gentile nations. This represented what amounted to a seismic shift in how God will now operate going forward, particularly with regard to His redemptive plan. God still wants to bring the Gentiles in. God's will, in that regard, never changed.

There are a few verses in Ezekiel 20 we will visit to help us understand God's final position with Israel as it related to His redemption plan. Ezekiel 20 summarized what happened, and *why* it happened the way it did, and set the stage for Plan B. Let's begin by looking at Ezekiel 20, which nicely details God's attitude, complaint, and standing with the nation.

While in captivity, the elders approached the prophet Ezekiel, in the seventh year of captivity, to seek counsel from God. No specific question is mentioned, but the assumption is they came to ask a question of God through the prophet Ezekiel. I, for one, don't think they got the chance to ask a single question. God spoke to Ezekiel in verse 2, and here's how God responded in Ezekiel 20:3-4:

> *"Son of man, speak unto the elders of Israel, and say unto them, Thus saith the Lord God; Are ye come to inquire of me? As I live, saith the Lord God, I will not be inquired of by you. Wilt thou judge them, son of man, wilt thou judge them? cause them to know the abominations of their fathers."*

Wow! God told them not to ask Him anything! It was a "talk to the hand, because the ears ain't listening" kind of moment. God would not hear them! God said "As I live", which is an incredible preface to the response He gave. That statement was designed to stop them in their tracks. God then told Ezekiel to remind them of the abominations their fathers had done ... some of which are mentioned at the beginning of this chapter. It sounds to me as though God had enough of that. What followed these verses was a discourse of Israel's history ... failings after failings after failings, despite God's deliverances, blessings, punishments and warnings. Sin had taken hold of Israel, and God dealt out punishment. The final punishment was eviction from the land into captivity ... just like He said He would do!

What this story should serve to do is remind us that God will not allow sin to continue unpunished forever. There comes a time when we must pay for our unrepentant sins. God is gracious in that He gives us room to repent before administering punishment for non-repentance. We like to believe that God's patience is endless, but it is not. Yes, God could punish us immediately. That's His right as Sovereign Lord and Creator. But the truth is: His patience does come to an end, His holiness does demand repentance, and His justice does require payment. As it was true in the days of the Old Testament, so it is true now. As Christians, God will not allow us to continue in sin. Check out this verse in 1 Corinthians 5:5:

> *"To deliver such an one unto Satan for the destruction of the flesh, that the spirit may be saved in the day of the Lord Jesus."*

Briefly, the verses that preceded this verse told the story of a Christian brother who was involved in an incestuous relationship with his father's wife. That, of course, was not allowed … and was sinful. Definitely not cool! In Old Testament times, this behavior was punishable by death (Leviticus 20:11). As punishment, this unrepentant brother was removed from the church so as to not influence the church body. The spiritual consequence of this eviction resulted in this brother being removed from under the protection of God, which would allow Satan to take this man's life. His body (flesh) could be destroyed, but his spirit would still be saved. The point here is that God did not allow sin to go unchecked in the Old Testament or the New Testament, and He will not allow sin to go unchecked now. Israel learned this lesson the hard way, and suffered the consequences. Prophetically, God's punishment of the world's sin is still to come. We will discuss much more on that when we get to the book of Revelation.

Returning to Ezekiel 20, God voiced His anger over Israel's failures in verses 8, 13, and 21. In each recitation, God wanted to pour out His fury against them, but He spared them so that His name would not be blasphemed (cursed or spoken irreverently of) before the heathen, meaning the Gentiles. That's you and me, unless you are Jewish. Even though God was justified in His refusal to listen to the elders and had cause to exact punishment, He remembered His covenant and, for His name's sake, spared the nation.

Here's what this means to me. God chose to build a nation, Israel, consecrated to Him, to accomplish His will. And God's will for them to be a nation of priest wasn't "just because". Israel was to lead the way to show the Gentile nations what it meant to serve the Lord God. More importantly, through the nation (Israel) would come the redemption of the Gentiles. Where's that in the Bible? Don't forget about God's promise to Abram in Genesis 12:3. Also, look at what Isaiah wrote in 42:6:

> *"I the Lord have called thee in righteousness, and will hold thine hand, and will keep thee, and give thee for a covenant of the people, for a light of the Gentiles."*

This verse is not only a prophecy of Christ, it also tells Isaiah and the people of Israel that they were to be a light to the Gentiles, to bring them into fellowship with the Lord! God made a great promise to and about

Israel—that through them the whole world would be blessed. Israel would benefit as well. They got divine protection and provision. Israel, however, failed. They acted like the Gentiles. But mankind's redemption meant so much to God that He promised to fulfill this covenant HIMSELF, no matter what Abram or his descendants did. And it's a good thing God did that! So what happened? Abram's descendants, Israel, rebelled. They did not keep their part of the agreement (the Mosaic Covenant). If the salvation of the Gentiles were, in any way, dependent on Abram walking through the sacrifice with God in Genesis 15, or on Israel keeping the covenant, then the Gentiles would be in pretty bad shape. God's foreknowledge and love of His creation was the reason He walked through the sacrifice by Himself! Can I get an AMEN?

Despite what Israel had done, God had to keep His word because He made a promise to Abram, and He walked through the sacrifice by Himself. God cannot lie ... He cannot utter anything that is not true or truth. That's not an option ... not even a possibility. If He destroyed all of Israel, as it sounded like He wanted to do in Ezekiel 20, He would have broken His promise to Abram, and His name would be blasphemed before the Gentiles, who knew of the God of Israel. (See the story of Rahab the harlot in Joshua chapter 2 if you don't believe me.) Who is going to honor God if God destroyed His own people, whom He promised an everlasting kingdom? God, in that case, would not be true to His word. How could man (the Gentiles) revere God if God did not keep His word? So God punished Israel, as He said He would do if they did not keep His commandments and statutes. But, He did spare Israel from destruction, and thus kept His word.

Here's the final point to consider. Clearly God reverences His word and His name, as indicated in Ezekiel 20:9, 14, 22, and 39. God told us not to use His name in vain in the Ten Commandments (Deuteronomy 5:11). The profaning of God's name before the Gentiles was mentioned again and again in Ezekiel 36. Let's look at a few choice verses to show just how seriously God valued His name, and how seriously Israel had offended Him.

Speaking of Israel in verse 20:

"...they profaned my holy name..."

Verse 21:

> "But I had pity for mine holy name, which the house of Israel had profaned among the heathen, whither they went."

Verse 22:

> "...I do not this for your sakes, O house of Israel, but for mine holy name's sake, which you have profaned among the heathen, whither you went."

Verse 23:

> "And I will sanctify my great name, which was profaned among the heathen, which ye have profaned in the midst of them; and the heathen shall know that I am the Lord, saith the Lord God, when I shall be sanctified in you before their eyes."

God intends to sanctify (to declare holy, or consecrate) His name which was blasphemed by Israel, through their actions, before the Gentile nations. As His chosen people on earth, how could Israel (or Christians for that matter) dishonor God through their disobedience, idolatry, or blasphemous representation of His name without some consequence? Israel should not have, and we should not either.

The question for you is how do you reverence God's name in your life? Or perhaps it's a more basic question: Do you reverence God in such a way that people see it is *Him* we serve? As Christians, we have an obligation to reverence God and His name before all people, particularly the unsaved. We (Christians) are in the same position Israel was once in. That is why asking forgiveness and repentance is so important. As Christians, we ought to honor God and His name; not dishonor, profane, or blaspheme God's name before the unsaved. Learn the lessons of Israel's past.

The good news is that despite His anger against Israel for blaspheming His name before the Gentiles, God once again demonstrated His grace by prophetically promising to redeem Israel. He still keeps His word. Beginning in Ezekiel 36, God prophesied a future step in His redemptive program. Israel was to be returned to their own land (verse 24), cleansed (verse 25), and given a "new heart" and a "new spirit" (verse 26). This same prophecy is found in Jeremiah 31:31-34. Because of its importance, here is the passage:

> *"Behold, the days come, saith the Lord, that I will make a new covenant with the house of Israel, and with the house of Judah: Not according to the covenant that I made with their fathers in the day that I took them by the hand to bring them out of the land of Egypt; which my covenant they brake, although I was an husband unto them, saith the Lord: But this shall be the covenant that I will make with the house of Israel; After those days, saith the Lord, I will put my law in their inward parts, and write it in their hearts; and will be their God, and they shall be my people. And they shall teach no more every man his neighbor, and every man his brother, saying, Know the Lord: for they shall all know me, from the least of them unto the greatest of them, saith the Lord: for I will forgive their iniquity, and I will remember their sin no more."*

This new covenant will replace the old Mosaic Covenant, which Israel broke. Further, the new covenant would be inward, meaning written on the heart, and not come by way of writing on a stone tablet as it had before. It will occur by the indwelling of the Holy Spirit (Ezekiel 36:24-32). There would no longer be a need for Israel to tell the world of God's goodness, holiness, and grace, for all the world will know. The world will be filled with the knowledge of the Lord (Isaiah 11:9; Habakkuk 2:14). The sins of Israel will be forgiven and forgotten—not because God will simply say "forget about it". Sin still requires payment. The sins would be forgiven and forgotten because the price to be paid has been paid by Jesus Christ, whom Israel will recognize. Of course, all of this will occur in the last days at Christ's Second Coming.

The prophet Jeremiah calls this the **New Covenant** in verse 31 above. Christ makes reference to the new covenant in Matthew 26:28 at the Last Supper when He said:

"For this is my blood of the new testament, which is shed for many for the remission of sins."

From this time forward, God's plan of redemption for man would not depend on Israel being the peculiar nation or nation of priests before the Gentiles. To sanctify His name, and not have it blasphemed by Israel before the Gentiles, God will employ a different approach to accomplish His program of redemption going forward. That approach is called the Church, which was ordained by Jesus Christ, the Son of God. Israel couldn't do it, so God sent His Son to do it. However, the redemptive and kingdom prophesies continue; they are not cancelled or dismissed. We'll see how God accomplished that when we talk about The Messiah.

God is not finished with Israel just yet, however. Remember, God promised the land to Israel, and in May 1948, the Jews were brought back to a portion of the land God had promised them. That was just a partial fulfillment of the prophecy. What's left to be fulfilled is their redemption, which is promised in Ezekiel 36 and Jeremiah 31. Until then, Israel is not in the redemption picture as they once were. God will deal with the Gentiles another way, because He walked through the sacrifice by Himself.

Lay-off of Israel

Let's not be too critical about Israel, or bad-talk them, or rejoice over their fall. Those nations that did were dealt with very harshly by God, who mentioned their treatment of Israel as the basis for His judgment. If you read through Ezekiel 25-32, you'll see God's judgments against those nations and peoples, which included the Ammonites, Tyre, the Philistines, Pharaoh of Egypt, and Egypt, just to name a few. Never forget … Israel is still a source of blessings for those bless them, and a curse to those who curse them according to Genesis 12. Further, the whole world is blessed because of them. Jesus Christ, the Savior of the world, is descended from Israel, so we should not go around bad-talking His family, or His people. Besides, you don't want people speaking ill of your family, do you?

The Apostle Paul also says in Romans 11:1 that God did not cast away His people. True, they are set aside, but not discarded. The purpose of Daniel's 70th Week, which is addressed under a separate heading, is to bring them back in the fold, under the Great Shepherd, Jesus Christ. But for now, their current position or status is temporary, not permanent. They are only partially blinded (Romans 11:7 and 25). Paul adds in Romans 11:11:

"I say then, Have they stumbled that they should fall? God forbid: but rather through their fall salvation is come unto the Gentiles, for to provoke them to jealousy."

While no one should be grateful or happy about the failure of another person, or group of people, to do or act righteously, one of the blessings of Israel's stumbling is that the Gentiles received salvation directly through an intimate relationship with Jesus Christ, the Son of God. Further, because of Christ, Gentiles do not have to go through the ritual practices of the Law. We are under grace, not the Law (Romans 6:14). That became evident when the veil in the temple was torn in two (Matthew 27:50-51) simultaneous with the death of Christ on the cross. Just so you understand this, within the temple was the Holy of Holies—a sacred, small, windowless, perfectly cubed room that contained the Ark of the Covenant. It was THE holy place in the temple. No one except the high priest could enter into the Holy of Holies, and even he was only allowed to enter into it but once a year—on the Day of Atonement (Yom Kippur). Any violation or transgression meant death by the hand of God (Leviticus 16:2). It was during this day that the presence of God filled the Holy of Holies to accept the sprinkled blood sacrifices on the Ark of the Covenant, offered by the high priest, for the sins of the people. The entry into the Holy of Holies was covered by a large thick veil. When Christ died on the cross, this veil was torn in two. The tearing of the veil symbolized unfettered access to God by all the faithful, not just the high priest, and at any time we want; not just once a year. How so? Because Jesus Christ, as our sacrifice, became our (Christians) great High Priest (Hebrews 4:14), and we can go to Him anytime we want!

As we have covered, and will cover some more, Paul also tells us that all of Israel (meaning a remnant from all tribes) shall be saved (Romans

11:26). We are to be brothers in the Lord. So instead of being critical of Israel's fall, pray for the partial blinders to come off. Indeed, some have come to a saving knowledge of Christ already, so we should thank God for their salvation. As a nation or people, pray for their restoration, and ignore the politics, practices and circumstances of the past and present.

Let's move on.

The Times of the Gentiles

As mentioned in the last section, today we are living in a period known among biblical scholars as "the Times of the Gentiles". What does that mean? What it means is the Gentiles have taken over. The Gentiles are in control because God put them in control, and placed Israel under their authority. God is no longer working with or through Israel in His redemptive plan for mankind. The Gentiles have taken over that role because of Israel's sins.

The term comes from the words spoken by Christ in Luke 21:24:

> *"...and Jerusalem shall be trodden down of the Gentiles, until the times of the Gentiles be fulfilled."*

This is the only place in the Bible where you will find that term. Christ quoted this verse in His discussion about the last days, which gives us an indication of how long the Times of the Gentiles will last.

Although God no longer planned to use Israel in His plan of redemption, He continued to reveal prophetic statements through them, or more correctly, through one of their prophets ... a man by the name of Daniel. Daniel is considered the last of the major prophets of the Old Testament. One of the more interesting things about the book of Daniel is that it is written in two languages, Aramaic and Hebrew. Aramaic was the language of the day in Babylon. One of the reasons the smartest and brightest of Judah were taken to Babylon in the first deportation was to learn their language (Daniel 1:4). For the curious of mind, Daniel 1:1-2:4a was written in Hebrew, Daniel 2:4b-7:28 was written in Aramaic, and the remaining chapters are all in Hebrew. It seems the target "audience" (Gentile or Hebrews) determined the language used.

The story of Daniel begins with him as a slave in Babylon. Daniel was of the king's seed (Daniel 1:3), a prince or nobleman, and served the Lord God since youth. King Nebuchadnezzar was impressed with Daniel and his three friends, commonly known to us as Meshach, Shadrach, and Abednego, and sought their counsel because of their God-given wisdom and understanding (Daniel 1:17-20).

Many of us know several of the more prominent stories or miracles recorded in the book of Daniel. For example, the stories of the fiery furnace (Daniel 3), the finger writing on the wall (Daniel 5), and the lion's den (Daniel 6) all involved Daniel and his three friends. However, what is not as widely understood is the prophetic chapters of this very important book, and the role Daniel played in its revelation.

Daniel's role in revealing God's introduction of the Gentiles into His redemptive plan began with the first of two related dreams. The first dream was by Nebuchadnezzar, which Daniel interpreted, but the second dream was by Daniel himself during the reign of king Belshazzar, Nebuchadnezzar's son. These dreams didn't happen on consecutive nights or years. Bible scholars estimate that Daniel was about 68 years old when he had his dream, but Neb's dream occurred early in his reign as king.

In the first dream, God revealed His will concerning the Gentile kingdoms to king Nebuchadnezzar. It's interesting to me that God would reveal His will to king Nebuchadnezzar. He was a heathen king who conquered Israel, raided their land, took their valuable possessions, and held them in captivity. Of course, God ordained it all, but Neb didn't know that. He thought it was all under his power. And as mentioned before, he had a high opinion of himself—something that would come back to bite him later on. But this does show that God will express Himself to the unsaved when it suits His purpose. That God revealed His will to Daniel, in the second dream, is not a surprise since Daniel was devoted to serving the Lord since the days of his youth.

Let's begin with chapter 2. In Daniel 2, Nebuchadnezzar had a dream. It is a recurring dream that kept him up at night. The king called for his astrologers, magicians, and sorcerers (the "wise men") to interpret the dream. Of course, they asked the king to tell them the dream, but he didn't tell them, or refused to tell them. I put it this way because many biblical scholars will tell you the king didn't tell them because he wanted to make sure the wise men weren't making stuff up. If they were indeed "wise men", they should know the dream, and interpret the dream. Hmm ... you have to admit, they were in a pretty tough spot. Verses 5 and 8, however, indicate that the king can't recall the dream ("the thing is gone from me"). The reason why he doesn't tell them is less important than their failure to interpret it.

To shorten the story, the king decreed that if they did not tell him the dream and its interpretation, all the wise men in the kingdom would be put to death (verse 5). Actually, the king said they would be cut in pieces. That's certainly not the best way to go out. Likewise, the king promised whomever could tell him the dream and its interpretation would be honored with gifts and rewards (verse 6).

As you might imagine, all the wise men were concerned about losing their lives, not to mention the agony of being chopped up in pieces. The decree came before Daniel, who along with his three friends, prayed to God (Daniel 2:17-18) and asked for the dream and the interpretation. Because Daniel was favored by God, the dream and its interpretation were revealed to him while he slept.

Before we get to the dream, notice what Daniel did immediately after these things were revealed to him. Beginning in verse 19:

> "...Then Daniel blessed the God of heaven..."

Verse 23:

> "I thank thee, and praise thee, O thou God of my fathers, who hast given me wisdom and might, and hast made known unto me now what we desired of thee: for thou hast now made known unto us the king's matter."

When God answers our prayers, we should acknowledge His sovereignty, and thank Him for His gifts. We are more than happy to do so if God grants our request, right? Even if God does not grant what we ask, however, we should still acknowledge and thank Him. Why? Because He is still God, and He answered our prayer, even if the answer was *no*.

Daniel went before the king, gave God the credit for revealing the dream, and then told the dream and the interpretation, as found in Daniel 2:31-45. Here's the shortened version of the dream and the interpretation. The king dreamed of a great image with a head of gold, breast and arms of silver, belly and thighs of brass, legs of iron, and feet of part iron and clay. Then the king saw a stone cut out without hands that smashed the feet of iron and clay, which led to the rest of the image falling and being blown away as the chaff. The stone then became a mountain, filling the whole earth.

The interpretation of this dream is very important, for it is God's prophecy concerning the four Gentile powers, or kingdoms, which will reign over all the earth.

1. The first kingdom, represented by the head of gold, is **Babylon,** which was then ruled by Nebuchadnezzar. He must have been pretty happy about being number one. Daniel also said that after Babylon there shall arise three other kingdoms that, although inferior to Babylon, would nonetheless reign on the earth.

2. The second kingdom, represented by the breast and arms of silver was the **Medes & Persians**;

3. The third kingdom, represented by the belly and thighs of brass, was **Greece**;

4. And finally, the fourth kingdom, represented by the legs of iron and feet of iron and clay was **Rome**.

To be clear, Daniel did not tell the king the names of the kingdoms to come. That wasn't revealed to him. We know the succession of kingdoms based on history.

Why these four kingdoms? Certainly there were other kingdoms of the world in existence at the time, and certainly there would be more kingdoms to come. These four were prophesied because they are the kingdoms that would rule over the land of Palestine, and the people of Israel. That keeps Israel front and center in biblical prophecy. I can't help but wonder if Israel had done what they were was supposed to do, the Gentiles would not rule over them, but serve them as God's anointed. But that too is pure speculation on my part.

Some will say the feet of part iron and part clay represented a fifth kingdom, but since Daniel's dream only mentions four kingdoms, and since both dreams represent the same thing, that means there is no fifth kingdom. However, it does have an unrealized, prophetic meaning, which we will get to in a moment.

If you know your world history, you know that Babylon was defeated by the Persians in 539 B.C. during a drunken feast held by king Belshazzar (Daniel 5: 1-2). During this drunken feast, the fingers of a man's hand suddenly appeared, and began writing on the wall. That put an end to the feast. Nobody felt like partying anymore. The king was so shaken by the sight of it, his knees were literally shaking, and he fell to the floor (Daniel 5:6). Imagine what that must have looked like! The Medes and Persian army dug underneath the city walls, entered the city, and took control without much of a fight. The kingdom of Greece, led by Alexander the Great, defeated the Medes and Persians around 334-330 B.C., and Rome defeated Greece in 63 B.C. The feet of iron and clay represent the weakness of Rome, oddly enough. Babylon, the Medes & Persians, and Greece were all defeated. But not Rome! If you know your history, you know Rome fell apart, but not by the force of any army or kingdom. Iron is the strongest of the metals in the dream, and properly reflects the might of Rome. But the fact that the toes are composed of iron and clay meant that Rome could not be maintained. It could not remain unified. Iron and clay don't mix ... and as such, Rome couldn't keep it all together.

The stone was the most important part of the dream because of what it represented. The interpretation of the stone is found in Daniel 2:44, which reads:

> *"And in the days of these kings shall the God of heaven set up a kingdom, which shall never be destroyed: and the kingdom shall not be left to other people, but it shall break in pieces and consume all these kingdoms, and it shall stand forever."*

The stone was cut out of the mountain without hands, meaning it was cut out by the Lord God of heaven. That the stone became a mountain and filled the whole earth is also meaningful. In scripture, kingdoms are often symbolized by mountains. So this stone grew and grew to become a mountain that filled the whole earth. This represents the kingdom of Jesus Christ, which started out as a stone, and will eventually rule the whole earth. Christ's kingdom will put down every rule, and every kingdom in the world, and He will establish His own kingdom here on earth. He will be truly recognized as the King of Kings! Amen to that!

While the Gentile kingdoms now rule the world, God is building His kingdom, which will rule forever. When is the realization of this prophecy? It will occur immediately following the Tribulation Period.

The second dream, this one dreamt by Daniel, occurred many years later during the reign of king Belshazzar, he of the shaken knees, as found in Daniel 7:1-3:

> *"In the first year of Belshazzar king of Babylon Daniel had a dream and visions of his head upon his bed: then he wrote the dream and told the sum of the matters. Daniel spake and said, I saw in my vision by night, and, behold, the four winds of the heavens strove upon the great sea. And four great beasts came from the sea, diverse one from another."*

The reference to "the four winds of the heavens" is a term of judgment as used here (see also Jeremiah 49:36, Zechariah 6:1-7, and Revelation 7:1). This is an indication that some unpleasant things are being revealed, or are about to happen. Daniel's dream was also about kings and kingdoms. How do we know this? The answer was provided to us. If we jump ahead a few verses, we find out what these beasts represented. Daniel 7:17 reads:

> *"These great beasts, which are four, are four kings, which shall arise out of the earth."*

In terms of subject matter, Daniel's dream was much like Nebuchadnezzar's. But there are some important differences in how each person viewed these kingdoms. Nebuchadnezzar dreamed of one great image or statue, something splendid, and embedded with gold, silver, brass, and iron. Each metal in the image represented a different kingdom. But what did Daniel see? He saw four beasts. Why the difference in representations in the two dreams? The answer is one of perspective. In the eyes of a godly man, like Daniel, the beasts represent things that are wild, untamed, vicious, or uncontrollable. Daniel looked at the kingdoms from God's perspective. Nebuchadnezzar, on the other hand, saw them from man's perspective. He saw them as glorious or precious. This is just another example of what man sees as precious or valuable, God sees as dangerous or harmful.

As we read further in chapter 7, you'll see that Daniel's dream also included much more in the way of content and completeness with respect to prophecy. We are given more descriptive information about these four beasts beginning in verse 4:

> *"The first was like a lion, and had eagle's wings: I beheld till the wings thereof were plucked, and it was lifted up from the earth, and made stand upon the feet as a man, and a man's heart was given to it."*

Remember, this dream occurred when Belshazzar was king, and after Daniel interpreted Nebuchadnezzar's dream in Daniel 2. Nebuchadnezzar is already out of the picture. Daniel knew Nebuchadnezzar's history. So this beast was clearly a reference to Nebuchadnezzar, who was the head of gold in the first dream. So you may ask, what's up with the plucked wings, and "made stand upon the feet as a man", and "a man's heart was given to it"? We didn't cover this before, but the story began in Daniel 3 and culminated in Daniel 4.

At some point during his reign, Nebuchadnezzar got a little big-headed. Actually, he got really big-headed ... too big-headed for his own good. In Daniel 3, the king got angry because Shadrach, Meshach, and Abednego would not bow down and worship his image when rap music came on surround sound throughout the province. Knowing Neb was an ego driven king, the song was probably something like "Can't Touch This". But the Hebrew boys wouldn't bow down, so he had them thrown in the fiery furnace. God miraculously spared them, however. It was, in fact, Neb who saw a fourth figure in the fiery furnace, and said to himself the fourth figure looked like the Son of God. Little did he know! You'd think the king would have learned a lesson from that experience. Don't mess with these boys or their God. Apparently, that wasn't enough.

Neb then had another disturbing dream that required Daniel's interpretation in chapter 4. When told of the dream, even Daniel had to pause (verse 19). Neb noticed Daniel was shaken by the dream and its interpretation, but was told to chill; everything would be cool. It's too much to write the details here, but in short, the meaning of the dream was to warn Neb of his high-mindedness. He was going too far in his thinking of himself. But of course, the best lessons taught and warnings given are sometimes forgotten, or ignored, especially if we don't immediately suffer or benefit from the experience.

Those of you with big egos, please read all of Daniel 4 and take notes! You don't want this to happen to you. One year later, Neb had forgotten or decided to ignore the warning from Daniel, and walked along the top of his palace, glorying in all that was Babylon, and the wonder of his palace. Then he made a critical mistake ... he gave himself the credit for it all, and said so (verse 30)! As soon as he had spoken these words, God fulfilled the warning of the dream. Neb was flying high up until now, but it was time to pluck his wings. Neb heard a voice from heaven saying (Daniel 4:31-32):

> *"...O king Nebuchadnezzar, to thee it is spoken; The kingdom is departed from thee. And they shall drive thee from men, and thy dwelling place shall be with the beast of the field: they shall make thee eat the grass as oxen, and seven times shall pass over thee, until thou know that the most High ruleth in the kingdom of men, and giveth it to whomsoever he will."*

Neb paid the price by living like an animal. Worse than that ... he lived with the animals ... and not like Dr. Dolittle either! He ate the grass like oxen, his hair became as feathers, and his nails as eagles claws (verse 33). He remained in that state for a full *seven years*! After the seven years God restored his sanity. Neb recognized that he wasn't what he thought he was. Then he blessed and praised God. His wings had been effectively plucked! He was made to realize he was just a man ... nothing more! Nebuchadnezzar's recognition, worship, and praise of God are recorded in Daniel 4:34-37. Great reading!

The second beast was described in Daniel 7:5:

> *"And behold another beast, a second, like to a bear, and it raised up itself on one side, and it had three ribs in the mouth of it between the teeth of it: and they said thus unto it, Arise, devour much flesh."*

This beast is compared to the breast and arms of silver in Neb's dream, which represented the kingdom of the Medes and Persians (Medo-Persia). Medo-Persia overcame Babylon during Belshazzar's reign. Historically, the Persians defeated the Medes, and the two united kingdoms defeated Egypt, Lydia, and Babylon. The three ribs in its mouth could represent the Medo-Persia defeat of those three kingdoms.

The third beast is found in Daniel 7:6:

> *"After this I beheld, and lo another, like a leopard, which had upon the back of it four wings of a fowl; the beast had also four heads; and dominion was given to it."*

This beast is compared to the belly and thigh of brass, which represented Greece, led by Alexander the Great. Alexander became king at the age of 20, and never lost a battle. History tells us that he died at a young age (32) in Babylon. Greece was known for its swiftness in battle, hence the leopard characterization with four wings. After Alexander's death, his kingdom was divided among four of his generals.

The granddaddy of them all, beast number four, is described in Daniel 7:7-8:

> *"After this I saw in the night visions, and behold a fourth beast, dreadful and terrible, and strong exceedingly; and it had great iron teeth: it devoured and brake into pieces, and stamped the residue with the feet of it: and it was diverse from all the*

beasts that were before it; and it had ten horns. I considered the horns, and, behold, there came up among them another little horn, before whom there were three of the first horns plucked up by the roots: and, behold, in this horn were eyes like the eyes of man, and a mouth speaking great things."

This beast is compared to the legs of iron, and feet part iron and part clay in Neb's dream. Daniel strongly reacted to this beast. He called it dreadful, terrible, and exceedingly strong. This beast is the Roman Empire. Rome was a juggernaut. They were brutal in their assaults against other countries and people. Again, iron was the strongest of the metals in Nebuchadnezzar's image, and it symbolized the might of Rome. It was the most powerful empire of its time and militarily could not be defeated. Each of the previous empires fell to the next empire. Not Rome. Rome was the last great empire. Rome imposed its will on all things not Roman. However, Rome could not maintain a unified nation. Because of its ambitions and military conquests, it became too big. In fact, it was so big it split in two, Eastern Rome and Western Rome, each with its own capital. However, internal problems of a political, economic and social nature festered. It over-reached in its military ambition, creating enemies on all sides, and as a result was economically unsustainable. It took a lot of money to have troops across the breath of the empire to keep the peace. Let's not forget, Christianity was born during this time, which contributed to its internal problems. Rome, with its many gods was no match for Christianity, and the Lord God! Can I get another Amen! All of these factors led to Rome's fall. Anyway, enough of Roman history—in the end they fell.

Daniel's dream, however, took on greater significance. Why? Because it expanded on what Neb had dreamt. God just gave Neb a peek of the Gentile kingdoms through the Rome of old. But God had given Daniel prophecy about each kingdom in more detail, the end time, and identified the person central to the end time. God clearly wanted Daniel to know more about this fourth beast.

Look carefully at the complete description of the beast. It is a beast with ten horns. Verse 7 told us what the beast was, and what it did. It was strong, terrible, with great iron teeth. It devoured, broke stuff in pieces, and stomped what was left over under its feet. That was Rome of old ... it destroyed and gobbled up everything in its path. That's what Neb saw. But then there are the horns. There are independent actions associated with these horns, as if they have minds of their own, and agendas. And they do! If you jump ahead a little bit, you'll see that the horns are kings (verse 24). Further, from out of these ten kings will come another king, who usurps, takes the place of, or otherwise subdues three of the ten kings. This little horn becomes a major player in the end times. But none of this has happened yet. It is yet future. If you know your history, then you know that when Rome of old fell apart it didn't have ten cents to its name, much less ten kingdoms. So when you hear or read about a revived Roman Empire, you know a reference is being made to these horns. And, since the horns are attached to the beast, and the beast is Rome, it is a continuation, or a revived Rome. Maybe it won't be known as Rome literally, but it certainly will be known as Rome figuratively, or more accurately, spiritually. Many people believe the European Community, and the euro dollar, is but the start of this unification.

Let's examine the horns in Daniel's dream a bit more closely. Daniel's beast has ten horns, which will become the political platform, or launch pad, for the little horn. Verse 8 tells us that from out of the ten horns a little horn arises. This little horn is described as having "eyes like the eyes of a man", a "mouth speaking great things", and that before it "three of the first horns are plucked up by the roots". Whatever does this mean?

Before we get the answers, let's continue with Daniel's dream for a moment. We'll see the answers. I promise. Daniel saw God seated on the throne in heaven (verse 9), and Christ given dominion and a kingdom. This is great! Can you imagine seeing God seated on His throne in heaven?!?! That will make you straighten up and fly right! Well, Daniel was already flying right, which is why he got to see God seated on the throne. Daniel saw the realization of God's prophecy, rule, and kingdom established on earth. That is something we should all look forward to seeing. The Lord's Prayer says, "Thy kingdom come". Well, in his dream, Daniels saw it ... at least the "as it is in heaven" part. What a blessing!

But Daniel was still troubled by the dream (verse 15) and wanted to know the meaning of it. He was told beginning in verse 17:

> *"These great beasts, which are four, are four kings, which shall arise out of the earth. But the saints of the most High shall take the kingdom, and possess the kingdom for ever, even for ever and ever."*

Well, at least the last part of it was great. The earth shall be under the control of these beasts, but in the end, the saints of God would take possession of it. Well, that's cool, but Daniel remained troubled by the fourth beast, as found in verse 19. He wanted to know the truth of the fourth beast. He wanted to know what it was because of how he saw it— exceedingly dreadful, teeth of iron, and nails of brass. This was something that clearly gave Daniel reason to pause. Daniel kept thinking, "What is that thing"?

He got his answer in verses 24-25:

> *"And the ten horns out of this kingdom are ten kings that shall arise: and another shall arise out after them: and he shall be diverse from the first, and he shall subdue three kings. And he shall speak great words against the most High, and shall wear out the saints of the most High, and think to change times and laws: and they shall be given into his hand until a time and times and the dividing of time."*

Daniel had already been told that the four beasts were four kings. Now, in verse 24, he was told that out of the fourth kingdom (Rome) shall come ten kings, symbolized by the ten horns. However, another little horn, a king, showed up and subdued three kings. This little king came out of nowhere, probably someplace insignificant since it was described as a "little horn". But it becomes prominent and will take over three kings. Let's look closely at the descriptions and actions of this little horn:

- The "eyes like the eyes of man" (verse 8) symbolize intelligence. This king will be powerful, but also brilliant, and will undoubtedly use his brilliance to take over the three kingdoms, and become more influential worldwide.

- He will be "diverse from the first" (kings). There will be no one like him, not before, and not after. He is unique. As we move along, it will become clearly evident exactly how unique this person will be.

- "A mouth speaking great things" symbolize boastful claims. He will make great (boastful) statements, like a trash talker. He will "mouth off" as the current saying goes. The problem is, he "mouths off" against the Lord God (the most High). That alone should tell you this guy is trouble.

- He will "wear out the saints of the most High". For a period of three and a half years ("a time" = one year; "times" = two years; and the "dividing of times" = one-half year), this little horn will persecute the saints of God. Some scholars believe the "saints" represent the people of Israel, while others believe it represents those who become Christians during this terrible time. I believe "saints" must represent Christians by definition. You can't be a "saint" unless you belong to God through acceptance of Jesus Christ. No one, Jew or Gentile, is a saint without Christ. But as we shall see later, this little horn will persecute Israel for certain, as well as anyone else who stands in his way. Undoubtedly, the Christians of that time will recognize Israel's importance to God and His prophecy, and will serve to aid and protect Israel in their time of persecution. These acts by Christians will make them an enemy to the little horn, and lead to their persecution as well.

- "Think to change the times and laws". He will have no regard for existing laws or practices, and will establish his own set of standards. What you say won't matter to him, and he will demonstrate that at the mid-point of the Tribulation Period.

This man, this "little horn", is a central character in Bible prophecy. He is mentioned several times throughout the Bible going forward, and is known by several names. In addition to the "little horn", Daniel referred to him as "the prince that shall come" (Daniel 9:26), and a "king" (Daniel 11:36). The Apostle Paul referred to him as "that man of sin" and "the son of perdition" in 2 Thessalonians 2:3, and "Wicked" (or "Lawless One" in some versions) in 2 Thessalonians 2:8. In Revelation 13:1, the Apostle John calls him the "beast". The most prominent name for this character is the Antichrist. We will cover more of this character and his activities under a separate heading.

So, in summary, the Times of the Gentiles began with Israel taking a back seat in God's redemptive plan. Israel is under the rule of the Gentile nations. God revealed the Gentile powers to Daniel through two dreams, Nebuchadnezzar's and his own. However, only Daniel got to see Gentile kingdoms *and* the last days. Nebuchadnezzar missed out on the last days. History has recorded the existence and passing of the Babylonian, Persian, Greek, and Roman empires. Thus, most of Daniel's prophetic vision has been fulfilled.

Still to come is the revived Roman Empire, the subsequent emergence of the little horn (the Antichrist), and the ushering in of God's kingdom.

The Seventy Weeks of Daniel

What is revealed next, in Daniel 9, is very important prophecy concerning Israel and God's redemptive program, so we are going to cover this chapter very carefully, and in a little more detail. This chapter was written in Hebrew, meaning they were the intended audience. One of the major aspects of this particular prophecy is it provided a timeline we can follow, and revealed the totality of God's redemptive program for Israel going forward. Thus, we must address each part of the prophecy we've been given in this chapter. However, while this prophecy is for Israel, we will see how the Church fits in its realization.

By this time, it is generally believed that Daniel had been in captivity for about 66 years or so, having been deported around 605 B.C. I question this date and age for reasons that will become obvious in just a second. Depending on the historical source, the date of captivity, and hence the time period of captivity, may not be certain, but the events of chapter 9 took place in the first year of Darius, king of the Medo-Persian Empire. The "changing of the guard" is also significant, but just bear with me for a second. Nebuchadnezzar is dust, and so is his son, Belshazzar who followed him on the throne. So obviously a significant amount of time had elapsed since Israel's captivity. If you remember, Daniel was among the first of those deported from Jerusalem, which suggest to me he's really much older than 66 years of age, but his age isn't the real issue here. What is more important is he and his people were under this new regime, the second of the Gentile powers.

At the beginning of chapter 9, Daniel was studying the scriptures, as recorded in verse 2:

> *"...I Daniel understood by books the number of years, whereof the word of the Lord came to Jeremiah the prophet, that he would accomplish seventy years in the desolations of Jerusalem."*

Among the books Daniel read was that of the prophet Jeremiah, which prophesized that God would accomplish 70 years of desolation in Jerusalem. This reference, found in Jeremiah 25:12, reads as follows:

> *"And it shall come to pass, when seventy years are accomplished, that I will punish the king of Babylon, and that nation, saith the Lord, for their iniquity, and the land of the Chaldeans, and will make it perpetual desolations."*

These two verses cover many things, one of which is the fact that Jerusalem would be uninhabited for 70 years. The seventy years was because Israel violated the Sabbath of the land (2 Chronicles 36:21). So the punishment (captivity) and the sentence (seventy years) go hand-in-hand.

But more importantly, Daniel recognized something else as he was reading. Daniel put two and two together when he realized that Babylon was no more ... it had ben overthrown by the Medo-Persia. King Darius of the Medes and Persians was running the show. According to the verse, Babylon was going to be punished when the seventy years were up. That meant the 70 years of captivity were up! It was the epiphany of epiphanies. Israel would be freed to go home. This was significant, so Daniel got down to business. Verse 3:

> *"And I set my face unto the Lord God, to seek by prayer and supplications, with fasting, and sackcloth, and ashes."*

When I read this verse, my first thought was "why did Daniel fast and do the sackcloth and ashes thing?" Israel was going home soon. I'd pray and thank God, but I'd be happy. But it looked to me that Daniel was about to grieve. Fasting ... sackcloth, really? He didn't like it there that much, did he? True, Daniel was big-time in the realm (Daniel 6:2), but he did want to go home, right? He should be happy about that. Instead, he prayed, fasted, and repented in sackcloth and ashes. He goes the whole nine yards. Why on earth did he do that?

Here's why. Daniel prayed for guidance and forgiveness for his people. He wanted God to know they (Israel) understood what got them in this mess in the first place. He wanted divine guidance so there would be no repeat of what got them in captivity. Daniel also understood repentance must come first, so on behalf of his people he acknowledged all of Israel had sinned, ignored the covenantal relationship with Almighty God, and failed to listen to God's prophets. As a consequence, they were punished, and Daniel acknowledged that God was just in His punishment (verse 14). Daniel also acknowledged God's deliverance from Egypt, begged God to turn away His anger from His people and Jerusalem, and hear his prayer. Daniel knew that God's blessings would not flow without repentance ... as was mentioned before. This is worth repeating. We cannot remain in defiance of God's requirements and expect God to bless us. Blessing only comes with repentance and obedience!

Daniel asked God to restore the sanctuary (the temple) and Jerusalem; not for the sake of Israel, but for His own name's sake (verses 17 and 19). Israel was a reproach among the nations around them (verse 16), and Daniel sought God's mercy. So Daniel also clearly understood the importance of representing God's name. And while he was praying, an amazing thing happened. The angel Gabriel appeared to him, as mentioned in verse 21:

> *"Yea, whiles I was speaking in prayer, even the man Gabriel, whom I had seen in the vision at the*

beginning, being caused to fly swiftly, touched me about the time of the evening oblation."

Imagine that! Not only did Daniel get an answer to his prayer, he got it while he was praying! Why did God respond to Daniel so quickly? Let's look at what Gabriel said in verse 23:

"At the beginning of thy supplications the commandment came forth, and I am come to shew thee; for thou art greatly beloved..."

When Daniel started praying, God started answering! This demonstrates how God responds to those who live to serve Him. Daniel rated in heaven. Today we would say, "Daniel, you the man!" What a blessing, and what an example of what God will do for us, if we live to serve Him.

Daniel was then given a prophecy specifically concerning *Israel* that was central to God's plan for their future, but will also greatly affect our future as Christians and His redemption program for man. This prophecy clearly demonstrated that God did not toss away Israel, He merely set them aside. Daniel was told beginning in verse 24:

"Seventy weeks are determined upon thy people and upon the holy city, to finish the transgression, and to make an end of sins, and to make reconciliation for iniquity, and to bring in everlasting righteousness, and to seal up the vision and prophecy, and to anoint the most Holy."

The first thing to understand is the 70 weeks mentioned in the verse are really 70 years of sevens. Some of the newer Bible translations have "seventy-sevens" instead of seventy weeks. This period of seventy-sevens, or 490 years, accomplishes the six points mentioned by the angel Gabriel. This first three points address sin; the last three points address the kingdom. Let's look at the meaning of each point, keeping in mind these points specifically address Israel:

- *To finish the transgression*. It's important to distinguish transgression from sin, which is the second point mentioned. So, what is transgression? A simple dictionary definition defines it as a breach or violation against a law or command. As it applies here, is transgression sin? Yes, of course it is. That's why this was a point in Gabriel's response. What was the transgression? Gabriel was responding to Daniel's prayer, so let's look at what Daniel was praying about with regard to transgression. Daniel, in verse 11, said that all of Israel (all 12 tribes, not just Judah) had transgressed God's law. Well, what law? It was undoubtedly the Law of Moses, the Mosaic Law, which was specifically stated in the verse.

Further, Daniel said therefore the curse was poured upon us. The curse was the removal of Israel from the Promise Land. That was the final step God would take if the punishments outlined in Leviticus 26 didn't result in Israel's repentance. Therefore, to *finish the transgression* means to bring an end to Israel's disobedience of the Law of Moses. The transgression will be finished when Israel accepts Jesus Christ, the Messiah, at the end of the last days, which occurs in the last week of the seventy-sevens. The transgression then will be finished, the curse lifted, and Israel will be fully restored to her land in the Millennium at the end of the seventieth week.

- *To make an end of sin.* An "end of sin" is different from "finish the transgression". Where transgression is an act of violation against the law, sin is much broader in scope. You know the expression "the letter of the law"? You can follow the law, be in strict adherence to it, and yet violate the spirit of the law. Daniel admitted, in verse 5, that "we have sinned and have committed iniquity". This goes beyond transgressions of the law.

Christ tells us in John 4:24 we must worship God in spirit and in truth. James 4:17 tells us that if we know to do good and don't do it, it is sin. No law there—just sin. Sin is a matter of the heart. So God will put away or end Israel's attitude of sin. This end of sins occurs when God enacts Ezekiel 36:26, which takes away their "stony heart" (the Law) and gives all of Israel a new heart (the Holy Spirit), under the new covenant, after they recognize Christ as the Messiah.

- *To make reconciliation for iniquity*. Reconciliation is the restoration of a broken relationship. The cause of the broken relationship is because the two sides are not in agreement with each other; the "partnership" is not moving in the same direction. In this case, Israel, because of her sins, has moved away from God, therefore reconciliation has to take place before the relationship can be restored.

  As we know, sin requires payment. God, because He is holy, cannot be reconciled to man; man has to be reconciled to God if there is going to be a relationship. Reconciliation to God was made possible by the death of Christ on the cross. When Christ died on the cross, He paid the price for sin that no other man, before or after, could pay. He was the perfect sacrifice. His death was in atonement for our sins. When Israel comes to recognize Jesus Christ as the Lamb of God, His shed blood will satisfy (atone) the payment for their sin, and reconcile them to God. Then Israel's relationship with God will be restored.

- *To bring in everlasting righteousness*. This refers to the righteous rule of God's kingdom on earth, with Christ sitting on the throne. This happens at the beginning in the Millennium, or the 1,000-year reign following the Tribulation Period. It is the realization of God's original plan for man to have dominion on earth, as stated in Genesis 1:28. Earth will be ruled *righteously and perpetually* by the man Jesus Christ (Revelation 20:4; 1 Timothy 6:15).

- *To seal up the vision and prophecy*. This is in reference to God fulfilling all His prophetic announcements concerning Israel and His covenantal promises with them. This goes back to His promise to Abraham, his seed (Genesis chapters 12, 15, and 17), and David's seed (2 Samuel 7).

- *To anoint the most Holy*. This is the anointing, or crowning, by God of Jesus Christ on the throne, and the establishment of

His kingdom that will last forever. Israel will recognize Christ as Messiah the King in fulfillment of the prophecies concerning God's kingdom, including what Daniel interpreted in Nebuchadnezzar's dream as well as his own!

The completion of the above six events will occur over 490 years, and is divided into three phases. The specific prophetic timetable related to these three phases is found in Daniel 9:25-27, the salient excerpts of which are below:

> *"Know therefore and understand, that from the going forth of the commandment to restore and to build Jerusalem unto the Messiah the Prince shall be seven weeks, and threescore and two weeks: the street shall be built again, and the wall, even in troublous times."*

> *"And after threescore and two weeks shall Messiah be cut off, but not for himself: and the people of the prince that shall come shall destroy the city and the sanctuary..."*

> *"And he shall confirm the covenant with many for one week: and in the midst of the week he shall cause the sacrifice and the oblation to cease, and for the overspreading of abominations he shall make it desolate..."*

Numerically, what we now have is:

1. The rebuilding of Jerusalem, the first phase, is seven sevens, or 7 x 7, which covers 49 years. We find the command to build Jerusalem in Nehemiah 2:1-8. It was issued by the Persian king Artaxerxes and given to Nehemiah in the month of Nissan (March) in 444 B.C. Many scholars have computed March 5, 444 B.C. as the exact date the decree was issued. I'm not in a position to confirm or reject that computation, but is does appear reasonable, especially since multiple sources have computed the same date. So, based on Nehemiah 2 and historical records, we

will use the March 5, 444 B.C. date. This started God's prophetic timetable toward the first phase of Gabriel's announcement. The completion of the city (Jerusalem) in 395 B.C. concluded this part of the prophetic timetable. Just so you're not confused, Persian kings Cyrus and Darius also issued decrees prior to that of Artaxerxes, but those were for the rebuilding of the temple, not Jerusalem.

2. The birth, rejection, and death of Messiah the Prince (Jesus Christ), the second phase, is 62 sevens, or 62 x 7, which covers 434 years. This phase follows the rebuilding of Jerusalem. This calculation is much more sophisticated because of the intricacies of the Jewish calendar and the conversion to the Gregorian calendar, so I'll leave that up to the scholars. Several sources have computed the timing of this portion of the prophecy as presented below. Regardless of the mathematical complexities, we know it was fulfilled 483 years following Artaxerxes' decree because the Bible said that's when it would be fulfilled. It is fact that Jerusalem was rebuilt, and history records Christ came, was crucified, and died without a kingdom. But for those interested, here's some of the basic math as computed by the scholars.

According to Nehemiah 2:1-8, we know the start date is Nissan (March 444 B.C.) on the Jewish calendar. The Jewish calendar is composed of 30-day months (360 days per year). The computed number of days associated with this prophecy ((7 x 7) + (62 x 7)), is 483 years, or 173,880 days. Counting forward 173,880 days from March 5, 444 B.C. gets you to March 30, 33 A.D., which is one of the recognized dates of Christ's death on the cross, something that I will comment further upon shortly.

When Christ was crucified, He had nothing, which goes back to Gabriel's announcement. The Jews had rejected Him, so no kingdom was ushered in. Christ was cut off, as was prophesied. He had no kingdom ... no anything. Further, after Christ's death, the second temple was destroyed in 49 A.D. by the Romans ("the people of the prince that shall come") in fulfillment of the prophecy concerning the destruction of the city and the temple (Daniel 9:26).

Now, to be honest, the most common opinion is no one really knows the exact date Christ died on the cross. April 3, 33 A.D. seems to be another commonly cited date, but other dates have been proffered based on various computations and interpretations of scripture. The March 30 or April 3 A.D. dates, however, are *at least* within a reasonable timeframe consistent with Daniel's prophecy. But since we have the March 5, 44 B.C. proffered date of the decree, I'd go with the March 30 date.

3. The covenant of peace with Israel, the third and final phase, is one year of sevens, or 1 x 7, which covers the last 7 of the total 490 years. This phase of the prophecy remains unfulfilled. This seven-year period is known as the 70th Week of Daniel. Christians generally refer to it as The Tribulation Period. The "he" in Daniel 9:27 is the same person Daniel spoke of in chapter 7—the "little horn", or the Antichrist. The Antichrist will broker an agreement with the nation Israel, which will provide them with the peace they've been longing for since coming back to their land. Yes, there have been many peace accords, and meetings, and more meetings, and more temporary truces, but none have been of a permanent nature. Attacks and skirmishes continue to this day. But the Antichrist will succeed where everyone else has failed because of his influence in the latter days. This will allow Israel to resume their sacrificial offerings in peace.

In the midst, or middle, of the week (three and a half years), however, the Antichrist will break the covenant and put an end to the sacrificial offerings. The middle part of Daniel 9:27 declared this. It is at this time the Antichrist will declare himself to be god, stop the sacrifices offered to the true God, and demand all to worship him. Of course, the Jews will not go for this and will have to flee Jerusalem, or else come under the thumb of this madman; hence the abomination (the Antichrist's declaring himself a god in the temple) and desolation (flight of Israel from Jerusalem).

The Book of Revelation details God's work with Israel and unrepentant man, and reveals His final effort to draw both into His grace. We will discuss this more under the Tribulation Period.

History has recorded the fulfillment of phases one and two of the timetable. However, there is a huge time gap between phase two, the death of Christ on the cross, and phase three, which begins the seventieth week. The most obvious question is: Why is there such a big break in the timetable? That is a perfectly legitimate question, for which there is a perfectly legitimate answer. The answer is there had to be a break in the timeline. Why? Going back to Ezekiel 36, God said He would sanctify His name before the Gentiles. Since Israel profaned God's name before the Gentiles, God couldn't use them to do that anymore. Who was going to listen to them? They were doing the same things the Gentiles were doing. So, God had to accomplish His will another way. That way would be the Church. It is through the Church God's name would be sanctified and the Gentiles would be brought under His grace.

Consider the alternative. Suppose there was no gap in the timetable? Suppose the kingdom came immediately after Christ died on the cross? If that were the case, the first thing is we wouldn't be here to talk about it. If the last seven years of Daniel's prophecy were fulfilled, the Tribulation Period would have come and been long gone, not to mention the Millennium. That suggestion would be absurd. And don't even think about this present world being eternity! That's even more absurd. The fact of the matter is the conditions under which the kingdom was to be ushered in never existed. The events prophesied to happen before the kingdom was to be ushered in hasn't happened. Christ never sat on His throne in Jerusalem, nor was the earth ever full of the knowledge of the Lord, as prophesied. Satan is still running around trying to trip everybody up. And don't forget, Israel still does not believe in Christ, the Messiah. So they would have been left out in the cold as well. So, if there were no break in the timeline, who would have been left out? Easy ... practically everybody! The kingdom would have included Christ, certainly, and probably the disciples, His mother, family members, and those few who repented after witnessing His miracles and those who responded to His message.

The world at large, meaning the Gentiles, would have been left out in the cold, which is something God clearly did not want! So there had to be a gap, or break in the timetable, so that you and I could be included. Don't you feel special now? You should, if you don't.

Understanding that, let's move on to this next phase of God's redemptive program to see how that came about.

The Messiah

Galatians 4:4-5:

> *"But when the fullness of the time was come, God sent forth his Son, made of a woman, made under the law, To redeem them that were under the law, that we might receive the adoption of sons."*

The next step in God's redemptive program begins with the Messiah, who was mentioned in the second phase of Daniel's prophecy of 70 weeks. We know from the timeline provided in Daniel 9 the Messiah was coming, and that He would both come and be "cut-off" within 434 years following the rebuilding of Jerusalem, which was the first phase (49 years) of Daniel's prophecy of 70 weeks.

The coming of the Messiah would also accomplish another purpose: He would sanctify God's name among the Gentiles, which is something God wanted all along. How? Have you been paying attention? Through the Church! The nation of Israel was to lead the way and bring the Gentiles in, but they didn't. Israel was to be a nation of priests, but they weren't. And because of their disobedience and idolatry, God's name was blasphemed by the very people whose job it was to be His representatives before the people God wanted to bring in. As we saw in Ezekiel, God expressed His anger to Israel about their conduct before the Gentiles, but He also said this in Ezekiel 36:23:

> *"And I will sanctify my great name, which was profaned among the heathen, which ye have profaned in the midst of them; and the heathen shall know that I am the Lord, saith the Lord God..."*

God promised to sanctify His name before the Gentiles. But as we learned in Daniel, it wouldn't be through Israel because they were being set aside. They will be restored, but not until the last days.

At the time of Christ, the nation of Israel had been in existence for over 1,800 years. They were used to having God's ear, so to speak, so stepping aside would probably not be the most natural thing for them to do. Perhaps this was another reason why they clashed with Christ, and weren't receptive to what He had to say. The Gentiles ruled over Israel, her people, and the Promise Land through the kingdoms discussed in Daniel chapters 2 and 7. Specifically, we are now in the period of the fourth kingdom, which is Rome. Rome, as you may recall, was represented in king Nebuchadnezzar's image as the legs of iron, and feet and toes of iron mixed with clay. Daniel represented Rome as the fourth beast, the most terrifying of them all. Regardless, the time had come for God to transition the program of redemption, from the Jews under the law, to adoption through His Son, Jesus Christ. It was under this regime, the *old* Roman Empire, that God sent His Son to sanctify His name and redeem the Gentile nations, and it will be under the *revived* Roman Empire that God will take up His program of redemption with Israel. What follows introduces the birth of Jesus Christ, the key to all mankind's redemption.

The Seed is Planted

One day, Mary, who was to become the mother of Jesus, was going about the daily concerns of her life when suddenly the angel Gabriel, who appeared before Daniel, now appeared before her. As you might imagine, Mary was understandably shaken when she saw him. Using current terminology, you might say she almost "freaked out". It is not hard to imagine why. But Gabriel settled her down with some great news (Luke 1:30-35):

> *"...Fear not, Mary: for thou hast found favor with God. And, behold, thou shalt conceive in thy womb, and bring forth a son, and shalt call his name JESUS. He shall be great, and shall be called the Son of the Highest: and the Lord God shall give unto him the throne of his father David: And he*

shall reign over the house of Jacob for ever; and of his kingdom there shall be no end. Then said Mary unto the angel, How shall this be, seeing I know not a man? And the angel answered and said unto her, The Holy Ghost shall come upon thee, and the power of the Highest shall overshadow thee: therefore also that holy thing which shall be born of thee shall be called the Son of God."

One of the most important declarations in these verses, and there are a few, is the virgin birth. Isaiah 7:14 prophesied this:

"Therefore the Lord himself shall give you a sign; Behold, a virgin shall conceive, and bear a son, and shall call his name Immanuel."

Though found in Isaiah, this prophecy goes back to Genesis 3:15, where God prophesied about the seed of the woman defeating the seed of the serpent. No man, no human male, was involved in this process! It was a divine and creative act of God, through His Holy Spirit, fulfilling His Word. It is through God from whom Jesus was born sinless, and not inherit the sinful nature of Adam. Said another way, the sin of Adam, through whom all sin is passed down, was not passed down to Jesus. Jesus is the Son of God!

According to the angel Gabriel's announcement, this child was born to be king of an everlasting kingdom. As you probably know, many, if not most of the kings of Israel were descendants from their fathers before them, with the obvious exceptions of Saul, the first king of Israel, who was subsequently rejected, and David, who was chosen by God to replace Saul. In our present day, there are kings in many countries, and the succession of kings follows that same pattern. But to be the beneficiary of the throne of David, Christ had to come from the line of Judah, through David … all of the prophesies say so. Not only that, both Joseph and Mary had to come through the same line, otherwise Christ could not be descended from David. He could not be the beneficiary of the throne if He was an heir through only one of them. That's why the genealogies of both Joseph and Mary are included in the Gospels. The genealogy of Jesus in the Gospel of Matthew 1 shows Jesus had rights to the throne through His adoption by

Joseph. The genealogy of Jesus in Luke 3 shows Mary's lineage, which also gave Jesus birth rights to the throne. Both genealogies trace back to David and Abraham. Interestingly, the genealogy of Joseph starts with David, the son of Abraham, and goes forward in time, while the genealogy of Mary begins with her father, Heli, and goes backward to David, Abraham, and Seth, who replaced Adam's son Abel, whom Cain murdered. This started the battle of the seeds, remember? So Jesus' right to sit on the throne of David was beyond question.

After Jesus was baptized by John the Baptist, the Holy Spirit led Him into the wilderness to be tempted by the devil (Matthew 4). The question is: Why did Jesus have go through the temptation? This is a question I've asked myself time and time again. I knew that Christ was led into the wilderness by the Holy Spirit specifically to be tempted, and He was obedient to the call. As we just read, Jesus was born of the Holy Spirit, so in that regard, He was and is fully God. As He was born of a woman, He was and is fully human. This position is supported by John 1:1 and John 1:14, which were quoted previously at the beginning of this book. John 1:1 speaks about Christ being with God in the beginning, and affirms that He is God. John 1:14 speaks of Christ becoming man in the flesh, born of a woman. These verses are valuable, so commit them to memory.

As God, Jesus could not be tempted (James 1:13). His divine nature precluded His being tempted to sin. Being fully human, however, He could feel the temptation just as you and I feel it when we are tempted (Hebrews 4:15). Earlier, we discussed the limitations of the physical versus the spiritual. The physical is at a distinct disadvantage. But, Jesus was as tied-in to the Father as one could be spiritually, and as God, He could not be tempted spiritually (with idolatry for example). Therefore, this temptation must be a test of the physical—an appeal to the flesh, or His humanity if you will. We have all faced this temptation at one time or another. What will you do at your weakest physical moment? You have to admit, it's easier to withstand temptation in church, especially since there shouldn't be any there, or right after hearing an inspired sermon. Everybody's all pumped up, filled with the Holy Ghost, and shouting "praise the Lord" all over the place. The question is can you do that when you're not in church, or when you're tired and beaten down, or aggravated? It's easier to be strong when you're strong. Can you be spiritually strong when you feel physically or mentally weak? Can you do that when some knucklehead with bad breath gets in your face and taunts you after a long day at school or work?

So it is here. Would Jesus, after forty days of fasting, continue to withstand the temptations thrown at him by Satan? Would He defeat Satan on his home turf? The outcome of this temptation would affect the whole of mankind. The answer was yes, because this was a spiritual issue (yield to the temptation, or remain sinless) with a spiritual purpose (sinless sacrifice)! It was part of that spiritual warfare mentioned at the beginning of this book. This was the first spiritual battle between THE seeds mentioned in Genesis 3:15. Christ demonstrated that even at His physically weakest point, He would not, and could not, allow a physical test to overcome His spiritual nature. I've often wondered why or how Christ could suffer the brutality of His physical punishment at the hands of the Romans, especially after seeing the movie *The Passion of the Christ*. After all, He could have stopped it at any time. Christ Himself told us He could call twelve legions of angels to free Him from capture (Matthew 26:53). But he didn't do that ... He didn't stop it. While the movie may have been a bit gratuitous with respect to the level of brutality, I believe it captures accurately the intensity of the physical suffering our Lord went through to accomplish the spiritual goal of paying the price for our salvation. The lesson for us, I believe, is that if we hold to our spiritual convictions, we too can overcome any temptation or testing. "God's will first" was Jesus' motivation, and it has to be our motivation not to give in to sin. So, just remember, "If you don't give in, you will not sin." Keep your heart and mind on the spiritual, not the physical. Jesus proved that point at the "temptation" and at the cross. Granted, it is easier said than done, but it *can* be done. Not enough, you say? Well, how about this?

Galatians 5:16

> **"... Walk in the Spirit, and ye shall not fulfil the lust of the flesh"**

That's straight from the Word, so its validity and efficacy cannot be questioned.

It is also worth mentioning that Satan's temptation of Christ was of the same nature as the temptation he used to entice Eve: lust of the flesh (bread to satisfy physical appetite), lust of the eyes (kingdoms of the world), and pride of life (throw himself down from the temple). Remember 1 John 2:15-16.

After the temptation, Jesus began His ministry with these words, recorded in Matthew 4:17:

"...Repent: for the kingdom of heaven is at hand."

There's that word again. As we've learned from our study in Daniel, and God's complaint about Israel's disobedience in Ezekiel 20 and 36, repentance is necessary before God bestows His blessings. In this case, Israel was given another chance to see the kingdom of God established on earth. That's why Christ quoted the kingdom. Repentance first, then the kingdom!

Following His testing by Satan, Jesus' fame began to grow as He taught in synagogues in Galilee and the region. Then He went home to Nazareth and attended service at the local synagogue, where He read the following scriptures before the congregation (Luke 4:18-19):

"The Spirit of the Lord is upon me, because he hath anointed me to preach the gospel to the poor; he hath sent me to heal the brokenhearted, to preach deliverance to the captives, and recovering of sight to the blind, to set at liberty them that are bruised, To preach the acceptable year of the Lord."

Once He read this passage, which was taken from Isaiah 61:1, Jesus sat down and announced (Luke 4:21):

"...This day is this scripture fulfilled in your ears."

The people in attendance were amazed at what He said. This was a very big statement by Jesus. This rocked the boat big time! The people in the synagogue knew what this meant. This is another situation I would love to have seen. Can't you see it? Congregants stared at Him, eyebrows were raised, mouths dropped open, deacons hyper-ventilated, ushers fanned the fainted, sisters jumped out of the pews, and brothers shouted "Say what!?!?" Pardon me, please. Imagination is a wonderful thing. Anyway, this statement created a bit of an uproar to put it mildly. Here was Jesus, a local kid, Joseph's son, claiming to be the Messiah (which means "The Anointed One"), prophesied by Isaiah, who was an honored prophet of God.

Jesus, however, perceived the hesitation by them in accepting His claim and cited two historical incidents as a comeback to their disbelief. The first involved the prophet Elijah and the widow woman at Zidon, found in 1 Kings 17:8-16. The second involved the prophet Elisha and the leper Naaman, a great captain in the Syrian army, found in 2 Kings 5:1-19. In both of these instances, these Gentiles (the widow woman and Naaman) were blessed because they believed, despite the incredible request made of them. They exercised faith. During both of these incidents however, Israel remained in hardship because of their unbelief. The congregants did not take this rebuke well, and tried to kill Jesus, who managed to escape. But Christ had staked His claim in telling the Jews that He was the Messiah they had been looking for. He was here to set up the Kingdom of God on earth, but repentance must come first and then acceptance of Jesus as the Messiah.

Christ began to validate His claim that He was the Messiah by performing the miracle of changing water into wine in John 2. He went on to perform many, many more miracles; so many more in fact that not all of them could be recorded (John 21:25). Christ visited synagogue after synagogue in Galilee, teaching, preaching, and healing (Matthew 4:23) to demonstrate to the Jews that He was the Messiah. His message was directed only to the Jewish people at the time, to let them know the kingdom would be ushered in if they would first repent. When Christ sent out His disciples in Matthew 10, He empowered them to heal the sick and cast out demons. But He specifically instructed them not to go to the Gentiles or Samaritans but rather to the lost sheep of the house of Israel (Matthew 10:5-6) and preach the kingdom of heaven was at hand. Christ was reinforcing the call for repentance to usher in the kingdom.

These miracles, however, began to present a problem to the Jewish leaders of the day. Jesus was drawing crowds of people wherever He went, telling them about the kingdom to come. The Jewish leaders were concerned about His teachings being in conflict with the Law (of Moses) and were afraid of how the Romans were going to react. So they did what most politicians do—they began to speak ill of Him. All the good He had done—such as healing the sick, casting out demons, recovering sight for the blind, even raising the dead—none of that mattered. In fact, the Pharisees accused Him of doing all of these miracles through Satan (Matthew 12:24). Later, in Matthew 21:23, the chief priests and elders asked Jesus by what authority did He do these miracles, as if He, The Son of God, needed their permission!

At one point the Jews asked Jesus directly if He was the Christ (John 10:24). Jesus responded (John 10:25):

> *"...I told you, and ye believed not: the works that I do in my Father's name, they bear witness of me."*

And how did the Jews do in respond to this? They tried to stone Him (John 10:31).

The *coup de grace*, however, came in John 11. In this chapter, Lazarus died and Jesus, after proclaiming Himself to be the resurrection and the life (John 11:25), raised a dead Lazarus back to life. As you might imagine, this news spread quickly to the Pharisees (John 11:46), who with the chief priests, convened a meeting to address this latest miracle. After deliberation, they arrived at a fateful conclusion, expressed in the following verses found in John 11:

Verse 47:

> *"...What do we? for this man doeth many miracles."*

In other words: How do we handle this? What are we going to do? This man is doing too many miracles, and this last one was a whopper!

Verse 48:

> *"If we let him thus alone, all men will believe on him: and the Romans shall come and take away both our place and nation."*

Translation: If He keeps doing these miracles and we don't do anything about it, EVERYBODY is going to believe in Him. The people will continue to follow Him, which will really stir up a problem with the Romans. Then we'll really be in trouble. The Romans will destroy us and our nation.

Verse 50:

"...it is expedient for us, that one man should die for the people, and the whole nation perish not."

Translation: To prevent the Romans from destroying us, this man must die. He must die to save our people and our way of life.

Verse 53:

"Then from that day forth they took counsel together for to put him to death."

So after Christ resurrected Lazarus, the chief priests and Pharisees plotted to take the life of the One who resurrects life. A little ironic, wouldn't you say?

This is truly an amazing conclusion on so many levels. First, the Jewish leaders were blinded by their desire to protect their own way of life, much like many people today who are in positions of power or influence. The truth and reality of what's actually happening, or has happened, is irrelevant to them. Here in John 11, a man was resurrected; a life was restored to one who was dead. There was no denying a real honest-to-God miracle had taken place. Yet, verse 48 tells us that they were concerned about the Romans' taking away "our place", meaning their leadership standing. They clearly missed the point.

Second, they were willing to ignore the miracles of Christ; miracles that were clearly effective in turning the people around and drawing them to Christ's point of view. The people were repenting. They were looking forward to the establishment of the kingdom of God as prophesied! The Sanhedrin (the ruling council of the Jewish people) acknowledged the effectiveness of the miracles in verse 48. For the Sanhedrin to suggest that the miracles were of Satan confirmed their blindness, hardness of heart, and protection of their parochial interest.

Third, they ignored the Old Testament prophecies concerning the Messiah and the Kingdom. Willing ignorance of God and His wishes, and disobedience will *always* give rise to such a result.

Fourth and finally, they were demonstrating absolutely no faith in the God of their fathers. How could the Sanhedrin possibly believe the Romans could stop God from establishing His kingdom? Daniel told them that in his interpretation of Nebuchadnezzar's dream. The stone became a mountain and filled the earth. Their eyes were clearly focused on their place and standing within the community in the here and now, and on the Romans, *not* on God and His kingdom.

John 11:51-52 really captures the irony and prophetic meaning best:

> *"And this spake he not of himself: but being high priest that year, he prophesied that Jesus should die for that nation; And not for that nation only, but that also he should gather together in one the children of God that were scattered abroad."*

The high priest, Caiaphas, didn't really understand that his vote of condemnation was leading to the fulfillment of multiple prophesies going back to Genesis 3:15 and God's first promise to Abram in Genesis 12. Caiaphas and those Pharisees who conspired with him did what they did for all the wrong reasons even though it was factored in God's redemptive plan. As opposed to working to achieve the plan of God, they rebelled *into* the will of God since God's will cannot be overcome. This is what happens when we stubbornly refuse to submit to God's will: We become blinded to the truth! What's the result in this case? No repentance and no kingdom. The Messiah was rejected, as prophesied in Daniel 9:26. He was cut off!

Of course, Jesus knew He would be rejected and the kingdom would not be ushered in, and said so to the Jews in Matthew 21:43:

> *"Therefore say I unto you, The kingdom of God shall be taken from you, and given to a nation bringing forth the fruits thereof."*

There are different interpretations of what this verse means, but it is my opinion that the nation given the kingdom of God was the Church, which produced fruits, and will continue to produce much fruit until the time it is taken away. Jesus said so in Matthew 16:19 in reference to the Church. Going back to Matthew 21:43, it is clear who is being addressed. Jesus was talking to the chief priest and elders of Israel. The question is what, if anything, does the "you" in the verse symbolize? The suggested answers include the nation of Israel as a whole, or the chief priest and elders themselves, or this specific generation? There are arguments on all sides of the table, but Matthew 21:19 cleared that up for me.

> *"And when he saw a fig tree in the way, he came to it, and found nothing thereon, but leaves only, and said unto it, Let no fruit grow on thee henceforward for ever. And presently the fig tree withered away."*

Fig trees normally produce fruit as its leaves appear. Jesus saw the leaves, and since He was hungry, went to it expecting to see figs. Since it didn't, Jesus cursed the fig tree because it didn't bear fruit even though it produced leaves. The nation Israel is represented here by the fig tree. They showed themselves to be fruitful, but in fact, did not bear fruit for the kingdom of God. Therefore, they too are under judgment. They would wither, just like the fig tree.

The Apostle Paul explains the problem of the Jews nicely in Romans 16:25-27:

> *"Now to him that is of power to stablish you according to my gospel, and the preaching of Jesus Christ, according to the revelation of the mystery, which was kept secret since the world began, But now is made manifest, and by the scriptures of the prophets, according to the commandment of the everlasting God, made known to all nations for the obedience of faith: To God only wise, be glory through Jesus Christ for ever. Amen."*

These verses are referred to as a doxology, which is a praise of God. Many doxologies are in the forms of hymns, like "Praise God From Whom All Blessing Flow", which you've probably heard once or twice. But many are scripture verses, such as the above. This particular doxology is more than just praise to God because it lets us know the revelation of Jesus Christ was a mystery to Old Testament prophets and saints. As used in the Bible, a mystery is defined as something not previously known, but is now revealed. This is a perfect example of the process of revelation, first mentioned under The Creation and Fall of Man. God now reveals this mystery; He unveils something new. The Old Testament prophets wrote about the coming Messiah, but didn't know He would be Jesus Christ. They just had faith God would send the Redeemer of Israel and the world. This was part of God's redemptive plan, kept secret since the world was created. The Jews were reliant on the Law, not the promise of the Redeemer, so they had trouble grasping who Jesus was since He was not spelled out specifically in the Old Testament scriptures. But despite the fact that Israel rejected the Messiah and, as a result, negated ushering in the kingdom, God's plan of redemption still moved forward, as we shall see next.

Parting Gifts

Jesus, realizing He must depart without establishing the kingdom, made several important announcements before His crucifixion, some of which we will cover here.

The Church

The first, and one of the most important of all the announcements, is found in Matthew 16:18-19:

> *"And I say also unto thee, That thou art Peter, and upon this rock I will build my church; and the gates of hell shall not prevail against it. And I will give unto thee the keys of the kingdom of heaven..."*

Christ announced a new program called the Church, a term taken from the Greek word "ecclesia", meaning "called out ones". The Church would be the vehicle that God would use to spread the gospel, or "good news" concerning the redemptive work of Christ.

Christ promised to build His Church upon this "rock" called Peter. The disciple Peter's given name was Simon. When he met Jesus for the first time, Christ renamed him Cephas (John 1:42), translated "stone" or "rock" from Aramaic, the common language in Jesus' day. The name Cephas is translated Petros in Greek and Peter in English.

Symbolically, the rock in John 1:42 and the stone in Daniel 2:45 represent the same thing; that being the beginning formation of the kingdom of God. Daniel prophesied the kingdom to come, and Christ told us how it would come—through the Church. This rock called Peter symbolically becomes the mountain or kingdom that Daniel prophesied. Thus, as the Church grows, it will fill the earth, and it will overcome all existing kingdoms, thrones, and rules. This will be realized at Christ's Second Coming, when He rules during the Millennium. True, the renaming of Simon to Peter is also a character reference for Peter, but I don't believe it is coincidental to Daniel 2, especially considering Christ mentioned "rock" and "Church" in the same sentence.

Remember, God's plan was to use the Jews to usher in the kingdom, but couldn't because of their continued idolatry and disobedience (as the Old Testament tells us), and their rejection of the Messiah (in the New Testament). Where the Jews failed as God's representative before the Gentiles, the Church would succeed, and it will all begin with this rock. The gates of Hell shall not prevail against it no matter how many times it tries, or how hard it tries. The Church will prevail because Jesus said so, and He cannot break His Word any more than God the Father can break His.

It is also through the Church that God's name would be sanctified and honored before the Gentiles. To make sure that happened, Jesus gave the disciples a direct command, as found in Mark 16:15:

"And he said unto them, Go ye into all the world, and preach the gospel to every creature."

This is how the Church would bring in the Gentiles. I think you have to admit the Church has been extremely successful in that endeavor. The proof is in the Church itself—it is composed primarily of Gentiles. No race, class, tongue, or groups of people are to miss out on this. If you remember, the miracles and preaching of Jesus was focused mainly in the Jewish communities, but they resisted. When the Jews rejected

Christ that changed, and the Gentiles were blessed! Thankfully, quite a few Jews have accepted Christ as the Messiah. Let's thank and praise God for that!

The Church was also given the keys to the kingdom of heaven (Matthew 16:19), which is a prelude to the discussion Christ had with the chief priests and elders back in Matthew 21:43.

Jesus spoke of this as a future program ("I will") that would occur following His death on the cross. The Acts of the Apostles record the beginnings of the Church, thus realizing the fulfillment of Christ's prophecy. The Church Age began at Pentecost (Acts 2), is still in the building phase, and will not cease building, or growing, until Christ comes back for it. The return of Christ is some very, very good news that we will get to very shortly.

This program is unique and personal to Christ. He calls it "my church". You can't get more personal than that. It is His creation to continue His redemptive work. Christians constitute the Church. The Church is so personal to Christ, it is known as the Bride of Christ, called as such based on the references comparing Christ's relationship with the Church to that of a husband to a wife. My favorite verses to demonstrate this comparison is found in Ephesians 5. The Apostle Paul, in his letter to the believers in Ephesus, discussed the relationship between husband and wife. At the end of the discussion, Paul revealed this relationship as another *mystery*. That means the Old Testament saints had no idea this was coming down the pike. That mystery and explanation are found in Ephesians 5:32:

> *"This is a great mystery: but I speak concerning Christ and the church."*

So while the topic is the marriage relationship, the comparison is clearly made to Christ and the Church. Husbands, love your wives as Christ loves the Church (Ephesians 5:25); wives, submit to your husbands as unto the Lord (Ephesians 5:22). I hope and pray you will keep this in mind as you begin to think about a potential marriage partner. Both partners have an obligation to the Lord under marriage. If one of the marriage partners is not a Christian, the relationship cannot reflect the intended meaning of marriage. They are unequally yoked (2 Corinthians 6:14). Other Bible passages that illustrate this relationship can be found in Romans 7:4, Ephesians 5:24-27, 2 Corinthians 11:2, Revelation 19:7-8, and Revelation 21:2, 9.

But it should be clear to you now that the Church becomes the primary vehicle through which God's redemptive plan, and mankind's means of salvation, takes root.

The Rapture of the Church

As His next parting gift before the crucifixion, Jesus made a promise to come back for His Church in John 14:2-3:

> *"...I go to prepare a place for you. And if I go and prepare a place for you, I will come again, and receive you unto myself; that where I am, there ye may be also."*

This is the first promise of the Rapture of the Church. When Christ ascended into heaven (Acts 1:9), He went home to be with God the Father (John 20:17). While there, He promised to prepare a place for us. Christ cannot be talking about the kingdom to come on earth, because He is talking about where He is going in verses 2 and 3. We will expand on this further when we discuss the Rapture of the Church.

The Holy Spirit

Christ also promised the arrival of the "Comforter," who we now know as the Holy Spirit, or Holy Ghost. In John 14:26 we read:

> *"But the Comforter, which is the Holy Ghost, whom the Father will send in my name, he shall teach you all things, and bring all things to your remembrance, whatsoever I have said unto you."*

Jesus gives us more detail on the functions of the Holy Spirit in John 16:7-14, which includes:

Verse 8:

> *"And when he is come, he will reprove the world of sin..."*

The Holy Spirit will convict the world, unsaved mankind, of their sin. Verse 9 further defines that sin as not believing in Jesus. Therefore, when a man, woman, boy, or girl is prompted to recognize his or her sin in response to the Word, it is the work of the Holy Spirit working within that person to recognize sin, and lead such a person to Christ.

Verse 13:

> *"...he will guide you into all truth..."*

The Holy Spirit provides us with guidance as to what is true. Think of it as God operating within us (for His Spirit does dwell within us— 1 Corinthians 3:16) to inform or instruct us regarding the truths of God. The Holy Spirit passes along the truths of the Godhead to the believer. In that regard, the Holy Spirit will lead us to do God's will. It is not our conscience because our conscience is led by our sinful nature.

Verse 14:

> *"He shall glorify me..."*

The Holy Spirit magnifies Jesus Christ and His work in our lives. He provided the apostles with understanding and remembrance of those things Jesus taught them while He was with them.

We see that the works of the Holy Spirit are multiple. It goes beyond just throwing up your hands and saying "praise the Lord" when things go our way and we feel good about it. We must recognize all that He does and praise Him for all that He does.

Holy Communion

The last of the announcements we'll cover is Christ's institution of a practice to replace the old Passover feast.

Matthew 26:26-28 tells us:

> *"And as they were eating, Jesus took bread, and blessed it, and brake it, and gave it to the disciples, and said, Take, eat; this is my body. And he took the cup, and gave thanks, and gave it to them, saying, Drink ye all of it; For this is my blood of the new*

testament, which is shed for many for the remission of sins."

The origin of the Passover is found in Exodus 12, and represented an annual feast to the Lord in observance of God's liberation of Israel from the bondage of Egyptian slavery. The ceremony required, among other things, the sacrifice of an unblemished lamb. On the night Israel was released from Egyptian captivity, the blood of the sacrificed lamb was poured into a bowl and then wiped along the doorposts of every Hebrew home. The destroyer (Exodus 12:23) "passed over" (hence, Passover) the homes marked with the blood of the lamb, but killed the firstborn (man and cattle) of all other families whose doorposts were not marked with blood.

In Matthew 26:26-28, Christ met with the disciples for the Passover meal and instituted a new practice that we now refer to as Holy Communion or The Lord's Supper. The breaking of bread and drinking of wine symbolize His broken body (a really battered body since no bones were broken) and shed blood for the remission of sins. We are to observe this sacred occasion in remembrance of the Lord until He returns. What are we to remember? The body and blood sacrifice of Jesus Christ, the Son of God. Jesus lived a sinless life, and like the unblemished lamb in Exodus 12, His shed blood can be applied to the doorpost of our lives to free us from the bondage of sin, and spare us from death and destruction—*if* we choose to apply it. His broken body paid the price of our sins; His shed blood forgave us of our sins and ushered in the new covenant. Jesus Christ as the Passover Lamb takes away the sin of the world! This sacrifice also addresses the prophecies of the New Covenant, which we covered Ezekiel 36:24-28 and Jeremiah 31:31-34. We are given God's Holy Spirit to keep and preserve us ... which is what Israel will receive when they accept the Messiah, as Ezekiel and Jeremiah promises.

By Now it Should be Obvious

With the nation Israel "on hold" so to speak, and under the rule of the Gentile kingdoms, God sent His Son, Christ Jesus, to offer the kingdom to the Jews, only to be rejected. Again, God knew this would happen as the testimony of the Old Testament prophets attest. Check out Isaiah 53, Daniel 9:26 (yes, again!), and Zechariah 12:10.

God keeps His Word—in this case the promise He made to Abram (who wasn't Abraham yet)—to fulfill the covenant by Himself. So, specifically, what did God do to fulfill His promise concerning all families of the earth?

John 3:16:

> *"For God so loved the world, that he gave his only begotten Son, that whosoever believeth in him shall not perish, but have everlasting life."*

This is real sacrifice. God gave up something very personal and something very valuable. God sent His Son, born of a woman, to fulfill the promise to bless all families of the earth ... to redeem mankind. God knew this is what it would take. No one else could do it. No one else could fit the bill. Whosoever believes will be blessed with everlasting life. This applies to all people and families of the earth, not just Israel.

John 3:16 is undoubtedly one of the first verses children learn in vacation Bible school, Sunday school, or Bible class. I learned it as a child in Bible class held at a home in my grandmother's neighborhood in Philadelphia. I hope it now makes more sense to you. God's redemptive program always included redeeming mankind to fellowship with Him through the sacrifice of His Son, Jesus Christ. It was a plan established from the foundation of the world (Revelation 13:8). It is a free gift available to all who claim it. Christ died for all men, that we might have everlasting life.

Satan tried to thwart the plan of God, but what Satan did not know, and was ineffective at preventing, was God would send His Son, Christ Jesus, to come down and die on the cross. The prophet Isaiah foretold this in Isaiah 9: 6:

> *"For unto us a child is born, unto us a son is given: and the government shall be upon his shoulder: and his name shall be called Wonderful, Counsellor, The mighty God, The everlasting Father, The Prince of Peace."*

The Son (of God) was given, born as the child, born from a virgin. After the last days, He will be the government of the people, ruling from His throne.

So now we know. God sent His Son, whom Israel rejected, to build His Church and preach the gospel to all men. That sacrifice would bring in the Gentiles and sanctify God's name before them. Aren't you glad about that?

After Christ's death, burial, resurrection, and ascension, the Church was launched, became established, and preached the gospel of Christ throughout the world ... to the Jews and Gentiles! The Comforter (the Holy Ghost), as promised, was sent in Acts chapters 1 and 2 and empowered the first disciples to go forth in power and boldly preach the Word to the world. The stone has become a mountain, and it will continue to grow until it fills the whole world.

To strengthen your walk with the Lord and grow in grace, I strongly encourage you to read Paul's letter to the Romans. It is a fascinating book that details the Christian life, what it means, and more. In my view, it contains more foundational statements about the gospel of Christ than any other book of the Bible. It is an awesome and inspirational read. It gives meaning and substance to the revelation of God to man, and covers topics such as sin, salvation, redemption, righteousness, faith, sanctification, our old and new nature, and much more. It tells us that as much of a blessing as it is to receive eternal life, that isn't *all* we receive. It also tells us who and what we are in Christ.

My final word to you about Paul's letter to the Romans is found in Romans 10:9-10:

> **"That if thou shalt confess with thy mouth the Lord Jesus, and shalt believe in thine heart that God hath raised him from the dead, thou shalt be saved. For with the heart man believeth unto righteousness; and with the mouth confession is made unto salvation."**

Confession is required, but belief is a matter of the heart. God cannot be fooled.

We've covered the things of the past and present. Let's move forward to understand the final steps in God's redemptive program. What follows are those things that will occur at the appointed time in the future. Depending on which side of the fence you're on, these things will either be exciting or dreadful. The choice, as always, is yours and yours alone to make.

The Rapture of the Church

The world today has many religions. Generally, the major religions include Islam, Hinduism, Judaism, Buddhism, and for sake of discussion, let's include Christianity, although Christians do not believe Christianity is a religion. Anyway, each of the non-Christian religions believes its way is the *right* way or *only* way to reach God, or it espouses the "right way" to live. However, an event is coming that will put all such discussions to an end. This event will be a pivotal point in all unfilled prophecy other than the physical return of Jesus Christ to set up His Millennial Kingdom.

The anticipation of this event is so great movies and television series have already been made about it. After this event, there will be no doubt the Bible will be validated in the eyes and ears of many religious and non-religious skeptics. This event is going to get everybody's attention ... so much so that I believe it will be a catalyst to make many of these same skeptics eager and receptive to the Word!

As previously covered, Christ promised to come back for His Church in John 14:2-3. We call the realization of this event "The Rapture". It is the next major prophetic event of the Bible. It is a time of great expectation for Christians everywhere. It is an event that will remove Christians from this present sin-laden earth to be with our Lord and Savior Jesus Christ in heaven, and thus shall we ever be with the Lord (1 Thessalonians 4:17). For Christians, it will be the beginning of a grand and glorious time in heaven with rewards being handed out and a marriage ceremony taking place, while on earth evil reigns and judgment rains.

Don't go looking for the word "rapture" in the Bible. You won't find it. We use this term to define the removal of the Church from the earth immediately prior to the Tribulation Period. This period is characterized by the pouring out of God's wrath on unrepentant man, the reign and domination of the Antichrist, and God's final dealing with the nation Israel. The word "rapture" comes from the Latin word "rapturo", which was translated "caught up" in 1 Thessalonians 4:17. Some dictionaries also translate it to mean "to snatch away".

While many Bible scholars disagree on *when* this event will occur, there is little disagreement that it *will* occur. Some believe the Rapture will occur before the Tribulation Period (pre-tribulation view), some believe it will occur at the mid-point of the Tribulation Period (mid-tribulation view)—just prior to the Great Tribulation Period, and others believe it will occur at the end of the Tribulation Period (post-tribulation view). I have to admit that I like door number one best, but I also believe that is what the Bible teaches.

We Have Lift-off!

References to the Rapture are taken from New Testament prophecies found in three passages:

John 14:2-3:

> *"In my Father's house are many mansions: if it were not so, I would have told you. I go to prepare a place for you. And if I go and prepare a place for you, I will come again, and receive you unto myself; that where I am, there ye may be also."*

1 Corinthians 15:51-52:

> *"Behold, I shew you a mystery; We shall not all sleep, but we shall all be changed, In a moment, in the twinkling of an eye, at the last trump: for the trumpet shall sound, and the dead shall be raised incorruptible, and we shall be changed."*

1 Thessalonians 4:16-17:

> *"For the Lord himself shall descend from heaven with a shout, with the voice of the archangel, and*

> *with the trumpet of God: and the dead in Christ shall rise first: Then we which are alive and remain shall be caught up together with them in the clouds, to meet the Lord in the air: and so shall we ever be with the Lord."*

There's a lot to these three verses, but the gist of the matter is all Christians will be reunited with Christ when He comes for His Church. This includes those who have died (or are "asleep", which is the term the Apostle Paul used for Christians who have died in the past) and those who remain alive. In short, *it includes every member of the Church*, past and present. This event, then, will fulfill the promise that Jesus made to His disciples in John 14:3. Paul provides us with more specifics, namely:

- Jesus is gonna come calling for His Church. He said *"I will come again"* ... not a substitute or proxy. Jesus leads the welcoming party, and either He or the archangel shouts to get our attention. We know for certain the archangel speaks, but we do not know from whom the shout comes. It could be Christ, or it could be the archangel. We also don't know what He will say. It could be something as simple as "come home" or "welcome home". But whatever it is, it will be an attention-getter, and quite dramatic for all who hear it.

- There will be a trumpet sound to augment to voice command. All eyes up! I'm sure that'll get our attention.

- We will undergo a dramatic, physical transformation from corruptible to incorruptible. Our bodies are changed from an earth-bound vessel to a heavenly vessel. There are perks that come with that, by the way. Wait until we get to the Millennium.

- The resurrected bodies of Christians who have passed on before us (those who are asleep) will precede those of us who are alive. Yep! They get first dibs on this great event. After all, most of them have been waiting a bit longer than those of us who will remain (are alive when the Rapture happens). So be prepared when someone zips up past you! The rapture does not apply to

Old Testament saints because they are not a part of the Church. They will be resurrected at the *end* of the Great Tribulation Period when Christ comes back (the Second Coming) to set up His millennial reign on earth (Daniel 12:1-2 and Revelation 20:4-5).

The Apostle Paul tells us in 1 Corinthians 15:51 that the Rapture of the Church is a new revelation, a mystery—another process of revelation. He also tells us we shall be changed from corruptible to incorruptible. We will not and cannot be raptured into heaven in our present sinful bodies. Our current bodies cannot handle the holiness and glory of heaven. So we'll get new *bodies;* bodies that are incorruptible, pure, and sinless. I don't know if they'll make the front of a Wheaties box, but they will be better than that. Read all of 1 Corinthians 15, particularly verses 39–54. Paul makes some great points and analogies about why this change must take place. You'll have a much better understanding of the point he was trying to make after you read this chapter.

Don't be confused about this. The *souls* or spirits (the terms are synonymous for our purposes) of saints who have died in Christ are present with the Lord now (2 Corinthians 5:6-8). Their departed spirits rest with Christ in heaven in the mansions (or apartments) Christ promised to prepare for us. It is the decayed degenerated bodies laid in the earth that are resurrected, incorruptible, to be rejoined with their spirits at the Rapture. So, rejoice! If they had, or you have any kind of physical ailment, they won't and you won't then. Perfect bodies! Think about it ... no eyeglasses, limps, aching hips, bad knees, bunions, hearing aids, pimples ... none of that stuff! No wigs, weaves, or walkers, as the old folks used to say when I was growing up.

As mentioned above, Bible scholars have proposed several interpretations on when the Rapture will occur. Here's the one I'd like to point out to you, found in 1 Thessalonians 5:1-5, which also supports the belief that the Church will not go through the Tribulation Period. It states:

> *"But of the times and the seasons, brethren, ye have no need that I write unto you. For yourselves know perfectly that the day of the Lord so cometh as a thief in the night. For when they shall say, Peace and*

> *safety; then sudden destruction cometh upon them, as travail upon a woman with child; and they shall not escape. But ye, brethren, are not in darkness, that that day should overtake you as a thief. Ye are all the children of light, and the children of the day: we are not of the night, nor of darkness."*

The primary purpose of these verses was to reinforce what these believers knew about the unpredictability of the day of the Lord. The "day of the Lord" has special meaning, which we will get to in the next few paragraphs. Anyway, Paul says they "know perfectly" that the day of the Lord will come unexpectedly, without notice, like a thief in the night.

Before we move further, allow me to digress for a moment. Many people, including some prominent personalities in Christian circles, have tried to predict exactly when the Rapture will occur, down to the day and date. This truly baffles me. The above makes it clear no one knows when the Rapture will occur because no one knows when the day of the Lord will begin. The Rapture precedes the day of the Lord, and the day of the Lord will come as a thief in the night, meaning no one knows when it will occur! A thief doesn't announce when he's coming, so why people would then proclaim to know when the Rapture will occur is just plain nonsense and not supportable from a biblical standpoint. Anyway, let's get back to the verse.

Prophetically, to get what Paul is talking about here, we must understand what is meant by the *"Day of the Lord"*. The Old Testament mentions the day of the Lord in several passages, and all indications were for dark days ahead. The meaning is replete with warnings of destruction, vengeance, darkness, and terror. It is a time of judgment! Check out Isaiah 2:12, 13:6, 34:8; Jeremiah 46:10; Joel 1:15; and Zephaniah 1:14—just to name just a few. Let's look at Zephaniah 1:14-18, which presents a complete picture of that day:

> *"The great day of the Lord is near, it is near, and hasteth greatly, even the voice of the day of the Lord: the mighty man shall cry there bitterly. That day is a day of wrath, a day of trouble and*

> *distress, a day of wasteness and desolation, a day of darkness and gloominess, a day of clouds and thick darkness, A day of the trumpet and alarm against the fenced cities, and against the high towers. And I will bring distress upon men, that they shall walk like blind men, because they have sinned against the Lord: and their blood shall be poured out as dust, and their flesh as the dung. Neither their silver nor their gold shall be able to deliver them in the day of the Lord's wrath; but the whole land shall be devoured by the fire of his jealousy: for he shall make even a speedy riddance of all them that dwell in the land."*

Clearly, this day is not a 24-hour day, but rather a period of time when God will pour out His wrath on unrepentant man. That period of wrath will occur during the Tribulation Period. The questions now become: Does God pour out His wrath on Christians during the day of the Lord? Does the Rapture occur after the Tribulation Period begins? The answer to both questions is *No!*

Paul was comforting the believers in Thessalonica with the good news that they (the Church) will not go through this period. Why? Because we are not on the receiving end of God's wrath! Paul says that in verse 9 of this chapter:

> *"For God hath not appointed us to wrath, but to obtain salvation by our Lord Jesus Christ."*

Christ took care of the wrath against us when we accepted His sacrifice for our sins! We are at peace with God through our Lord Jesus Christ (Romans 5:1). Why, then, would the Church experience God's wrath, as poured out during the Tribulation Period, if we are at peace with Him? The answer is we wouldn't. Paul also says that we are not of the darkness, and thus that day cannot overtake, or include, us. 1 Thessalonians 5:5 tells us we are children of the light, not the darkness. Further, Paul, in addressing who will not escape the day of the Lord uses the pronoun "they" in verse 3 ("they shall not escape"), therefore excluding himself, and us.

A good parallel to demonstrate this consistency is found in Genesis 18:23:

> *"...Wilt thou also destroy the righteous with the wicked?"*

This was Abraham's plea upon learning of God's plan to destroy Sodom and Gomorrah because of their extreme wickedness (Genesis 18:20 and 19:13). Lot, the nephew of Abraham, Lot's wife, and his children were in Sodom. Abraham knew they were there, so he had a personal interest in their salvation from this destruction. So he stated his case before the Lord God and got a partial victory. God still passed His judgment on the cities and carried out His sentence, but made a provision for Lot and his family to escape Sodom's judgment.

The destroying angels told Lot to remove himself, and his family, from Sodom to avoid being destroyed along with the city. Lot obeyed, and his family was spared from the destruction, although his wife disobeyed the warning of the angels after leaving Sodom, and was turned into a pillar of salt (Genesis 19:26). How does this relate to the Church and the Rapture? Just as God made a provision for Lot and his family to be removed from the pending destruction in Sodom, He also makes a provision to spare the Church from the judgments and destructions to come upon unbelievers during the Tribulation Period. That provision is The Rapture. The righteous will not suffer with the unrighteous. Yet another example of God sparing the righteous is His deliverance of Noah and his family from the flood.

Let's look back to 1 Thessalonians 5 for a moment. Paul's letter also states that since we can't predict when the Rapture will occur, he encourages us to be vigilant in our behavior and activities. He encourages holy living. Think about holy living and what that means, and then ask yourself this question: Would you change your plans knowing you'd be staring Christ in the face tomorrow? Don't answer out loud. Somebody might be listening and start eye-balling you. That's why Paul said we are to be watchful (verse 6)! Said another way, since we don't know exactly when Christ will return to gather His Church, we do know He is coming, and we must prepare. There is nothing worse than knowing something is about to occur and not prepare for it ... especially if that something is a real big something. If you remember what it was like preparing for a major test in high school, or college mid-terms or finals, then you understand the importance of preparation if you care about your grades. And this something is of an eternal magnitude, so we must prepare for His coming and live our lives like we know He is coming. Don't live and act in ignorance of the fact that you may stand before the Lord tonight or tomorrow.

The actual occurrence of the Rapture will be a signal to mankind that some pretty strange (at a minimum) or horrifying stuff (at a maximum) is about to happen. It will be the latter if you have any doubts. Imagine it ... hundreds of millions, or perhaps billions of Christians throughout the world will disappear without warning. Mass confusion and hysteria will rule. Undoubtedly it will be the cause of great commotion across the globe. Can you imagine the response here in the United States? Without a doubt, there will be skeptics. Somebody has to come up with a rational explanation of what happened to Christians. Scientists will blame it on some pseudo-rational scientific phenomena that cannot be observed; politicians will blame it on members of the other political parties; and communists will claim it's a subversive plot hatched by western imperialist countries designed to overthrow their government. It will be a heyday for all such "he said-she said" group nonsense.

I do believe, however, that some people who have attended Church regularly and heard about the Rapture, but never accepted Jesus Christ, will realize exactly what happened. They will have heard about it ... probably didn't believe it ... and will then know the truth about it. These will be the same people who've heard the miracles of the Bible and asked sarcastically, "You mean to tell me you really believe Jesus walked on water?" Well, the miraculous will suddenly seem not so farfetched, and they will believe.

In addition, the disappearances will probably result in some destruction, carnage, extreme fright and hysteria. Manned conveyances like cars, airplanes, buses, trains, and other vehicles operated by Christians will suddenly be unmanned, leading to accidents all over the place. Loved ones or acquaintances will disappear in the middle of a conversation, or dinner, or at work. Imagine the mob scene at a sporting or theatrical event when this happens. It will be the start of a very chaotic time. And it is during just such a time that people will be looking for answers; someone to lead them and provide some sense of order, security and stability—someone who promises to bring order out of the chaos. Peace and safety will be the buzz words of the day. Enter the Antichrist.

The Antichrist

Following the Rapture of the Church and amid the ensuing chaos, a charismatic leader will emerge. He will appear to be the "answer man" everyone is looking for to help stabilize the world. This person will be on the scene long before the Rapture, but he will not be understood to be the Antichrist until later. How much later is the real question! What do I mean by that? Depending on your interpretation of certain terms found in 2 Thessalonians 2, many people will know and understand him to be *the* central character of the Tribulation Period before the actual Tribulation Period begins. We'll examine this issue in just a minute.

As we've mentioned before, this person is presently known by many names. One of the more common names is the beast, so called from the description John gave to him in Revelation 13:1, as shown below:

> *"And I stood upon the sand of the sea, and saw a beast rise up out of the sea, having seven heads and ten horns, and upon his horns ten crowns, and upon his heads the name of blasphemy."*

Unless you play power-forward in the NBA or are a professional football player, this is not a complimentary description. This is a heinous, evil, brutal man—a *beast* as John put it. John saw it like Daniel saw it ... from God's perspective. But that's not all.

> *"And the beast which I saw was like unto a leopard, and his feet were as the feet of a bear, and his mouth as the mouth of a lion..."*

These descriptions are similar to the descriptions given to three of the Gentile kingdoms in Daniel's dream (Daniel 7:4-6), which not only provides us with an indication of his world-wide dominance, but of his power and persona as well.

The most common name or term of reference for this person, however, is the Antichrist. He is called that because he is literally *against Christ*. He represents the opposite of everything Christ stood for, lived for, and died for. He is a polar opposite! That the beast is described as rising up out of the sea means he is a Gentile, as opposed to rising up out of the land, which would make him of Jewish descent. The sea referenced here is probably the Great Sea, also known as the Mediterranean Sea. This gives us an indication of his place of origin. In this case, it suggests he is European.

The term Antichrist is familiar to most people nowadays and is synonymous with the numerical 666. If you mention either term, people are likely to know, however limited their understanding, what these terms refer to. A lot of people have come to know of this character through movies or television shows that portray him as a creepy, dark, sinister person empowered by demons of darkness, hell's angels, or Casper the unfriendly ghost. But 666 is definitely taken more seriously within the Christian community, and is a source of great speculation with regard to understanding what it means. This 666 is taken from Revelation 13:18, which states:

> **"Here is wisdom. Let him that hath understanding count the number of the beast: for it is the number of a man; and his number is Six hundred threescore and six."**

First, let me say up front that I have no special understanding about what this number means, other than it represents the Antichrist. But there is plenty of speculation out there concerning what this number means. There's a lot of talk about the number six. Yes, man was created on the sixth day, and yes, man was to work six days and rest on the seventh, and yes, since the number seven represents perfection and man's number is six, it means man falls short of perfection. All of these facts may be interesting, but they aren't meaningful or necessarily have any relevance to the 666. Or maybe they do. I just haven't heard one yet. One of the theories out there suggests that 666 represents Satan, the Antichrist, and the False Prophet, together often referred to as the unholy trinity. As the unholy trinity, they certainly fall short of the perfection that is true of the Holy Trinity, which of course is God the Father, God the Son (Jesus), and God the Holy Spirit. While I agree that the true Trinity is perfect and the unholy trinity falls short of perfection by a long shot, the only problem I see with that interpretation is 666 is ascribed solely to the Antichrist, as we are told in the preceding verse (Revelation 13:17). Verse 18 (above) also states "it is the number of a man". It is the number of his name, not a representation of the unholy trinity. The 666 is a sum representation of the name of the Antichrist. It does not represent individual numbers (6-6-6 or 6,6,6).

All of this speculation, while interesting, cannot be accepted as fact. There are many other suggestions about what 666 means, and many people have opined on the matter. At one point someone suggested it was a former president of the United States because of the six letters in his first, middle and last names. I thought that was pretty funny, but also pretty weak. I also remember reading something long ago that connected 666 with the word "computer". If you take the English alphabet and assign incremental values of 6 to each letter (A=6; B=12, C=18, etc.), then sum the values in the word "computer", it adds up to 666. Now I thought that was really interesting ... not particularly meaningful, just interesting. The Book of Revelation was written in the Greek alphabet (which had 22 letters then; now it has 24), not in English (which has 26), so that application doesn't cut the mustard, so to speak.

The point is no one knows what 666 means. Or perhaps God has revealed it to some. Perhaps there are some modern-day Daniels or Apostle Johns out there who understand what it means. But I haven't heard an explanation or read one that leads me to accept any of these interpretations as fact, or as something plausible. At some point in the future, the meaning will be clear and understood worldwide—but not today. When God wants the number to be understood, He will reveal it, just as He has revealed His redemptive plan over the years.

Laying Low — For Now

Speaking of revealing, another prevailing question seems to be: *Has the Antichrist arrived on the scene yet?* Well, we can't really say for sure that he is not here. Whether he is alive or not, we do know he is powerless to do anything until a couple of things happen.

Let's look at 2 Thessalonians 2 where Paul gives us an indication of when the Antichrist will be revealed—not in terms of what calendar date or year, but rather the circumstances under which he will be revealed. To understand the context of the verses, believers during this time were not only going through their own version of tribulation and hardship, but were also being subjected to false teaching concerning the day of the Lord. This false teaching may have led some believers to think the day of the Lord was immediate. Paul wrote this letter to correct that false teaching, and told the Christians in Thessalonica not to worry about the day of the Lord.

In addition to correcting false teaching, Paul also gave them insight about the introduction of the Antichrist. Paul told these Christians the following in 2 Thessalonians 2:1-3:

> *"Now we beseech you, brethren, by the coming of our Lord Jesus Christ, and by our gathering together unto him, That ye be not soon shaken in mind, or be troubled, neither by spirit, nor by word, nor by letter as from us, as that the day of Christ is at hand. Let no man deceive you by any means: for that day shall not come, except there come a falling away first, and that man of sin be revealed, the son of perdition."*

Before we expand on these verses in 2 Thessalonians 2, there is an interpretive matter I want to discuss that centers on what the "day of Christ" means. Some of the newer Bible versions translate the "day of Christ" found in the original language (Hebrew and Greek), from where we get the King James Version, to "day of the Lord". This is very significant, in my opinion, as these two terms mean very different things. We have already covered the "day of the Lord" when we discussed the Rapture of the Church. Go back to Zephaniah 1:14-18 to refresh your memory. The "day of the Lord" is clearly a day of wrath. There is no dispute concerning that.

The references to the "day of Christ", however, are unique to the Apostle Paul, and are found only in the New Testament in the following verses: 1 Corinthians 1:8, 5:5; 2 Corinthians 1:14; and Philippians 1:6, 10, 2:16. As you read these verses, you will notice that none of them makes reference to the wrath of God. Instead, each makes reference to the return of Jesus Christ, whether it is for the Church (the Rapture), or His second coming when He establishes His throne at the start of His 1,000 year reign (the Millennium). With the exception of the guy who was acting crazy, i.e., immorally with his stepmother in 1 Corinthians 5, all of these verses provide words of encouragement.

Using the "day of Christ" as the reference point, these verses in 2 Thessalonians 2:1-3 tell us is two things will happen before Christ returns for His Church (the Rapture, or "our gathering together unto him" as the verse puts it):

1. **There will be a falling away; that is, an apostasy.** The day of Christ will be preceded by a period of apostasy, broadly defined as an abandonment or renunciation of the faith. In this case it represents a falling away, or a rejection of Christianity (those who *profess*, not confess, to be Christians), a rebellion of people against recognizing God, or a departure from religion in general. This type of rebellion reminds me of what Jesus said to his disciples in Matthew 24:37-38 where he mentioned "as the days of Noah were". People then were acting like anything goes; completely unconcerned about God ... and God was watching. If you keep your eyes and ears on current events, you can't miss the signs that show this world is, once again, headed in the same direction. They are turning away from God and acting like they can do whatever they want. And God is still watching!

   Getting back to the point of the verse, I think it highly probable that many of these apostates are habitual church-goers. However, they are not Christians. They merely attend church because that's how they were reared by their parents or relatives, or see it as the right thing to do to be "spiritual". Revelation 7:9 tells us that a great many people will be saved during the Tribulation Period, and I think (and pray), many of these people will wake up and be among those who will then accept Christ knowing they missed the Rapture.

2. **The Antichrist will be revealed.** While I do believe this will occur prior to the Rapture, I'm going to present two options with this one because of the different interpretations out there surrounding what the "day of Christ" means. If the "day of Christ" is in reference to the timing of the Rapture, then the Antichrist, this man of sin, will be known to us prior to the Rapture because that's what the verse tells us. If that's the proper interpretation, then what you have is:

Apostasy / Revealing → Rapture → Tribulation Period

However, if the "day of Christ" is His second coming, or if it is the same as the "day of the Lord" (and personally I do not believe either to be the case), then clearly we will not know him prior to the Rapture. Christ's second coming *follows* the Tribulation Period, and the day of the Lord occurs *during* the Tribulation Period. The Church will not be around to witness the "day of the Lord", as we've already covered. If that's the proper interpretation, then you have:

Rapture → Apostasy / Revealing → Tribulation Period

Under each scenario, the Tribulation Period is not triggered until the treaty is signed by Israel. Having said that, what is clear is the Antichrist is introduced onto the scene, and the timing of his introduction is centered around 2 Thessalonians 2:2. That is not in dispute or subject to different interpretation.

As a matter of full disclosure, many Christians believe that the Antichrist will not be revealed until after the Rapture of the Church, which is the second option mentioned. Whichever option or interpretation you subscribe to, the point is the advent of the Antichrist surrounds, and is integral to, the day of Christ, however defined, as spelled out in verse 2.

Let's also look at 2 Thessalonians 2:7-8:

> *"For the mystery of iniquity doth already work: only he who now letteth will let, until he be taken out of the way. And then shall that Wicked be revealed..."*

The appearance of the Antichrist is also precluded, or held back, by "he who now letteth" or restrains his appearance (or revelation). Most scholars attribute the identity of the "he" in this verse to the Holy Spirit who indwells each believer and convicts the world of sin. There is zero doubt in my mind that the Holy Spirit, as one of the Trinity, has the power to restrain. Further, since one of His tasks is to reprove the world of sin, and since the work of the Antichrist is in direct opposition to what the Holy Spirit does, it does make some sense that the Antichrist cannot be revealed or empowered to do his dirty work until after the Holy Spirit is removed.

Let's think about the consequences of the Holy Spirit's removal. Because of man's sinful nature, evil does occur. However, the evil that could occur, because of man's sinful nature, does not always occur. Why? It does not occur because of the restraining power of the Holy Spirit working through man in general and Christians in particular. The Holy Spirit and Christians, doing God's will, helps keep a lid on things—all the evil that could take place. The injustices that could occur don't, because we speak out against it. The evil that men could do doesn't happen because Christians would (and should) be up in arms, bringing light to bear. Once the Holy Spirit and Christians are removed, however, the potential and propensity to sin, and therefore propagate evil, would abound. I am reminded of a quote I once read from Martin Luther King, Jr., who said, "Darkness cannot drive out darkness; only light can do that. Hate cannot drive out hate; only love can do that". Without the light in the world through the Holy Spirit and the Church, darkness and evil will reign through the Antichrist, who will then be unrestrained.

A Wolf in Sheep's Clothing

The previous discussion focused on the conditions that introduce the Antichrist's appearance. Now we'll look at what this person will do once he arrives on the scene. We have already covered some of what follows, but in this section we'll present as complete a picture as we can.

The first thing you need to understand is the source of his power and authority, as described in Revelation 13:2:

> *"...and the dragon gave him his power, and his seat, and great authority."*

And who is the dragon? Revelation 12:9 says:

> *"And the great dragon was cast out, that old serpent, called the Devil, and Satan, which deceiveth the whole world..."*

2 Thessalonians 2:9 tells us:

> *"Even him, whose coming is after the working of Satan with all power and signs and lying wonders."*

The Antichrist, this beast, is in league with Satan. Keep these verses in mind as you read about him. These verses make it clear. The Antichrist is empowered and given his authority by Satan. That is what makes him unique, as Daniel said in 7:7 and 7:24 of his book. He, along with Satan and the False Prophet (Revelation 13:11), operate under the same umbrella. And what is their purpose? To be worshipped!

As previously covered, during the last days, a revived Roman Empire will emerge, consisting of ten previously sovereign nations (Daniel 7:7, 24). Since old Rome was broken up into what we know today as Europe, it is probable that a reconsolidation will occur. Out of this revived empire will emerge what Daniel called a "little horn" (Daniel 7:8). He will be a relatively unknown personality who will suddenly uproot, or control, three of the ten horns, or kingdoms. According to Wikipedia, there are approximately 56 sovereign states and 12 monarchies in Europe, so the Antichrist could be hiding in plain sight, and we might not even notice him if he's presently among us. At any rate, he will rise to power through three of the ten nations. Since he will be empowered by Satan (Revelation 13:2), this is not an unrealistic probability. We've already discovered, in Daniel 10, that nations can be controlled by demonic forces.

Also as mentioned earlier, this person will be brilliant. Daniel 7:8 described this little horn as having "eyes like the eyes of a man", meaning intelligence. Although John describes him as a beast in Revelation 13:1, he won't be instinctual like a brute beast or wild animal. He is governed by brutal or evil intelligence, not beastly instinct. That is not hard to surmise when we consider who it is that supports him (Satan), as well as what it is he will do prophetically. I think it's fair to say most people are attracted to intelligence at some level, or at least somewhat fascinated by it. On the negative side, some might be jealous of it at a deeper level. I've met some highly intelligent people who were pleasant and mesmerizing, and others who were downright nasty and arrogant. The point is, we are sometimes amazed at how they grasp the most complex issues, and then simplify them to explain it to us common everyday folks. Perhaps the attraction to intelligence is the wonder of how these people absorb tons of information and regurgitate it all at a moment's notice. These are the people who blow the test curve and make it difficult for everybody else to get higher grades. I remember those days ... they weren't fun. Anyway, this beast is one of those people. He will be highly intelligent. And when he speaks, the world will listen. The issue with him is how he put this intelligence to use.

Daniel 9:27 tells us that he will reach a covenantal agreement with Israel for one week, or seven years; something no one else has been able to do, by the way. So his introduction to the world will be benign relative to his end objectives. Israel will no doubt be happy. From their perspective, there will be no more acts of aggression against them from other nations seeking to take away their land. Further, they will be able to reinstitute their sacrificial practices in a new temple that we presume will be built since it is from the "holy place" that the Antichrist will commit the abomination.

Peace and safety ... noble goals on the part of the Antichrist. Crafting a peace treaty and taking over three kings is certainly not the accomplishment of a stupid person, or even one of average intelligence. Crafting an agreement to protect Israel and taking over three kingdoms will, I believe, place this person front and center in the news and in world political circles ... all under the guise of doing good. Such feats will leave his intelligence and leadership beyond question.

Assuming the Antichrist is revealed before the Rapture, he either brokers this agreement prior to the Rapture (less likely) or immediately thereafter (more likely). I believe it will be immediately thereafter since the brokered agreement starts the Tribulation Period, and we have already demonstrated that we (Christians) won't be here when that occurs. At any rate, the Antichrist undoubtedly will have created a name for himself in doing so, making it easier to consolidate his influence and power among the revived Roman Empire (Europe) and the rest of the world.

Now let's move on into spiritual issues. In the absence of the raptured Church, the Antichrist will support an ecumenical movement to foster spiritual comfort via a one-world religious "church" (aka The False Church). The most obvious problem with this is it leaves out God. Revelation 17:1 goes so far as to call this movement or system "The Great Whore" because it drives mankind into false worship. The use of the term "The Great Whore" defines acts of gross immorality, unfaithfulness, and idolatry. I believe the period of apostasy is a lead-in to facilitate this abomination.

Revelation 17 also makes it clear that this false religious system sits upon the beast, meaning it also is supported by the beast. So early on in the Tribulation Period, the Antichrist engages in activities that broaden his base of support worldwide in political and religious matters. Other big events will be going on at the same time, such as the judgments, but here we are talking only about the Antichrist and his activities.

Let's see what happens at the mid-point, when the tide turns.

On the Prowl

The introduction of the beast, as described in Revelation 13, reflects his character leading into the last three and a half years of the Tribulation Period. It is during this time the world will see his true colors. The Apostle John saw a beast, something wild, untamed and powerful, just like what Daniel saw in his visions (in Daniel 7). They are not coincidental. Daniel 7:25 tells us that he will "think to change times and laws", meaning he will have no regard for established customs, principles, or laws. He will do as he pleases and institute his own system, reinforcing his character as someone wild and untamed.

I believe around this time, or just prior to the start of the last three and a half years, something will occur to shock the world. The Antichrist is riding high in popularity; his influence is worldwide or perhaps wildly growing. John in Revelation 13:3 tells us what happens then:

> *"And I saw one of his heads as it were wounded to death; and his deadly wound was healed: and all the world wondered after the beast."*

The Antichrist (or one of the ten heads) will receive a fatal wound from which he, or one of the other (ten) heads, will recover. This could be interpreted a few ways. The first is that one of the heads (a kingdom) receives a symbolically fatal wound; something that compares to a death blow. It could be that a kingdom falls but is revived in some miraculous way. The other, more common interpretation is the Antichrist himself is slain, but somehow is revived in a miraculous way. This interpretation, then, presents the Antichrist as a type of messiah—one who is raised from the dead or revived to life. Either way, the recovery will be a wonder or astonishment to many people, to such an extent it will cause many to worship him.

Revelation 13:4 says:

> *"And they worshipped the dragon which gave power unto the beast: and they worshipped the beast, saying, Who is like unto the beast? who is able to make war with him?"*

This is exactly what the Antichrist wants. After this, things will get really nasty. This is the point when he starts to do his thing.

One of the first things he does in the second half of the Tribulation Period is break the treaty with Israel (Daniel 9:27). Jesus made mention of this in Matthew 24:15 when he referenced the "abomination of desolation" spoken of by Daniel. It is at this point the Antichrist's true agenda becomes clear. No more Mr. Nice Guy. In fact, at this point he doesn't consider himself a *guy* at all ... he thinks he's God. An excerpt from 2 Thessalonians 2:4 makes this clear. Paul, speaking about the Antichrist, said:

> *"...so that he as God sitteth in the temple of God, shewing himself that he is God."*

If his recovery from the fatal wound precedes this, then perhaps he feels empowered following the recovery. Granted, the timing of the fatal wound is speculative, but it will happen as prophesied. The Antichrist will commit "the abomination of desolation", i.e., the act of proclaiming himself to be God in "the holy place" (Matthew 24:15), which is located in the temple, as referenced in the above verse. He breaks the treaty with Israel, and forces an end to their sacrificial offerings to the Lord God because he refuses not to be recognized as God. In his mind, if a sacrifice is to be made, it better be to him. Any recognition of another God, other than Satan, is a big no-no. This is the fulfillment of Daniel 9:27. By the way, this act signals the start of the Great Tribulation, which will usher in the worst time period mankind will ever know.

The Antichrist then goes on a search-and-destroy mission. An excerpt from Daniel 7:25 tells us:

> *"...and they shall be given into his hand until a time and times and the dividing of time."*

The "they" in the above verse are the saints of God, whom the Antichrist will persecute and kill. Unfortunately, this will represent a time of unprecedented persecution for those who convert to Christianity in acknowledgment of God's call for repentance. This is, therefore, all the more reason to respond to God's grace now! Don't wait. You won't have to go through this.

The time (one year), times (two years), and dividing of time (one-half year) is a total of three and one-half years, which represents the length of the Great Tribulation period. So, the abomination and the Great Tribulation go hand-in-hand. Likewise, Revelation 13:5 reveals the same timetable:

> *"...and power was given unto him to continue forty and two months."*

These forty two months are the same three and one-half years of Great Tribulation.

Christians won't be the only ones in the cross-hairs of the beast. Holding himself out as God, the Antichrist won't tolerate the worship of anything other than himself. So guess who he targets next? The one-world religious "church", aka spiritual Babylon, he set up in the first half of the Tribulation Period. He works with the "kings of the earth" (Revelation 17:12-16), who are the leaders within his political empire, to destroy the one-world religious system. The Bible devotes two whole chapters to the destruction of Babylon in Revelation 17 and 18, so its role and impact during the Tribulation Period is as heinous as it is noteworthy. We'll cover much more of this later. But for now, with the elimination of the one-world religious system, the Antichrist assumes total control as the world's political and spiritual leader.

Daniel 7:8 and Revelation 13:5-6 also tell us that he has a "mouth speaking great things". With an ego unchecked and empowered by Satan, he will blaspheme the name of God, the only One truly worthy of receiving worship. Why does he blaspheme God's name? Although the Bible doesn't provide an answer to that question, it's not hard to figure out. He follows Satan, who has been at odds with God since before man can remember. He is empowered by Satan, so naturally he is inclined to think and do what Satan thinks and does. He's clearly out to damage God's reputation and name, and perhaps even curse God for the carnage brought on by the judgments, which will be spelled out in the upcoming chapters. I believe his blasphemies are also to direct others to an alternative to God, namely himself and Satan. There always seem to be a "what's in it for me" when others are spoken ill of. Or perhaps he has simply taken on Satan's mantra against God.

There's an expression "absolute power corrupts absolutely". That attitude will define the Antichrist, particularly during the last three and one-half years. This guy will be on a roll! He's got the world on a string, Satan has his back, and the kings of the earth to do his bidding. With all of those things in his back pocket, he will say and do as he pleases. While the Antichrist will be recognized for his intelligence, he clearly has no spiritual wisdom as evidenced by his alliance with Satan and blasphemy against Almighty God.

With the aid of the False Prophet, who we will discuss later, the Antichrist will institute a system requiring all men to receive a mark or number (aka the "mark of the beast") in order to buy or sell anything (Revelation 13:16-17). This will give him absolute control of the world's economy. This is of critical importance and presents an enormous problem for all who live during this time. Revelation 14:9-10 tells us why:

> *"...If any man worships the beast and his image, and receive his mark in his forehead, or in his hand, The same shall drink of the wine of the wrath of God, which is poured out without mixture into the cup of his indignation; and he shall be tormented with fire and brimstone in the presence of the holy angels, and in the presence of the Lamb."*

In other words, whoever takes the mark of the beast cannot be saved! Taking the mark seals your eternal damnation. Taking the mark eternally separates you from God and condemns you to the Lake of Fire ... *forever*. Think about that for a minute. If you believe in God, then it's really a simple question with an obvious answer. Do you want to be eternally separated from God? I would hope your answer is "of course not!" For those people around during that time, the decision to take the mark, or not take the mark, will be the last and most important decision they will ever have to make.

Some people will willingly take the mark because they have been deceived, and as a consequence will worship the Antichrist. These are people who have been taken in by his brilliance, his status, his accomplishments, and undoubtedly by the miraculous recovery from the fatal wound. However, there will be those on the fence faced with starvation, in need of medical care, or in need of other services that require money. They will be made to suffer if they choose not to accept the mark of the beast. Their decision, then, will be to take the mark or else starve, die of hunger, not receive medical care, or not get the services they require. I am reminded of what Jesus said to the masses in Matthew 6:25:

> *"Therefore I say unto you, Take no thought for your life, what ye shall eat, or what ye shall drink; nor yet for your body, what ye shall put on. Is not the life more than meat, and the body more than raiment?"*

This will be decision time for those in the Tribulation Period. But you must know nothing is worth more than the loss of your eternal soul—not food, not clothing, nor anything in between (Matthew 16:26). It is better to suffer for a moment than to suffer for an eternity.

Clearly this man, the Antichrist, is against God and God's program. His alliance with Satan, as well as the prophecies that foretell what he will do, confirm that. But don't get bent out of shape about this. Good news is on the way. As with any and all who oppose Almighty God, the reign of the Antichrist is ordained to end when he leads the armies of the world against Jerusalem (Zechariah 12; Revelation 16:13-14, 19:17-19) in what is commonly known as the Battle of Armageddon. This battle will occur at the end of the Tribulation Period, so let's see what else will happen during that time.

Hebrews 10:31

"It is a fearful thing to fall into the hands of the living God."

The Tribulation Period

> *"But as the days of Noe were, so shall also the coming of the Son of man be. For as in the days that were before the flood they were eating and drinking, marrying and giving in marriage, until the day that Noe entered into the ark."*
>
> Matthew 24:37-38

These verses were spoken by Jesus Christ, so you really should listen. "As the days of Noah were..." What do you think that means? Jesus said in the days of Noah, people were eating and drinking, marrying and giving in marriage. Does that sound bad to you? It doesn't to me if I ignore what I know and what we've covered about the timeframe. There's nothing inherently bad about eating and drinking, as long as you don't do either too much. People were marrying and being given in marriage. At that time, these were the routine things of the day. You know what? People are doing the same kinds of things today. Actually, if you combine the eating and drinking with the marrying, it kind of sounds like a party or wedding reception, doesn't it? Sounds like fun? Well, it may have been at that time too ... *until* Noah entered the ark. Then the party was over. I mean really over. And there wasn't going to be a party next week either ... or the week after that, for that matter. Matthew 24:39 tells us they "knew not until the flood came", which implies it caught them by surprise. On the surface, those days may have seemed kind of harmless, but we know those days were evil, as Genesis 6:5 tells us:

> *"And God saw that the wickedness of man was great in the earth, and that every imagination of the thoughts of his heart was only evil continually."*

This was obviously a fatal indictment against that generation. *Every imagination was only evil ... always.* This was the battle of the seeds, as we discussed earlier. But what should concern the unsaved of today is this present world is headed in the same direction. People are concerned with eating well, drinking the good stuff, and marrying whomever for whatever reason ... all in the absence of what God must be thinking. The end result won't be quite the same as the days of Noah because God covenanted never to destroy man again with a flood. But His holiness still demands payment for sin. The point is that in the times and days yet to come, however normal those days might seem, God will once again execute judgment. Only this time, instead of a flood, God's wrath will rain down upon mankind through multiple series of judgments, and man will suffer greatly ... as in the days of Noah.

Moving toward the end of things to come, immediately after the Rapture of the Church, the unsaved are going to get a serious spanking, to put it mildly. It's not going to be a "time out" where you get to sit around and think about what you've done. Instead, God is taking man out to the woodshed for a whupping. It will not be pleasant. In fact, it will be terrifying! Mankind has talked back to God in a sassy tone, rolled his eyes, and defied God's command to stop the sin stuff. And when God offered love and mercy, man looked Him dead in the eye (figuratively speaking, of course), sneered, and said "yeah, right!" He has ignored God's warnings, again and again and again. How did God warn man? Well, God put man on notice through His written Word, the Bible, which tells man repeatedly of his wrath to come. God also warned man throughout the ages by the prophets, pastors and preachers. I believe God also made His will known through nature, or natural occurrences. God has been patient and gracious. However, since man hasn't responded to God's call by grace during the present Church Age, all that's left are the spankings to get man's attention, much like what God did with Israel. When that time comes, man will not be able to ignore God anymore due to the cascade of judgments that will fall. It will be God's final call of action to man, and the book of Revelation tells the whole story.

Volumes of books, commentaries, and study materials have been written about this time period. I invite you—in fact *urge* you—to read what's available. Just make sure what you read is Bible-based. Do a little research. Don't worry; it won't hurt my feelings. I am under no illusion that a few will not reach some of the same conclusions I have, particularly on the interpretations of the symbolism cited in Revelation, and perhaps one or two of the timing issues as well. It is good for you to be well-rounded and fully aware of the many issues surrounding the interpretation of the last days, as prophesied in Revelation. Just keep in mind it is part of God's redemptive plan.

There are many names for this period of time ... the most common term is the *Tribulation Period*, probably because that's how Christ referred to those days in Matthew 24:29. It is a period of intense tribulation for the world. Some people call it the *70th Week of Daniel*, in reference to the last of the 70 weeks in Daniel's prophecy. A few people will refer to it as *"the time of Jacob's trouble"*, according to the verse found in Jeremiah 30:7. Zephaniah's rendering is rarely referred to at all when and if you hear talk of the last days. No one came up with a catchy term for his description, but his description is frightening! But, no matter how you wish to refer to the latter days to come, big-time trouble is on the horizon.

The book of Revelation covers many unique aspects of the end times other than God's wrath. It is, in fact, the last of Daniel's seventy weeks, which makes this book supplemental to Daniel 9. Because it is the 70th week, it will also be the time God takes up His program with Israel; a plan revealed in a direct response to Daniel's prayer in Daniel 9. Israel will not enjoy this period either. "The time of Jacob's trouble" is definitely a reference for the Jews. They will experience the same wrath that God will lay upon all mankind, plus some. But God will save them out of it, as Jeremiah 30:4-7 tells us:

> *"And these are the words that the Lord spake concerning Israel and concerning Judah. For thus saith the Lord; We have heard a voice of trembling, of fear, and not of peace. Ask ye now, and see whether a man doth travail with child? wherefore do I see every man with his hands on his loins, as a woman in travail, and all faces are turned into paleness? Alas! for that day is great, so that none is*

> *like it: it is even the time of Jacob's trouble; but he shall be saved out of it."*

All of Israel (all 12 tribes) will experience great trials and hardships, akin to a woman in labor. I have yet to hear any woman call this travail (birth pains or labor) pleasant! I once heard a woman compare the pain of childbirth to pinching your top lip as hard as you can until it gets to the point where you just can't stand it anymore—and then rip it over your head! Absolutely gruesome! To reinforce the pains that Israel will have to endure, Jeremiah 30:11 says:

> *"For I am with thee, saith the Lord, to save thee: though I make a full end of all nations whither I have scattered thee, yet will I not make a full end of thee: but I will correct thee in measure, and will not leave thee altogether unpunished."*

So Israel will have to endure this period just like everyone else. They will be corrected (punished) for their sin and disobedience. But God will save the nation, as He promised He would. And He will still offer to save the unsaved.

Another unique aspect about this period is it represents the only time in world history that mankind is absent the righteous. All the people who enter the Tribulation Period are unsaved ... every single one of them. There's not a saved person among them, which makes what God will do even more amazing. But we'll get to that later. The Church is the vehicle God uses to call the Gentiles and Jews, and has been since the New Testament days. That continues to this day. However, not everyone has heeded the call. Those who did and are alive will be raptured out of here before this period begins. The people who did not heed the call are the unsaved. They did not come by grace. Now, during this period, the call to come will be by wrath. Those of you who don't believe in spankings as punishments will be disappointed God doesn't share your views on this matter. Get over it! Leviticus 26 should be ringing in your ears.

The final aspect I want to point out about Revelation is it unveils the final realization of God's prophetic plan. This is the end game. Everything gets wrapped up in this important book. But don't forget what this book is really all about. Need a hint? Since this book is prophetic, let's go back over some of the related prophecies. The very first prophesy in the Bible was pronounced by God, and it was about the seed that would become Christ (Genesis 3:15). All prophecy concerning the everlasting kingdom to come was about Christ. The prophecies concerning the blood sacrifice, and the atonement and redemption of man were about the sacrifice of Christ, the Lamb. So guess what Revelation is about? Christ, the King! It all points to Jesus Christ and His kingdom rule. Thy kingdom come! Thy will be done! Well, it's coming ... and God still wants you to be a part of it. The first advent of Christ was as the sacrificial lamb. His second coming will be as the conquering King. Revelation tells us how it all finally comes to a head.

Since the flood, the world has yet to experience the level and intensity of tribulation that will come in these days. How bad will it be?

Jesus said in Matthew 24:22:

> **"And except those days should be shortened, there should no flesh be saved..."**

Jesus said that, and He knew about the flood and everything in between. Now that's bad. It is the day of the Lord, a period of wrath.

The Tribulation Period begins with a covenant agreement brokered by the Antichrist, as we've previously covered in Daniel 9. So following the rapture and the ensuing chaos, there will be a glimmer of hope for peace, or maybe even a brief moment of peace. This is merely the proverbial eye of the hurricane. It won't last long. This seven year period can be further divided into two periods of three and one-half years each. As a whole, it is known as the Tribulation Period, but *the last three and half years* are absolutely terrifying in terms of the death, destruction, plagues, and the like, and it has its own name—the *Great Tribulation*.

The book of Revelation provides great detail concerning the many destructive events that will occur, as well as God's final and miraculous efforts to get mankind to repent ... Jews and Gentiles alike. It is mankind's last best chance, for after this your final residency is forever "etched in stone", as the saying goes. There are only two options for these people, just like there are only two options for everyone now. Option one is hanging out with the Lord, in fellowship, throughout eternity. You have to pick this option. It will not be granted or bestowed upon you. Option two is to be separated from God ... forever ... in torment ... in the Lake of Fire, not Hell as we are so often led to think. You don't have to pick this option because that's where you're headed if you don't pick option number one. So, it's your choice. Pick option one, or default to option two. Your final destination in either case does not hinge on how good a person you are, or think you are, or how good a life you have led up to this point. Your final destination will be based on your repentance, acknowledgment of your sin, and then accepting Jesus Christ as the only redeemer for your sins (aka option one). Your final destination is determined by you ... by the choice you make! No one else can make it for you. There's a big risk, however, waiting for those who go through the Tribulation Period. The risk assumes those who enter this period live through any of the judgments long enough to choose option one. That's a huge risk.

Before we get heavy into Revelation, let's settle on a few points as a preface to this study.

1. To start out, there is a blessing to those who read and hear the words of this prophetic book (Revelation 1:3).

   > *"Blessed is he that readeth, and they that hear the words of this prophecy, and keep those things which are written therein: for the time is at hand."*

   So read and study a lot ... get those blessings! Despite the inherent difficulty in understanding Revelation, we are encouraged to read it, hear it, and abide in it (take it to heart). This is a blessing looking for a place to happen. So if you're not hearing about it through sermons, tell your pastor, in a loving manner of course, that he is missing out on an opportunity to impart a blessing to the congregation.

2. Revelation was written to the seven churches named in Revelation 1:11. Christ tells John:

> *"...What thou seest, write in a book, and send it unto the seven churches which are in Asia; unto Ephesus, and unto Smyrna, and unto Pergamos, and unto Thyatira, and unto Sardis, and unto Philadelphia, and unto Laodicea."*

Jesus sent a personal message to each of these churches, which represent the types of churches in the world then, today, and tomorrow. I pray you are worshipping at a church like Smyrna or Philadelphia. When you read about these churches in chapters 2 and 3, you will understand why. They were the only churches Jesus did not rebuke. Jesus is telling the other five churches to get their act together. He even tells them their problem so they can fix it. It is interesting, and unfortunate, that I remember hearing very few sermons about these churches, particularly in my adult years. Considering that most of what is spoken in the first three chapters are the words of Jesus, I would have expected more sermons to focus on them, but no matter. And, yes, I was paying attention, in case you're wondering.

Also, there have been very few sermons on Revelation itself, which is also unfortunate, particularly since there are blessings associated with reading and hearing it, as we just learned. But, it would be very unwise to dismiss the prophecies or judgments as fantasy, or intentionally misrepresent them, because there are curses on those who do (Revelation 22:19). Admittedly, Revelation can be difficult to understand because of the symbolism, and hard for many to accept because of the incredible nature of the judgments, but this leads me to the next point.

3. The book of Revelation is heavy in symbolism for a very simple reason. John was attempting to explain the things he saw, but had no way of communicating in a way that makes sense to modern man. He clearly saw things beyond his age. He may even have seen things beyond our present age. We don't know. To us, there is no basis of comparison or experience John had to help us understand all that God revealed to him. Further, I

believe John may have understood the meaning of what God showed him, but not necessarily all the details of his vision; hence the symbolism. The difficulty for us, then, is in attempting to interpret, accurately, all of what he saw. Imagine someone in the time of Adam, or the time of Christ for that matter, attempting to describe an airplane, submarine, or armored tank. After freaking out, maybe the person, after his hands stopped shaking, would describe something that might make us laugh. As a consequence, the substance of what John saw, as expressed through symbolism, is open to many interpretations. There are, however, some things that are concrete and not subject to interpretation, as you will see.

4. The chapters in the book of Revelation are not chronologically arranged. Certain chapters and verses are *parenthetical*, meaning some of the information (chapters and/or verses) presented represent a break in the flow of the judgments to convey concurrent or supplemental information to what John had already seen. So while you are reading Revelation, think of the chronology of the judgments of God—the seals, the trumpets, and the vials (bowls). You will find some chapters and verses that break into the chronology of the judgments to talk about other stuff. For example, Revelation 6 begins with the breaking of the seal judgments. The next series of judgments (the trumpets), however, doesn't begin until chapter 8, making chapter 7 parenthetical. That means everything reported in chapter 7 occurs during the opening of the seals. Recognizing these parenthetical insertions facilitates understanding the order of Revelation. It helps you place the major events in the proper sequence and timeframe.

5. This bears repeating. There is no shortage of opinions that offer alternate interpretations on what some of this means, particularly when it comes to the symbolism and the timing of the events described in Revelation. In that regard, a minor comparison can be made to how the writers of the Gospels wrote about the life of Christ. They all witnessed what Jesus did on this earth, but there are distinct differences in how each of those writers depicted and related His life in each of those books of the Bible.

Of course, the difference now is godly people (hopefully) are trying to interpret what will happen as opposed to Matthew, Mark, Luke and John, who told us what did happen. People who are a lot smarter and better versed than I can provide you with more insight on how to put this all together. I pray you will seek such people out. I sincerely and humbly bow to their expertise and Christian experience. I also encourage you to seek out other literature on this topic. I'm not trying to present an authoritative or exhaustive work on this book. Rather, what I am trying to do is present you with a "working knowledge" of the contents of Revelation, and how they relate to God's redemptive program.

6. This also bears repeating. Always remember this is the period when God reinstitutes His redemptive program with Israel, and bring them to repentance and acceptance of Jesus Christ, the Messiah. In many ways, Israel is one of the keys, just not *the* key ... Christ is *THE KEY* to God's redemptive plan. Although Israel failed from the Christian perspective, the prophecy nonetheless revolves around them. To understand how God does this, look for chapters and verses that highlight Israel specifically. So even though this time period represents the "day of the Lord", and God's wrath is poured out on all of mankind, Israel will receive special, and in some instances, unwanted attention. The flip-side is they will also receive divine protection and deliverance.

7. There is a lot of punishment going on—a whole lot of punishment. So much so that you might think this seems like a lot just to get someone's attention. Doesn't all this wrath stuff seem a bit extreme? Okay, I understand how someone might think that, but first consider this. Think of the relationship between parent and a disobedient child. Perhaps some of you have been on the receiving end of something like this when you were much younger, probably around the 5-10 years of age range. Most children of that age range know what a parent means when they say "do this" or "don't do that". However, suppose the child repeatedly demonstrates a propensity to do the opposite *and* place himself or herself in danger in the process? What do you

think a parent should do to capture the attention of a wayward child? Would you just smack him or her upside the head? With today's laws, you'd probably end up convicted as a child-abuser and sent to jail if you were caught doing it.

But let's say the parent told the child to stay on the sidewalk or the grassy area, stay clear of the curb, and not go into the street. Those are reasonable instructions, right? No parent wants to see their child in danger, or face potential danger. The instructions are meant to protect the child from the danger of being hit by a car, truck, or bus. The child might not understand the potential danger, but the parent does. The child says ok, and after a moment, inches toward the curb. The parent might say it again, only a little bit louder with a bit of an edge to the voice ... like they might mean it. The child stops for a few minutes ... you know ... because mom or dad had that tone in their voice to let you know they might mean it this time. But because there was no punishment, moments after the parent turned their back, the child moves closer and closer to that curb. The parent's next warning will undoubtedly get louder still, maybe become even more stern, with more tension ... you know ... because this time the parent has "had it up to here" with the child's disobedience.

What do you think a parent would do if the child was about to run out into the street, and a car was coming? The startled parent would probably yell to get the child's attention, particularly if there was too much distance between the child and parent. But, if the parent were close enough, he or she might even grab or snatch the child with enough force to cause some physical discomfort, pain, and maybe leave a bruise. That's kind of like those scenes you've seen on television shows or in the movies when a hysterical person is slapped in the face in order to get him or her to calm down in a crisis and get them to focus. The pain of grabbing, or the slap, is incidental to pulling the child out of danger, or calming down the hysterical person.

Up until now, this is exactly what God has been doing. God has been warning and warning, and getting louder all the time, but mankind hasn't taken the hint. All of mankind is in danger, and God is yelling at mankind to stop doing what it has been doing and repent. Mankind, in a figurative way, is running out into the street, without a care in the world, footloose and fancy-free, but not looking for oncoming traffic. Most people do not enjoy being scolded and lectured by anyone; probably much less by some God they're iffy about. But, it is a warning. And we certainly don't want almighty God yelling at us, do we? This is a trick question in case you haven't caught on yet. The answer is *Yes!* If it is to save our lives, we should welcome the yelling. Why? Because, based on what we know about the days of Noah and Israel's history, God will dispense punishment. Unrepentant sin will be punished. Count on it! We should all know that by now.

8. One more thing before we move forward. The judgments are as mind-boggling as they are plenteous. You'll read about epic celestial events that contribute to disastrous consequences to earth's natural elements. You'll read about demonic attacks on a grand scale. There are natural disasters galore; and death all over the place brought on by the judgments. Reading about them from the safe distance of time is one thing—experiencing them is another. I, for one, would much rather read about them in the here and now than actually to experience them later. This is one experience you don't want. But unless you take this seriously, it can be easy to dismiss these judgments as fantasy. Before you do, let me ask you something. Do you believe God created the heavens and the earth? Do you believe the flood really happened? Do you believe God destroyed Sodom and Gomorrah? Do you believe in the plagues of Egypt? Do you believe God parted the Red Sea? Did you know God wiped out an army that fought against Israel with hailstones (Joshua 10:11)? Did you know in the days of Samuel the Prophet, the Philistines captured the Ark of the Covenant and took it home? Big mistake! God, after striking down a statue of their false god, struck the town's people

with a plague of emerods "in their secret parts" (1 Samuel 5:9). I don't even want to know where that might be. Emerods were believed to be a plague of hemorrhoidal tumors. Based on that, I have a pretty good idea where the "secret parts" are located. Sounds painful ... and gross! Everywhere they took the Ark, the people were smitten. They finally wised up and gave it back to Israel. How about the handwriting on the wall? You should have no question about that. Babylon was overthrown right after that. Do you believe in Christ's resurrection? Do you believe these things? These were all supernatural acts performed for a purpose. So are the judgments in Revelation. If you believe those acts of God, and I hope you do, then Revelation won't be a problem.

We will discuss some of the details in Revelation, but not all of them. We will focus on the major points. We will cover all of the judgments, but only some in detail. The seven seals are particularly interesting as you will see, as are one or two of the trumpet and vial judgments. But we will not cover all of the other judgments in the same amount of detail because they represent more of the same, only intensified. That's pretty scary if you really think about it.

Jesus Said It, I Believe It

Now that we've gotten that out of the way, I can think of no better way to go forward than to look back at what Jesus told His disciples about this period of time. Jesus spoke of the Tribulation Period in Matthew 24 (also in Mark 13:4-37 and Luke 21:7-36) in response to questions asked by His disciples, as found in Matthew 24:3:

> *"And as he sat upon the mount of Olives, the disciples came unto him privately, saying, Tell us, when shall these things be? and what shall be the sign of thy coming, and of the end of the world?"*

First, notice the questions address three points:

1. When shall these things be?
2. What is the sign of His coming?
3. Sign of the end of the world?

From a top down perspective, these questions relate to the end time, and Jesus told His disciples in Matthew 24:4-31 that some serious stuff is going to happen in the last days. In addition to detailing some of the signs and describing the terror of those times, Christ included a few markers that transition the order in which things will occur. Let's examine what Jesus had to say.

The Destruction of the Temple

The first question was related to the destruction of the temple. At the end of Matthew 23, Jesus said the temple would be left desolate. In Matthew 24:2, Jesus then said the temple would be torn down, with not one stone left upon another. It would be completely decimated. The disciples wanted to know when that would happen. Jesus' answer to this question is not in the book of Matthew, but in Luke 21:20-24. In short, Christ told them Jerusalem would come under assault by the armies of the Antichrist, who will wage a vicious campaign aimed at destroying Jerusalem, which is where the temple is located. Jerusalem will take a major hit, including the taking of captives until the Times of the Gentiles (remember that?) are fulfilled. We will cover this, as well as God's deliverance of Jerusalem, in a bit more detail when we discuss the second coming of Christ.

Signs of Christ's Second Coming

The second question asked for a sign of Christ's second coming. Instead of providing a sign (singular), Jesus launched into signs (plural) that will occur leading to His second coming. Many people, including me, believe the events Jesus described here correlate with the opening of the seven seals, which begins in Revelation 6. Not surprisingly, some people believe all of the events Christ described in Matthew 24 will occur in the second half of the Tribulation Period. But if that's the case, then I wonder what "tribulation" will occur in the first half. Since I don't believe that's the case, I don't think on it too much. I just think the correlation between what Jesus described in Matthew 24:5-14 and the seal judgments described in Revelation 6 are too strong to draw any other conclusion. But again, either way, I (and hopefully you) won't be there when all that happens, and those who are left behind will experience the order of these events in the time period as intended.

Here is what Jesus had to say about the signs of His coming.

Matthew 24:5:

"For many shall come in my name, saying, I am Christ; and shall deceive many."

Jesus said that *many* false christs shall appear and deceive a lot of people. Since the time of Christ, many frauds have come forward claiming to be the Messiah, or a reincarnation of Christ. I found a list of self-proclaimed messiahs by doing a simple Internet search. Many of these people have had followers who were led astray. Paul told the Christians at Thessalonica that the *mystery of iniquity*, in reference to the Antichrist, is already at work (2 Thessalonians 2:7), so it should be no surprise to anyone that false christs have appeared and will appear. While this trend will undoubtedly continue, I believe Christ was prophesying of events that will occur during the last days, meaning those days following the Rapture of the Church. The most notable of the false christs to appear will, of course, be the Antichrist. I believe he will have his own band of merry men who will proclaim his deity. The one-world church to come, referred to earlier as The Great Whore, or spiritual Babylon, is also part of the meaning of this verse.

Matthew 24:6-7:

"And ye shall hear of wars and rumours of wars..."

"For nation shall rise against nation, and kingdom against kingdom..."

Quite a few wars will occur, leading up to and during this time. Jesus was talking about wars and unrest (rumors) on a global scale. Remember, the Rapture would have already taken place, so I have to believe there will be massive social and governmental (political) instability, which lends itself to an environment of mistrust, unease, and military aggression.

Matthew 24:7:

"...and there shall be famines, and pestilences, and earthquakes, in divers places."

Some of these things are a natural consequence of wars, although, again, these will occur on a global basis—in divers, or many, places. Of course, famines are a lack of food, and pestilence is rampant disease and illness, just like the stuff God imposed on the Egyptians in the days of Moses. As if that's not enough to shake you in your shoes or wet your pants, earthquakes will occur globally.

So now you've got wars on top of wars, global famine, global pestilence, and global earthquakes. Seems like a lot? Jesus said ...

"All these are the beginning of sorrows."

This verse, as found in Matthew 24:8, tells us these things are just the beginning. That makes this verse a marker and a warning. Jesus was correlating and describing those signs as sorrows, or birth pains; analogous to a woman entering labor. This is a repeat of what God told Jeremiah (Jeremiah 30:6-7), which we have already quoted. Christ was, therefore, affirming the pain analogy and the time period.

As every expectant mother and father knows (should know, and will know—much to His delight, I'm sure!), pregnant women experience symptoms just prior to giving birth. At or just before the time of delivery, her water breaks and she experiences contractions. The contractions become both more severe and frequent as the time of delivery draws closer and closer. It's like a countdown. Things will only become more intense in terms of the pain threshold. Everybody gets more excited; the drama increases; expectations rise; and sometimes, just sometimes, people get a little crazy. A few women have been known to tell their husbands just what they really think of them while going through this pain, but we won't discuss those unpleasant occurrences. The point is things get amped up in terms of frequency and intensity. Ask any mother who has gone through natural childbirth. The labor pains are one thing, but the actual pains of childbirth are something quite different ... and not in a good way. By the way, there will be nothing akin to epidurals or pain-killers to offset the judgments.

Anyone who regularly watches news broadcasts on television, or surfs the news on the Internet can clearly see the onset of many of these signs. The frequency and intensity of earthquakes, floods, droughts, and other natural disasters are clearly seen. There seems to be no end to conflicts between nations. Some within the Islamic nations or factions thereof wage war against non-Islamic nations and peoples with regularity. Suicide bombers strike with regularity, and militant Islamic groups have declared *jihad, or* conduct a self-described "holy war" against "infidels" (non-Muslims). The development and infestation of new strands of germs and infections (including AIDS, SARS, MRSA, Ebola, and others) affect millions of people globally each year. If you think it's bad now, just wait ... it gets a lot worse. Based on Christ's response to the disciples' question, these things will occur with *increasing frequency*, just as the pregnant woman's contractions become more frequent and intense as she gets closer to delivery.

After the birth pangs, or sorrows, as Jesus put it, things get a lot dicier because the world is moving closer to the second half of the Tribulation Period. The signs Christ then mentioned shift from global judgments to judgments that affect people at a more personal or intimate level. Jesus issued a warning to Jews and Christians. They will experience an intensity of persecution. Jesus presented a litany of events that will occur following the birth pains, like this one.

Matthew 24:9:

"Then shall they delivery you up to be afflicted, and shall kill you: and ye shall be hated of all nations for my name's sake."

I believe those "delivered up to be afflicted" in this verse refers to Jews and Christians. Both groups will be delivered up (turned in) to be afflicted (persecuted), killed, and hated worldwide. Jews and Christians will be persecuted big time. Go to Luke 21:12, which is Luke's take on what Christ told them. You will see there that it references "delivering you up to the synagogues" (as does Mark 13:9). This is a specific reference to the Jews, not the Gentiles, who do not worship in synagogues. Further, Jews are not delivered up "for my name's sake" ... only Christians. And, Christ was talking to His disciples, who would become the first Christians. So I believe Jesus was talking about both groups.

Notice that the scope of this hate will be world-wide. Many non-Christians will take offense at the stand Christians take, which is to not worship, acknowledge the deity of, or otherwise bow before the Antichrist. Neither will they worship in the False Church. Because of that stand, they will be betrayed to the world governments run by the Antichrist. I think it highly probable the Antichrist will be promoting his "deity" at this time, which may be one of the reasons Christians are targets. I don't think the Antichrist acts impulsively and suddenly decides he is god. He's been thinking that all along. But, it won't be until he makes his move in the temple that the Jews get a whiff of his intentions.

Luke 21:16 tells us the betrayers will include parents, brethren, kinfolks, and friends. Clearly, the old saying "blood is thicker than water" will not apply at this time. Those who are aligned with the Antichrist will be against those who are not. This is a continuation of the battle of the seeds, and demonstrates the hold or influence the Antichrist will have on the world during these times.

Matthew 24:11:

> "And many false prophets shall rise, and shall deceive many."

As the Antichrist's grip on the world tightens, his followers and the one-world religion will spread their own word and beliefs, *not* the true Word of the Gospel. Unfortunately, many will believe and follow them.

Matthew 24:12:

> "And because iniquity shall abound, the love of many shall wax cold."

Because iniquity (sin) will abound, people's hearts will turn cold. Allow me to make a point here. This relates to, and is a consequence of, the removal of the Holy Spirit and the introduction of the Antichrist as told to us in 2 Thessalonians 2:7-8. Jesus made the statement that iniquity will abound (increase), and Paul tells us why it's going to happen. Iniquity is sin of course, but to a much greater degree. It is gross sin, wickedness and evil—the kind that makes you shake your head, or breaks your heart, and cause you to wonder "what on earth is going on?" Christians certainly would be appalled at it ... most non-Christians would too in today's time. If you listen to or watch the news, you've heard numerous reports of people walking into churches, schools or other places where people congregate and start shooting up the place. That's iniquity—the degradation of sin unchecked in the human heart. It's not what anybody would call a "white lie" kind of thing. Iniquity doesn't have to manifest itself in physical violence. It can also be an adopted lifestyle that incorporates sin to such a degree it creates a hardening of the heart toward God and what He expects of us. Jesus is telling us this type of behavior will be the norm. Understanding that's the way it's going to be should send shivers down your spine. Once the Holy Spirit is gone, there will be nothing to convict man of his sin; nothing withholding man from reaching his sin potential. Therefore wickedness, unchecked, will abound. People will seek to do only what satisfies them in an ultimate expression of "if it feels good, do it". As wickedness sets in, love for the truth and for others will lessen.

Despite all of this, a great thing will happen as well.

Matthew 24:14:

"And this gospel of the kingdom shall be preached in all the world for a witness unto all nations; and then shall the end come."

This is another specific reference to the Jews, who understand the meaning of "the kingdom". This is the everlasting kingdom promised to David, and prophesied by Daniel. During the Tribulation Period, God will send 144,000 Jewish evangelists to preach the kingdom (of God and Christ) throughout the world. Since the gospel of Christ will be preached in the entire world, this verse is not limited to the Jews only. The world benefits, and is blessed by what these witnesses accomplish. Many people will be saved. Praise the Lord for that! While I am happy to know that I will not be in the world at this time, I am very happy to know the Word of God will still be preached during those terrible times. We will definitely touch on this very shortly.

All of these things will happen before the mid-point of the Tribulation Period and will conclude the signs related to the second matter (the sign of His coming), as Christ clearly pointed out when He stated "then shall the end come."

The Great Tribulation

We now move to the third question by the disciples, which asked about the end of the world. The signs Christ presented introduce the Great Tribulation and the end of the world. How do we know this?

Matthew 24:15:

> *"When ye therefore shall see the abomination of desolation, spoken of by Daniel the prophet, stand in the holy place..."*

This is a *very big* marker. Recall that Daniel said in 9:27 the Antichrist will cause the sacrifices and offerings to cease. That is the act which will break the seven-year covenant. In the above verse, Christ was referring to that specific portion of Daniel's prophecy, so we know He was talking about what will happen at the mid-point of the Tribulation Period. Therefore, all of the previous signs Christ mentioned will occur in the first half. Christ described the period that will follow the mid-point in Matthew 24:21:

> *"For then shall be great tribulation, such as was not since the beginning of the world to this time, no, nor ever shall be."*

Jesus said subsequent to the previous signs then there will be *great tribulation*. Again, the analogy is like a woman in labor versus a woman giving birth. Both are painful, but the actual process of childbirth is much more painful. Using that analogy, what's about to happen is the childbirth. The Great Tribulation is, therefore, the sign of the end of the world. The subsequent verses identify the signs of Christ's second coming and the end of the world.

Matthew 24:16-17:

> *"Then let them which be in Judea flee into the mountains: Let him which is on the housetop not come down to take any thing out of his house."*

This isn't a sign as much as it is an instruction given as an imperative. The sign was the Antichrist committing the abomination mentioned in Matthew 24:15, followed by the instruction in Matthew 24:16-17. It tells the Jews (Judea) to head for the hills. Run ... flee, for destruction is coming. Don't even go back for your clothes! Leave everything behind! The Antichrist has stepped into the holy place in the temple and declared himself to be god (the abomination that causes desolation). The attacks and persecutions against Israel will then become front and center.

Christ then issued more solemn warnings in Matthew 24:22-29:

1. Except those days be shortened, no flesh would be saved.

2. For the elect's sake, those days will be shortened.

3. There shall arise false christs and false prophets who will show great signs and wonders.

4. Immediately after the tribulation of those days, the sun shall be darkened and the moon will not give her light. The stars will fall from heaven and the powers of the heavens will be shaken.

Notice the Great Tribulation is cut short for two reasons. The first is that nobody would survive. The world would absolutely end. The judgments are that severe! The second reason is for the sake of the elect. You should know there is a bit of disagreement on what Jesus meant by "the elect". Some interpret the elect as the Jews; others don't. Some interpret the elect as only Christians; others don't. This can be an extended discussion, but not one we will have here. For purposes of this book and for common understanding, let's agree for now that the elect, as Jesus used it here in this context, includes both Jews and Christians. Why should it include the Jews? It should include the Jews because God made a promise to Abraham in Genesis 17:7 and repeated it to David in 2 Samuel 7:12-16. If the Jews don't survive, then God breaks His promise. That, of course, can't happen. Why should it include Christians? Take a look at Romans 11:7, Colossians 3:11-12, and 1 Peter 1:1-2. In these verses, Paul and Peter were addressing Christians, whom both call the elect. Further, I think it includes Christians because there will be a repopulation on earth from the nations (Matthew 25:32). If it's only the Jews that survive, there are no "nations". So the elect in the Tribulation Period are Jews and those who come to Christ and survive that period, both of whom are special in the eyes of the Lord God. The Jews are special to God because of their relationship to the covenant; the Christians are special to Jesus Christ because of our relationship to Him as His bride. Therefore, as it relates to what Christ said, the tribulation of those days will be cut short to spare both from total destruction.

The false christ, false prophet, great signs and wonders refer to the Antichrist and False Prophet (Revelation 13), and their activities. The signs and wonders from these two characters will be so convincing many people will be deceived into believing in them, which of course will lead to the destruction of all involved.

The most immediate and final sign of Christ's return is the darkening of the sun and moon, stars falling to the earth and a commotion in the heavens. Darkness is a sign of judgment, and Jesus is coming to judge. This final event coincides with Christ's second coming with His holy angels, and celestial activity responding to His arrival. You'll see what leads up to this when we discuss Christ's seconding coming.

Against that backdrop, let's return to the book of Revelation and see how it compares with the shorter version Jesus told His disciples.

Time to Pay the Bills

Isaiah 13:6-8:

> *"Howl ye; for the day of the Lord is at hand; it shall come as a destruction from the Almighty. Therefore shall all hands be faint, and every man's heart shall melt; And they shall be afraid: pangs and sorrows shall take hold of them; they shall be in pain as a woman that travaileth..."*

Isaiah 13:11:

> *"And I will punish the world for their evil, and the wicked for their iniquity; and I will cause the arrogancy of the proud to cease, and will lay low the haughtiness of the terrible."*

Now I have to tell you, if I believed in God and wasn't a Christian, these verses would scare the life out of me! Isaiah sets the timeframe of these events with his reference to the "day of the Lord". We know the "day of the Lord" means God's undiluted punishment of the world in the end times. Add to this what was read in Zephaniah 1:14-18, which provided a more complete description of how terrible a time the "day of the Lord" will be, and there can be no doubt God will execute judgment against mankind for their evil and wickedness. And the price will be very, very high.

Many of you have seen your parents pull out their checkbook or do their online banking at least once a month to pay their bills—be it the house payment, rent, electricity, groceries, clothing, tithes (can't forget that!), etc., that have accrued since the previous month or more. If they're anything like me, they probably don't have a good time paying for most of that stuff, but are probably grateful that they can pay. Some things we might enjoy paying, like tithes, right? The Lord loves a cheerful giver (2 Corinthians 9:7). Or perhaps we'll enjoy paying for a gift for that special someone, or make a selfless donation that just helps a brother out, or aids someone in need.

God says a pretty big bill is way past due, and it is time for unsaved mankind to pay the debt owed for the sins that have accrued since the days of Noah. Clearly, God has been waiting for a very long time. Wanna talk about the patience of Job? Well, he's got nothing on God. God has been waiting much longer than that. He's even sent someone to pay the bill, but *noooo*, man has insisted on paying the bills his way. Better yet, some say they don't owe anything. It's a really big bill and, as they say, the Landlord has come to collect! Don't reach for your wallets or purses though, because all the cash and gold in the world can't pay this bill. Credit cards will do you no good, no matter how high your limit is, or the color of your credit card, be it gold or platinum. Leave your AMEX card at home. There's no bartering. Neither you, your momma, nor your daddy can call a buddy in government for a favor. He's in as much trouble as you are, if not more. Don't go crying to momma. She can't help you, either.

Let me tell you about one guy who can definitely pay your bills. This is the same person God sent to pay your bills long before you were born. Yes,

He still lives, and He can still pay your bills. Jesus offered to pay your bill because He knows you can't. During the destructive time that is about to be unleashed, He is still offering to pay your bills. Just read and pay attention.

The price of sin is high, and the unsaved begin to pay dearly beginning in Revelation 6. In today's slang, God begins to *flex*. I believe it is here Christ's prophecy in Matthew 24 begins to be fulfilled. God expresses Himself to Israel and unrepentant man through a series of punishments called judgments. Remember Leviticus 26? The curses became more severe if Israel failed to heed God and continued in their sin. So it is here. The longer we go into the Tribulation Period, the more severe the judgments become. In fact, many of the judgments overlap one another. These judgments are administered or released through the breaking of the seven seals (Revelation 6:1), the sounding of the seven trumpets (Revelation 8:6), and the pouring out of the seven vials (or bowls in some translations; Revelation 15:7).

First, let's look at who initiates these judgments. An excerpt from Revelation 6:1 says:

"And I saw when the Lamb opened one of the seals..."

This is interesting. Jesus Christ returns at the end of the Tribulation Period as the King of Kings and Lord of Lords, a conqueror, and in judgment (Revelation 19:11-16). In Revelation 6, however, it is Jesus as the Lamb who opens the seals. Revelation 5:9 tells us only the Lamb is worthy to take the book and open the seals, which makes sense since Jesus is the only one who ever lived a sinless life. However, it is Christ as the Lamb who opens the seals. I mention this because recently I heard a sermon that posed the question (paraphrased) "Why does Christ, the Lamb, open the seals?" I must admit, this is a question I never thought to ask. Based on my research on the seals, I can say apparently no one else thought about it either. I haven't been able to find a single comment on why it is the Lamb opens the seals, other than Revelation 5:9. Because Christ has not yet come back as King of Kings to rule, He is still the Lamb at this point in Revelation. But He is also the risen Lord, even though He is not presented as such here in Revelation 6. Here, He is the Lamb. Dr. Tony Evans, the speaker, in his series "Prophecy: God's Eternal Drama", offers an opinion that I find unique and compelling in terms of spiritual insight. His explanation, paraphrased, is this: Jesus Christ is described as the Lamb in His capacity as the sin-bearer, or sacrifice for man. As such, Christ, as the Lamb, is still seeking to save, despite the judgments that are to follow. He came to seek and save the lost (Luke 19:10), and He still desires to seek and save the lost even in the times presented in Revelation. Of course, you can argue that this is merely a timing issue, but I believe that Dr. Evans' insight on Christ, presented as the Lamb, has merit.

The Seven Seal Judgments

Let me add something before we move forward. I want to remind you that God sees everything in the present tense, which fits with His omniscience. God knows all because everything is right in front of Him, which, if you really think about it, is a testament to His power! But that's also why, to God, a day is as a thousand years, and a thousand years as one day (2 Peter 3:8). Why do I say this? I say it because what God reveals to the Apostle John in Revelation has already happened in God's eyes. When God tells us something which hasn't happened yet in man's history, or time, it is called prophecy. Therefore, these things that John wrote about have occurred before God, but will occur to man. They are inevitable! It would be senseless to ponder "what if". There is no "what if" when it comes to the judgments, the redemptive actions, and the final outcome. The only question is where you fall within the scheme of things based on the choice you make. Because God knows what decision you will make doesn't render what will happen fatalism. In fatalism, you have no choice. Here, you do.

Moving on, Jesus opens the seals to introduce the day of the Lord, the day of wrath. Let's look at what happens when the seals are opened.

Revelation 6:2, *the first seal*:

> *"And I saw, and behold a white horse: and he that sat on him had a bow; and a crown was given unto him: and he went forth conquering and to conquer."*

This corresponds to Christ's first sign (Matthew 24:4-5) of the last days. The rider on this horse is the Antichrist. The white horse is symbolic of victory, indicating that he will have some success as he goes forth conquering and to conquer, that is, to wage war against God's program and God's people. Remember, Daniel 7:25 tells us he will "wear out the saints of the most High". But he does not conquer! Only Christ conquers all! We know the Antichrist is already on the scene given the conditions under which he will be revealed in 2 Thessalonians 2:1-3. Based on Daniel's visions in chapter 7 of his book, and what John says in the above verse, the ambition of the Antichrist is to conquer. He wants total domination. The opening of the first seal introduces him in the role as the Antichrist, despite his initial appearance to the world as a peace maker. Some have identified the rider in this verse as Christ. But since it is Christ who opens all of the seals, it doesn't quite follow, to me, that He would also be the rider on the white horse. I think the better interpretation is the rider is the Antichrist, which fits one of the signs Christ mentioned.

Revelation 6:3 reports the opening of *the second seal*, the results of which are reported in verse 4:

> *"And there went out another horse that was red: and power was given to him that sat thereon to take peace from the earth, and that they should kill one another: and there was given unto him a great sword."*

This refers to Christ's second sign in Matthew 24:6-7, which predicts discord brought on by rumors of wars followed by actuals wars between nations. There will be global unrest and, as a consequence, wars between nations will spread. This will be a time of great upheaval. As I've already mentioned, on the heels of the Rapture I believe much social, political and spiritual anxiety will already exist, which will make matters worse. Millions of people can't just disappear and leave the world operating as though nothing happened. The opening of this seal will exacerbate this condition. The fact that the horse is red (symbolizing blood) and the rider is carrying a sword (symbolizing war) is further confirmation of what Christ said.

Revelation 6:5-6, *the third seal*:

> *"...And I beheld, and lo a black horse; and he that sat on him had a pair of balances in his hand. And*

I heard a voice in the midst of the four beasts say, A measure of wheat for a penny, and three measures of barley for a penny; and see thou hurt not the oil and the wine."

This is the third sign that Christ mentioned in Matthew 24:7. This is a depiction of famine throughout the world. Black, the color of the horse, is symbolic of death. The measurements of wheat and barley are in reference to a day's wages which was required to buy or prepare a meal in John's day. This is not the case in today's world where a day's wages is sufficient to purchase or prepare meals for more than a day, particularly for those who are not making minimum wage. Even so, in the last days, many may die from starvation.

Revelation 6:7-8 reports the opening of *the fourth seal*:

"And I looked, and behold a pale horse: and his name that sat on him was Death, and Hell followed with him. And power was given unto them over the fourth part of the earth, to kill with sword, and with hunger, and with death, and with the beast of the earth."

This also relates to the second and third signs Jesus spoke of in Matthew 24:6-7. The pale color, or ashen, also is symbolic of death, disease (sickly), or famine. If you think of someone being "deathly pale", you might conjure up images of someone about to die or of those zombies you see in the movies. No, I'm not saying zombies will be walking around! Don't go around telling people I said that or anything about a zombie apocalypse. What I am saying is if you consider what has occurred from the opening of the second and third seals, there should be little doubt that death and disease follow. This verse also tells us death and hell are let loose, and the toll on man will be great. How great? Verse 8 tells us a whopping 25% (the fourth part) of the world's population will die as a result of the opening of this seal. According to Worldometers world clock, as of June 3, 2014, there are approximately 7.3 billion people on earth. Based on that population number, approximately 1.8 billion people will die within the space of three and one-half years. Imagine the horror of it all! The United States of

America has a population of about 322 million. While there is no indication the 25% will be spread ratably across each nation or continent, imagine 80.5 million fellow Americans dying within that relatively short period of time. That works outs to greater than 63 thousand deaths per day in the United States alone! If you think those numbers are big, Europe has a population of approximately 742 million, and Asia's is 4.3 billion. That has to make you shutter when you consider the death toll. With wars raging, famine and pestilence festering, and the earthquakes ravaging, death will occur on a worldwide scale. The verse also mentions beasts, real animals in this case, not the kings, contributing to the death rate.

You may have heard of the Four Horsemen of the Apocalypse. That term originates from the four horsemen mentioned in Revelation 6.

Revelation 6:9 reports the opening of *the fifth seal*:

> *"...I saw under the altar the souls of them that were slain for the word of God, and for the testimony which they held..."*

This also relates to the fourth sign. Many saints will die "for His name's sake", as Jesus put it. In John's vision, this one occurring in heaven, he sees the souls of martyred saints in heaven who come out of the first half of the Tribulation Period. These do not, unfortunately, represent all of the saints who will be killed during the Tribulation Period. We know this from the response to the question asked by the martyred saints in verse 10:

> *"...How long, O Lord, holy and true, dost thou not judge and avenge our blood on them that dwell on the earth?"*

They are given the answer in verse 11:

> *"...and it was said unto them, that they should rest yet for a little season, until their fellowservants also and their brethren, that should be killed as they were, should be fulfilled."*

This makes it clear that many more deaths of the saints are yet to come, and further supports what Jesus prophesied in Matthew 24:9-14.

I've pondered this seal for quite a while because I didn't understand why this was a seal. The seals represent God's judgment on unrepentant man. That being the case, why or how are the martyred saints a seal? These saints aren't doing anything wrong. In fact, they did something right—they repented and accepted Christ. They responded to the message that was preached. Yet they die. These deaths are the direct result of their decision to accept Christ. They have taken a stand against the world order.

The answer to the question "why this is a seal?" is not the death of the saints per se, as much as it is a judgment against the Antichrist and his world order for the murders of these saints. This judgment is to be fulfilled at the second coming of Christ. The good news out of this seal, however, is that many souls will be saved.

Revelation 6:12-14 reports the opening of the *sixth seal*:

> "...*there was a great earthquake; and the sun became black as sackcloth of hair, and the moon became as blood; And the stars of heaven fell to the earth...*"
>
> "*And the heaven departed as a scroll when it is rolled together...*"

Jesus mentioned the occurrences of earthquakes in Matthew 24:7, so there is consistency with that prophecy. Jesus also said celestial disturbances would occur immediately prior to His coming (Matthew 24:29), but those mentioned by Christ don't occur at this stage because the judgments of the trumpets and vials are still to come. Besides, the Antichrist has not made his way into the temple yet, so the events in Revelation 6:12-14 must be first-half Tribulation Period events.

But look at what else happens according to the verse. On the heels of a great earthquake, wars, famine, pestilence, and untold deaths, how do you suppose would you feel if you looked up and saw a darkened sun, or a blood-red moon? Pretty unnerved, I think. Astrologers are going to freak and many people will be frightened.

Revelation certainly includes more details about the devastations to come versus the few things Christ shared with His disciples. Clearly

Christ's intentions were not to give a blow-by-blow account of everything that is to happen, but rather provide a sense of, or signs of, some of the things that will occur prior to the end time. For example, Christ does not mention the animals turning the tables on mankind, but Revelation 6:8 clearly tells us it will happen.

If you read the remainder of Revelation 6, you will find that man becomes terrified at these events ... and he should be. I certainly wouldn't want to be there! Things become so bad, man will beg for death. Why? Because man will have suffered greatly just from four of the seals—the second (wars), third (famine), fourth (death caused by various circumstances) and sixth (earthquakes). What's more incredible is *man will know these judgments are from God (Revelation 6:16)*. Filled with fear, they will cry out and attempt to hide from the Lord's wrath, which is just silly. They'd do better to simply repent!

Think that is terrible? There is one more seal judgment to come—the one that introduces the sounding of the seven trumpet judgments, which are then followed by the pouring out of the seven vials (bowls) judgments in rapid succession! The angels know what's coming, and issue yet another warning. Look at Revelation 6:17:

> *"For the great day of his wrath is come; and who shall be able to stand?"*

This is ominous. The words "the great day of His wrath" introduce the Lord God's judgment during the Great Tribulation. Just as the entire seven-year period is known as the Tribulation Period and the last three and one-half years are known as the Great Tribulation, so there is the "day of wrath" and the "great day of His wrath". The final halves of each period are correlated, and are in order of magnitude much greater than the first half. So we are told here the last three and a half years are being ushered in.

The seventh seal will introduce the first trumpet, and the seventh trumpet will introduce the first vial (bowl). Neither will be good for those who remain after the Rapture of the Church and *survive* the first half of the Tribulation Period. The results of the trumpet and vial judgments are much more destructive than the seal judgments. The sounding of the seven trumpets begins in Revelation 8:6, and the pouring of the seven vials begins in Revelation 16. Again, because Revelation is heavy in symbolism, I have found no consensus when it comes to interpreting all of the descriptions of the actual judgments uniformly, but some of them can be interpreted literally. Almost all of the results, however, are literal and can be plainly understood.

God is Still in the Saving Business—Part 1

Revelation 7 is an interesting chapter for a couple of reasons. It is the first of those parenthetical insertions mentioned at the beginning of this chapter. And, this parenthetical chapter is necessary if we are to get a full and accurate picture of all that will occur in the first half of the Tribulation Period. John chronicles the opening of the first six seals in Revelation 6, and then chapter 7 begins with the prepositional phrase "after these things". You might think John would continue chronicling the next set of judgments. But he doesn't. "After these things", God then shows John the things that take place concurrent with the opening of the seals, not the next series of judgments. These parenthetical insertions are one of the reasons Revelation is difficult to understand. It's like talking to someone and all of a sudden they say something completely off topic. The expression my generation uses when something like that happens is to say "they're coming out of left field on you". I don't know how that expression came to be, but most adults understand what that means. So it is here. Without telling you, Revelation 7 comes out of left field, but it is revealing something of critical importance that happens within the timeframe of the seals. It's just adding to the story in this case.

Second, and more importantly, this chapter demonstrates that despite the judgments being poured out, and the horrifying results in chapter 6, we see that God is still in the saving business. But remember, our holy God must deal with sin, which is one of the purposes of the judgments. As such, God is just and consistent when He punishes sin. From the time of Noah, man has continued in sin. Again, God recognized this in Genesis 8:21:

> "...for the imagination of man's heart is evil from his youth..."

However, now, a transition is taking place. Now mankind has to pay the price for its sin, rebellion, and evil in the sight of God. But even in His anger, God still wants to save. Ezekiel 33:11 emphasizes this:

> *"Say unto them, As I live, saith the Lord God, I have no pleasure in the death of the wicked; but that the wicked turn from his way and live; turn ye, turn ye from your evil ways; for why will ye die O house of Israel?"*

In this verse, God is speaking to Israel, but He pleads with all men to turn from evil and live. God implores, He begs: "turn ye, turn ye from your evil ways!" You do not have to die in your sins! God is saying the same thing during the Tribulation Period. Even though God has removed His Holy Spirit from the earth, He still makes a way for all to turn from their wicked ways and live! God is still gracious; God still saves!

So you may ask yourself, *how will God save during the time of the six seals?* Here's how. Either before or during the breaking of the seals, an angel tells some of his buddies to hold off on certain punishments, as Revelation 7:3-4 tells us:

> *"...Hurt not the earth, neither the sea, nor the trees, till we have sealed the servants of our God in their foreheads. And I heard the number of them which were sealed: and there were sealed an hundred and forty and four thousand of all the tribes of the children of Israel."*

These 144,000 are all Jews, 12,000 from each tribe of Israel, whom God will use to continue His redemptive program during the Tribulation Period. They are to be witnesses of Christ throughout the world, preaching the kingdom to come and attesting salvation through Jesus Christ. They will be sealed, that is, set apart, protected, and dedicated to do God's will, which remains the redemption of man. And they will be wildly successful. John tells us what he saw in Revelation 7:9-10:

> *"After this I beheld, and lo, a great multitude, which no man could number, of all nations, and kindreds, and people, and tongues, stood before the throne,*

and before the Lamb, clothed with white robes, and palms in their hands; And cried with a loud voice, saying, Salvation to our God which sitteth upon the throne, and unto the Lamb."

What a vision and what praise! From this we know a great multitude of people from all walks of life, nations, and tongues will be saved during the time the seals are opened. From this we know God does not love one nation, race of people, or class of people more or less than another. God sends the 144,000 out to the whole world. How anyone, or any race of people can believe they are better than someone else of another race, or another race of people, is beyond me. God wants to save all! No one person or class of people is better than anyone else, or any other class of people! Enough of that, though. Let's get back on point.

Although martyred, these saints will come out of great tribulation (Revelation 7:14) from every place on earth praising God and Christ (the Lamb). For such a small number, the 144,000 does a great job of getting the party started. I believe others who become saved will help out, but these 144,000 are the switch that "turned on the lights", so to speak. So many people will be saved! Revelation describes it as a number no man can number … from all walks of life, from every nation, and from every tongue. This is yet another great example of God using the lesser, in this case the 144,000, to accomplish His will—the salvation of millions of people.

Now you might wonder where the 144,000 comes from. The Bible does not specifically answer that question. But, the omniscient God of heaven has held a remnant of Israel in times past (1 Kings 19:18), so it's certainly no surprise that He can do it again. Perhaps Christ reveals Himself to the 144,000 as He did with the Apostle Paul. As Saul, Paul persecuted Christians big-time (Acts 8) until Christ revealed Himself to him. After being knocked off his high horse in Acts 9, Saul became Paul, and did great things for the Lord. The 144,000 will do the same thing. Revelation 14:4 provides us with some information about the 144,000:

"These are they which were not defiled with women; for they are virgins. These are they which follow the Lamb withersoever he goeth. These were redeemed

> *from among men, being the firstfruits unto God and to the Lamb."*

I believe the "not defiled with women" reference means the 144,000 maintain their spiritual purity from the onset of the Tribulation Period. They were not defiled because they did not worship idols, or submit to the ravings of the false christs, nor were drawn into worship of the "Great Whore" mentioned in Revelation 17. The bottom line is they were redeemed! Being the firstfruits indicate they were among the first people saved during the Tribulation Period. I believe the 144,000 understood what happened at the Rapture and came to believe, and accept, Jesus Christ as the Messiah. And on that basis, God anointed and sealed them to accomplish His redemptive plan of salvation for all men who remained during this turbulent time. They then went forth to spread the Word, which led to the salvation of many. Of course, there are dissenting opinions about the number and its meaning. Some people believe the number is symbolic of all those who are saved, and is not just a literal number. I think, though, since there are specifics concerning the 144,000 (i.e., the tribes of Israel, and the number from each tribe), we should take the writing literally.

It's Crunch Time

After these things, to borrow from John's expression, we are out of the parenthetical period and back into "real time", prophetically speaking. The Great Tribulation begins with the opening of *the seventh seal* in Revelation 8:1:

> *"And when he opened the seventh seal, there was silence in heaven about the space of half an hour."*

Have you ever really given any thought to what heaven is like, or what goes on up there? If not, you should know heaven is not a quiet place. It is a place where God is worshipped non-stop, 24/7 according to man's time. Revelation 4:8 tells us that there's a whole lot of praising going on up there:

> *"...and they rest not day and night, saying, Holy, holy, holy, Lord God Almighty, which was, and is, and is to come."*

The closest comparison I can make that you might understand is it's like a non-stop party or celebration. Young people, hopefully not too many, understand what that's like. Maybe some not-so-young people do too ... hopefully even less. The significant difference is this celebration is in heaven, where everything is perfect, and not in a banquet hall, pool hall, or someone's basement. The prophet Isaiah, in his book, also recounted a vision of God seated on His throne in heaven. In his vision (Isaiah 6:2-3), Isaiah talks about the seraphim who circle the throne:

> *"Above it stood the seraphims: each one had six wings; with twain he covered his face, and with twain he covered his feet, and with twain he did fly. And one cried unto another, and said, Holy, holy, holy, is the Lord of host..."*

The scene here is around the throne of God. Seraphims are praising God with shouts of "holy, holy, holy". Nonstop! Lest you think a few angels don't a party make, in Revelation 5:11, John saw and heard the voices of over 100,000,000 angels around the throne of God. How's that for a worship party? But suddenly, according to Revelation 8:1, heaven falls silent. The heavenly worship party is put on hold. For God not to be worshipped in heaven 24/7 is clearly not normal, so this has got to be serious. The question has to be: *What causes all of heaven to be silent?* In this case, logic (and this is a logical inference on my part) dictates that the opening of the seventh seal must be the cause. Revelation does not provide any other information about the silence in heaven. However, we know God is angry. We know He is about to pour out His wrath and punish mankind in a major way. My suspicion is God is not in a partying kind of mood, and heaven's silence reflects that mood. It's almost like knowing your parents are angry, so you steer clear until they're in a better mood. And no, I'm not suggesting God is moody. I am saying heaven reflects the seriousness of what's about to happen.

That's what so special about the opening of the seventh seal. It starts the Great Tribulation beginning with the trumpet judgments. God's undiluted wrath is about to be poured out on sinful man. The last time God got this upset and acted, it started raining and raining and raining. Already at least 25% of the population is dead because of the six seals. Heaven knows there are six more judgments associated with the trumpets and seven more judgments related to the seven vials. So we have 13 more judgments that man must endure in the last three and a half years, versus six judgments in the first three and a half years. It's no wonder heaven paused! No wonder it is called the *Great* Tribulation. No wonder it is referred to as the great day of God's wrath. Remember, Jesus said that unless those days be shortened, no one would survive (Matthew 24:22).

Truly much more devastation, by way of plagues, earthquakes, celestial disturbances, and death, is about to rain down on man ... because the seventh seal ushers in the great wrath of God.

The Seven Trumpet Judgments

The trumpet judgments, which begin in chapter 8, are summarized below.

1. Revelation 8:7, the *1st trumpet judgment*—hail and fire mingled with blood descend from heaven resulting in one-third of all the trees being burned up and all green grass being burned up. The hail and fire is a re-occurrence of what happened in Exodus 9:23. With a third of the trees burned and all the grass burned, global warming will take on an entirely new meaning and sense of urgency.

2. Revelation 8:8, the *2nd trumpet judgment*—"a great mountain", perhaps a huge asteroid, burning with fire is cast into the sea. One-third of the seas become blood, one-third of all sea life dies, and one-third of all ships upon the seas are destroyed. The "great mountain" is interpreted as an asteroid, but no interpretation is needed for the results. Scientists and astrophysicists have been harping on the likelihood of another asteroid or comet hitting the earth sometime in the future. Well, they might be right about that.

3. Revelation 8:10, the *3rd trumpet judgment* – a great star falls from heaven upon the rivers and fountains (springs) of water causing drinking water to become bitter. Many people will die from drinking this water. The Bible goes so far as to give this

star a name ... Wormwood, which means bitter! So you know that can't be good.

4. Revelation 8:12, the **4th trumpet judgment** – a celestial disturbance causes the sun, moon, and stars to be darkened by one-third below their normal illumination.

As if things won't be bad enough already, an angel makes an even more ominous announcement between the 4th and 5th trumpets by telling the world things are about to get much worse. The angel calls them "woes", which will be incorporated within the remaining three trumpet judgments. After you read and consider the remaining three trumpet judgments, you'll understand why the angel pronounced them as woes. You may have noticed that trumpets 1-4 directly affect the natural world. They affect mankind greatly, but only indirectly. But the trumpet judgments to follow will affect mankind directly, and in a much more personal way. There will be a lot of "woe is me" following these judgments.

5. Revelation 9:1, the **5th trumpet judgment** – a star falls to earth. This one is a bit unique. As we covered earlier, angels are sometimes referred to as stars. There's no doubt that is the case here. The use of the pronoun "him" in verse 1 and "he" in verse 2, in reference to this star, clearly negates any idea this star is an inanimate celestial object. This star is Satan, who is, in fact, sometimes referred to as a fallen star. He was also given the key to the bottomless pit (or "abyss" in some versions).

There are important parenthetical comments related to this particular judgment in Revelation 12. Satan, this star, will do more than just fall to earth. He will have no more heavenly access. That's what the "fall" is all about. One of the consequences of Satan's fall is he gets really angry, throws a temper tantrum, and takes it out on the citizens of earth. And it all starts when he hits his new home ... the bottomless pit.

He immediately starts his assault against mankind when he opens the abyss with his key, releasing smoke dense enough to cause a darkening of the sun and air. Out of the smoke or darkness, locust-like creatures (really demons) with stingers like scorpions come forth to *torture* mankind for five months. Real locusts can be devastating to farm crops. Ask Egypt (Exodus 10) or any current day farmer. But these locusts aren't like real locusts. They have stingers like scorpions which they use to attack people. Verse 4 specifically prohibits them from attacking anything green, like grass. In fact, they are only permitted to attack those who do not have the seal of God. Now how would you like to face that each and every day for five months? Well, the world at large during this time won't like it much either. But that's not the worst of it.

Aside from limiting their attack to people, there are two aspects of this judgment that make it more terrifying. The first is there will be no deaths ... just torture ... for five months! Many people have wished for death for lots of reasons, including debilitating or painful illnesses, the loss of loved ones, depression, or simply being tired of living a difficult life. But because of this judgment and the pain and agony associated with it, man will seek death, but there will be none (Revelation 9:6). There is no relief! The unsaved will continue to be stung; over and over and over again ... but death will elude them. Why no death? The reason why is because God will not allow these demons to take life by stinging someone to death (Revelation 9:5). It might seem to be a fate worse than death, but it does allow for those stung to repent and be spared from further punishment. The second aspect is it's just plain scary. John describes these creatures in Revelation 9:7-10, and it is monstrous by any perspective. The fact that John saw them and was able to describe them suggests those to be stung will see these creatures coming. That's not a sight I'd want to see or the kind of pain I'd want to experience. This is the first of the three woes.

There is some good news with this judgment, however, depending on the choice you make, of course. If you're not a Christian, and the judgments mentioned so far haven't done it for you, perhaps this will provide some extra motivation. Although the Bible does not state it specifically, most scholars and students of the Bible, including me, believe that *all saints*, not just the 144,000 in Revelation 7, will be sealed. What this means is all those who come to God during this period will have the seal of God on their foreheads, just like the 144,000, and consequently cannot be harmed by these locust-like creatures. Why do we believe this? It comes from understanding how God has operated historically. God has always spared His people from judgment upon repentance. Christ paid the penalty for our sin; hence, no more penalty is to be paid; no more judgment. The people who accept Christ during this time have repented. Ephesians 1:13 tells us that believers are sealed with the Holy Spirit of promise. Thus, the inherent purpose for the "sting" (punishment) has been removed. This "seal of God" may be literal in the sense that an imprint or impression on the body may appear, or maybe not. Maybe we'll see it, maybe we won't. Either way, it is real. No doubt spiritual beings will see it, just as the angels saw the mark in Ezekiel 9, and those who had the mark were spared from destruction.

6. Revelation 9:13, **the 6th trumpet judgment** – this is another important judgment because two things happen when this trumpet sounds.

First, four angels, previously bound in the river Euphrates, are now released. These angels are really demons because the holy angels are not bound. We saw an example of bound angels in 2 Peter 2 and in Jude. These demons, in Revelation 9:14, were bound and held captive for this precise moment. Why are they now being released? It is for the expressed purpose of killing one-third of all mankind (verses 14-15)! How will they accomplish this? That leads to the second point.

Second, John sees an army of horsemen numbering two hundred million (200,000,000), according to verse 16. John was told the number, presumably by an angel, so this is not guesswork. This army is the means by which the one-third deaths will come. That must mean this army is controlled by the four demons. An army of this size is more than just a blip on the radar. By comparison, the U.S military numbered approximately 1,370,000 as of December 31, 2013, according to the U.S. Department of Defense. According to the National WWII Museum website, the highest number of active duty U.S. military personnel was 12.2 million, and that was in 1945. So by comparison, the 200,000,000 is obviously a ridiculously huge army.

The description of these riders and horses is, in my opinion, less threatening and less scary than that of the locust-like creatures. But let's not forget, there is no common ground for John to describe something that you and I can relate to. Also, Revelation 9:18 tells us the deaths come by way of fire, smoke, and brimstone coming out of the mouths of horses, not the horsemen. That's all the relevant information we're given about these horses, but they do the damage. They do not appear or are referenced anywhere else in Revelation, so we may not know the true interpretation of the description John provided until it actually happens.

Some people believe the 200,000,000 million horsemen are demons, while others believe them to be John's attempt to describe an army with futuristic weaponry. I tend to lean toward the latter interpretation because there is no indication that they are demons, unlike the locust-like creatures that come out of the abyss, nor is there any indication they were bound, or fall out of the sky or heavens like the star mentioned in the 5th trumpet judgment.

With respect to this judgment, there's no consensus on the symbolism used to describe how people will die. Should the smoke, fire and brimstone out of the mouths of the horses be interpreted figuratively or literally? Again, I vote literal, with the understanding that the smoke, fire and brimstone are emissions from what would be futuristic weaponry to John. It sounds like chemical weapons, tanks or armored vehicles to the active imagination, but no one really knows. One thing is certain: The deaths of one-third of remaining humanity that result from this judgment are definitely literal and real! This is the second of the three woes.

Again, I want to point out man's response to these judgments. At this point, almost 50% of those who entered the Tribulation Period have died or are well on their way! Using the world's population numbers cited earlier (7.3 billion people), that means almost 3,650,000,000 deaths have occurred. After all that man has witnessed, the natural catastrophes on land and sea, and those caused by celestial bodies, many still refuse to repent, as we are told in Revelation 9:20-21:

"And the rest of the men which were not killed by these plagues yet repented not of the works of their hands, that they should not worship devils, and idols of gold, and silver, and brass, and stone, and of wood: which neither can see, nor hear, nor walk: Neither repent they of their murders, nor of their sorceries, nor of their fornication, nor of their thefts."

Amazingly, those who survive remain defiant of God's call to repent. This means they continued to worship Satan and the Antichrist. They continued to commit spiritual adultery with the Great Whore. They continued in their persecution of the saints and Israel. Instead of pursing God, they chased after the things that drive men away from God. They were not willing to recognize the sin and rebellion in their lives. This is true hardness of heart and rejection of the truth.

The 7th trumpet judgment does not immediately follow the 6th trumpet judgment. That's because there is a pause here at the end of chapter 9—a very big pause. In fact, except for Revelation 11:14-19, which is the sounding of the 7th trumpet, everything from Revelation 10 through the end of chapter 15 is parenthetical. John begins to write of the events which are concurrent with the sounding of the trumpets. Obviously, he has a lot to write about. A lot of very important events happens.

The events that transpire concurrent with the trumpet judgments include the following pivotal events.

1. Two Witnesses are introduced in Revelation 11. These witnesses are on the scene for three and one-half years, which suggests that they arrive at the same time the Antichrist breaks the peace treaty with Israel.
2. Satan, having been cast to earth at the 5th trumpet judgment in Revelation 9:1, pursues Israel with the intent of destroying them (Revelation 12).
3. The high profile activities of the beast (Antichrist) are introduced beginning in Revelation 13.
4. A second beast, known as the False Prophet, is introduced in Revelation 13:11.

Let's look a little more closely at these events.

God is Still in the Saving Business—Part 2 (aka The Two Witnesses)

God continues reaching out to save man, and His next step will be a doozy and a testament to His grace! This event represents the next clear intervention of Almighty God in the redemption of man during the Tribulation Period. How anyone can deny God's love and intention to redeem mankind after what He is about to do with this move just doesn't make sense.

Revelation 11:3 states:

> *"And I will give power unto my two witnesses, and they shall prophesy a thousand two hundred and threescore days, clothed in sackcloth."*

God will send two supernaturally empowered witnesses to preach the Word and witness for three and one-half years (time period sound familiar?). These men will be dressed old style. No, I'm not talking about like the old heads in the neighborhood or your grandfathers. I mean old, old, old style … wearing sackcloth. Yes, as in sackcloth and ashes old. They may even appear to be like some of the prophets in Old Testament times. As I understand it, sackcloth is a coarse fabric made of goat or camel hair. John the Baptist wore such clothing (Matthew 3:4)—not exactly the threads modern-day preachers wear, at least here in the United States. I think if you saw someone preaching on the streets today wearing sackcloth you might be inclined to dismiss him, or perhaps even think he was a little nuts. No one, however, will be able to dismiss these two witnesses. They might try, but it will be impossible for no other reason than these two witnesses have a divine hookup. They are divinely connected and protected! And to demonstrate that, God empowers these two witnesses with divine protection, and I don't mean with angelic bodyguards or a supernatural ability to perform kung-fu moves like Bruce Lee or Jackie Chan.

Revelation 11:5 says:

> *"And if any man will hurt them, fire proceedeth out of their mouth, and devoureth their enemies: and if any man will hurt them, he must in this manner be killed."*

To make sure these witnesses get the message of salvation across to the world, God will not allow them to be harmed for the entire three-and-a-half-year period of their ministry. It wouldn't surprise me if mankind tried to dismiss the asteroids, meteors, water contaminations, and other judgments as natural disasters. They have to come up with some kind of explanation, right? However, there will be no way the miracles performed by these two witnesses can be dismissed as natural disasters or freakish occurrences. These witnesses are in total control of what they do. If you mess with them or get in their way, you're toast! That should tell you something about the importance of their mission. You can't tell me with a straight face that God does not care about man's redemption! In the midst of all of these judgments, God reaches out, yet again, to save! God is throwing out a lifeline to those who are drowning. But let's go back to the verse.

For the entire three and one-half years, these witnesses cannot to be harmed. Anyone foolish enough to interfere with their mission by attempting to harm them will be killed. But you are old enough to know by now that there is always someone who will try. Someone is always looking for their 15 minutes of fame. They want to get on YouTube or become an

Internet sensation. Undoubtedly many will try, especially in the beginning of their ministry. Those who try to capture or kill these witnesses will have the honor of an unpleasant, once-in-a-lifetime experience. Then they will be on YouTube! The Antichrist will probably blow a gasket wondering who has the nerve to challenge his deity and preach salvation from God, whom he has already denounced. The Antichrist will likely send some of his little minions over there to take care of these two guys, but, as the saying goes: "another one bites the dust". Well, maybe not dust in this case—just ashes. Whether it is by literal fire coming out of their mouths or whether the fire is symbolic really doesn't matter. They will be killed. But, I do believe it will be a spoken word from the witnesses that causes any attacker to be set on fire. Fire is a sign of judgment, so it makes sense to me that it would be used in these circumstances.

These two witnesses have other God-given, supernatural abilities as well, as found in Revelation 11:6:

> *"These have power to shut heaven, that it rain not in the days of their prophecy: and have power over waters to turn them to blood, and to smite the earth with all plagues, as often as they will."*

They have the power to stop it from raining, turn water into blood, and inflict the earth with plagues. Think about the ten plagues of Egypt in the days of Moses (who, by the way, many people speculate will be one of these two witnesses). Would you have wanted to live in Egypt during that time and suffered through those plagues? My own answer is an unequivocal *no*. Thrill-seekers might think differently.

It's clear these witnesses will put their talents to use, and make things difficult for many people and the world at large. Verse 10 tells us they tormented the earth, so I'm pretty sure they didn't have a fan club outside of Christian circles.

Because of the disruption these two witnesses will cause, they will get a lot of press coverage. This revolution will be televised! They will get television coverage like nothing else! I think the world will be glued to television sets just to see what happens next. Wouldn't you?

At the end of their public service, Satan shows up, as reported in Revelation 11:7:

> *"And when they shall have finished their testimony, the beast that ascendeth out of the bottomless pit shall make war against them, and shall overcome them, and kill them."*

You should recognize that Satan was impotent to do anything about these witnesses until God accomplished His plan with respect to those who would respond to His redemptive call, and become saved. So does Satan win this particular battle? Absolutely not! This is a victory for God. Many people were saved. That's what God wanted, not Satan. Satan thinks he's minimized the damage. But just wait … this is going to be fun.

The Antichrist and people of the earth are going to celebrate the deaths of the two witnesses, who were so reviled their dead bodies will be left out in the streets to rot. That's degenerate thinking. These witnesses, who are doing God's work, are so reviled and hated, their bodies are left out in the street so a perversion of pleasure can be gained from their deaths. Not only that, now there's a party going on to celebrate those deaths.

Revelation 11:10 adds:

> *"And they that dwell upon the earth shall rejoice over them, and make merry, and shall send gifts one to another; because these two prophets tormented them that dwelt on the earth."*

Because of the plagues the witnesses cast forth, for ruining everyone's drinking water, and lighting up a few people, the world will celebrate their deaths. People will be *oh so happy* when they die. For three and a half days, people will be exchanging gifts and having a good time celebrating the deaths of these two "tormentors".

Then comes the *uh-oh* moment.

Revelation 11:11 says:

> *"After three days and an half, the Spirit of life from God entered into them, and they stood upon*

> *their feet; and great fear fell upon them which saw them."*

I'll bet they didn't see that one coming! And they will hear it too (Revelation 11:12). But really ... is there anything too hard for the Lord (Genesis 18:14)? People have been raised from the dead before. Remember Lazarus? He's just one of many. Needless to say, people will freak out! Then they will be even more astonished as the two are raptured out of here. A voice from heaven will say "Come up hither" (Revelation 11:12). Turn off the lights ... the party's over! Verse 13 says the remnant was frightened, and gave glory to God. There are many interpretations on what that really means, but at least they did give glory to God this time!

If you remember the 5th seal (Revelation 6:9), you will recall the martyred saints of the first half of the Tribulation Period asking when their blood would be avenged. They were told to wait until their fellow servants and brethren who were to be killed, were killed. I believe they were waiting for the deaths of those who would accept Christ through the testimony of these two witnesses. After all, Isaiah 55:11 prophetically tells us:

> *"So shall my word be that goeth forth out of my mouth: it shall not return unto me void, but it shall accomplish that which I please, and it shall prosper in the thing whereto I sent it."*

Many people will be saved as a result of the work of God's two witnesses—hearing their testimonies and the prophecies of the Lord, and seeing God's power through the plagues brought down upon the earth. Those saved become the enemy of Antichrist and of those who worship him. Many of these converted saints will be martyred by the Antichrist (Daniel 7:25; Revelation 13:7) and the False Church (Revelation 17:6).

Despite the drama of it all, the point of this is to reinforce the will of God that all men be saved. That's why the two witnesses appear in the first place.

The Antichrist

We've covered this character in a previous section, so we won't rehash the details of his role during this period. Revelation 13 reintroduces him because of his heinous activities during the Great Tribulation. During this three-and-a-half-year period he does the following:

- Makes his move into the temple and demands to be worshipped (Daniel 9:27; Matthew 24:15; 2 Thessalonians 2:4).
- Is killed and then resurrected (Revelation 13:3-4).
- Openly blasphemes Almighty God (Daniel 7:25; Daniel 11:36; Revelation 13:6).
- Raises his level of persecution against the saints of God (Daniel 7:25; Revelation 13:7).
- Destroys the one-world church (Revelation 17:13-16). More to come on this point.
- Assumes complete and total control of this world (Daniel 7:23-24; Daniel 11:43).
- Leads the armies of the world against Israel and Jerusalem (Zechariah 12:9; Daniel 11:41; Revelation 19:19). More to come on this point under The Second Coming of Christ.

He becomes the political, economic, and spiritual god of this world order. But as the saying goes, be careful what you ask for!

The False Prophet

The Antichrist will have a right-hand man. You know, like Hitler had Goering, Jesse James had Frank, and Dr. Evil had Mini-me (at least they were funny). Revelation 13:11-12 gives a description of this false prophet:

> *"And I beheld another beast coming up out of the earth; and he had two horns like a lamb, and he spake as a dragon. And he exerciseth all the power of the first beast before him, and causeth the earth and them that dwell therein to worship the first beast, whose deadly wound was healed."*

The best way to describe the nature of this character, who is a religious person, is that he is to the Antichrist as the Holy Spirit is to Christ.

That is to say, just as the Holy Spirit leads others to Christ, the False Prophet leads others to worship the beast. Terrible, isn't it?

Although he is introduced in Revelation 13, the False Prophet has probably already been on the scene, just like the Antichrist. His impact, however, is obviously more significant during the last three and one-half years. Characterized as a lamb, he will appear to be a non-threatening, humble, persuasive person, just like the Antichrist. He will undoubtedly be smooth and charismatic, like many influential preachers of today, but he will extol the "virtues" of the Antichrist. Remember, the Antichrist will be "resurrected", which will make it easier for the False Prophet to sway and deceive many people. He will speak as the dragon, just like the Antichrist, meaning with authority and power behind his words. This is yet another reason to know your Bible. And he will do things to make it difficult for man to ignore.

Revelation 13:13 says this of him:

> *"And he doeth great wonders, so that he maketh fire come down from heaven on the earth in the sight of men..."*

By this and other miracles (verse 14), he will deceive many. However, just because someone performs miracles or wonders does *not* mean they, or the miracles they perform, are from God. As in the days of Moses and beyond, people have always performed "signs and miracles". The magicians in Moses' time turned staffs into snakes (Exodus 7:11). Simon the magician in Acts 8 is another example. John, knowing these kinds of "great wonders" occur in the world, tells us in his first letter (1 John 4:1-2):

> *"Beloved, believe not every spirit, but try the spirits whether they are of God: because many false prophets are gone out into the world. Hereby know ye the Spirit of God: Every spirit that confesseth that Jesus Christ is come in the flesh is of God."*

In John's day, he expressed concern about false teachers and antichrists coming into the Church and poisoning Christians with heretical teachings. John says "they went out from us, but were not of us" (1 John

2:19). What was true in those days, as in current days, will be especially true during the Tribulation Period. The False Prophet is going to put some stuff out there that will not only cause people to wonder, but convince many that what he is doing is true. He will perform many miracles, but these miracles are not of God. Paul called them "lying wonders" in 2 Thessalonians 2:9. Don't let these tricks fool you, for he is one of the many false messiahs Jesus mentioned in Matthew 24.

The False Prophet's crowning achievement, however, will be the creation of an *image of the beast,* and the implementation of the *mark of the beast,* as described in Revelation 13:14-16:

> *"...saying to them that dwell on the earth, that they should make an image to the beast, which had the wound by the sword, and did live. And he had power to give life unto the image of the beast, that the image of the beast should both speak, and cause that as many as would not worship the image of the beast should be killed. And he causeth all, both small and great, rich and poor, free and bond, to receive a mark in their right hand, or in their foreheads..."*

The False Prophet will give this image the power to speak, and require all to worship the image, or be killed. All those people looking for a sign are now stuck between a rock and a hard place. You worship or you die! As mentioned earlier, once a person takes the mark, he or she cannot be saved (Revelation 14:9-10). There is no more hope for the person who worships the image of the beast and accepts the mark of the beast.

Does this seem unfair? Let me put it this way. These people had a choice, and they *chose* to believe the lie. How did that come to be the case? It came to be because they chose to ignore the truth, and disregarded the evidence and realities presented. Where to start? Let's see. Hundreds of millions, perhaps billions, of Christians all over the world have disappeared suddenly! That kind of thing happens every day ... not! How can anyone possibly rationalize those disappearances? What about the Bible? It's not a fantasy story ... and was, still is, and will always be available. Better yet, it will tell the story of what happened, and what is still to come, even in these times. How about the judgments? Are those just coincidences? Hardly! Rather than acknowledge and worship Almighty God, they still elected to ignore Him or dispute His existence. Defiantly, they chose to worship the Antichrist. The truth was presented to them by way of the 144,000 witnesses in the first half of the Tribulation Period, the two witnesses in the second half, and the judgments throughout both halves. D*espite all of that, they still rejected the truth.* What's the conclusion? When the objective truth of the Bible is rejected, all that remains are lies. It reminds me of some politicians who reject the truth in favor of some unstated, hidden agenda. But they will advance any lie, misrepresent any fact, or remain silent when they know the truth of a matter, just to defeat a bill before a legislative body, or defeat an opponent. The truth is ignored because they believe it is not in their best interest and it does not serve their agenda. The same can be said about business leaders, who will do anything, no matter how deceitful, to gain power or create wealth for themselves—all the while ignoring the truth.

In the last days, the truth will still be presented for all to acknowledge and embrace. It will not be screened, hidden, debatable, restricted to a limited few, or subjective. However, many will choose not to acknowledge or embrace it. These are people who are evil, self-serving, and determined to see and do things their way, no matter what the cost, no matter what evidence exists to the contrary, or even what common sense might dictate. They have no humility and are thus not willing to submit to the truth. They reject the truth outright because it is not in their self-interest. They have no sense of righteousness and deny the truth of our Holy God. They operate according to a self-appointed privilege to do their own thing, and hold to their own standing or rank. They don't want to hear the truth, and will slap you backward and talk about your momma if you insist on presenting the truth to them.

But the truth of the Gospel is still available and still preached during this time. This is evidenced by the fact that many people *will choose to believe the truth* during this time at the risk of being martyred ... and many *will* be martyred. Those who choose to take the mark of the beast and worship him will not be martyred. They get to "live", only to die. Let's look at what Paul has to say about those who are determined not to receive the truth.

In 2 Thessalonians 2:11-12 he says:

"And for this cause God shall send them a strong delusion, that they should believe a lie: That they all might be damned who believed not the truth, but had pleasure in unrighteousness."

The translation is this. If you reject the truth, if you choose to believe the lie, God will not only allow you to believe the lie, but will make it easier for you to do so, and be confirmed in the lie. That may seem harsh to you, but it is not unprecedented. Romans 1 speaks a lot about this. Romans 1:18 says:

"For the wrath of God is revealed from heaven against all ungodliness and unrighteousness of men, who hold the truth in unrighteousness."

The latter part of this verse means the truth was perverted and used in a way that produced unrighteousness. It was a rejection of what God made manifest in them (Romans 1:19), which was Himself! When this happened, the slippery slope became steeper. Romans 1:21 tells us:

"Because that, when they knew God, they glorified him not as God, neither were thankful..."

Then, Romans 1:25:

"Who changed the truth of God into a lie..."

This is utter perversion. It is malicious. Paul then speaks of God unrestraining people to their own uncleanness (Romans 1:24), vile affections (Romans 1:26), and reprobate minds (Romans 1:28) because they rejected the truth of God, and who He is. For these people it was not a question of knowing the truth. It was a decision to reject the truth in order to do what pleased them. The situation is the same in Revelation. The truth is presented, and many will reject it in favor of the lie!

Head for the High Ground

Revelation 12 is important because it begins to highlight Israel, and her activities. Both Satan and the Antichrist turn their attention to Israel. But God will step in to protect and redeem Israel from their persecution and elimination. This chapter is also parenthetical, providing supplemental information occurring during the sounding of the trumpets. Let's see how this unfolds.

As you now know, Israel gets to resume their sacrifices under an umbrella of peace and safety, made by way of the Antichrist. We are now at that point in the time yet to come, when the Antichrist breaks the treaty. As a consequence, Israel becomes front and center.

Verses 1-5 of this chapter recaps what already occurred in history.

Revelation 12:1-2 says:

> *"And there appeared a great wonder in heaven; a woman clothed with the sun, and the moon under her feet, and upon her head a crown of twelve stars: And she being with child cried, travailing in birth, and pained to be delivered."*

"A great wonder" is more accurately interpreted as a great sign from God—something that made John sit up and take notice. This sign, although seen in heaven, is something that occurred on earth. Symbolically, the woman clothed with the sun and about to give birth is Israel, identified by the 12 stars (going way back to Joseph's dream in Genesis 37:9; Joseph was the twelfth star). The sun and moon represents Joseph's parents. The baby to be born is Jesus Christ, an offspring of Israel.

Revelation 12:3:

> *"And there appeared another wonder in heaven; and behold a great red dragon, having seven heads and ten horns, and seven crowns upon his head."*

This second sign is of a great red dragon, which of course is Satan, who is described as having seven heads, ten horns and seven crowns. The heads, horns, and crowns are symbols of power, authority, or dominance. In this case, they represent Satan's authority over kings, kingdoms, and governments. Scholars believe these seven kingdoms, like those prophesied in Daniel's vision, represent nations that either controlled the land of Palestine or enslaved the people of Israel. These nations include:

1. Egypt, who held Israel in bondage, but were freed by the power of God through His servant, Moses.

2. Assyria, who conquered the Northern Kingdom after they fell into the sin of Jeroboam, and failed to follow the commands of God.

3. Babylon, who conquered the Southern Kingdom

4. Medes & Persia, who conquered Babylon

5. Greece, who conquered Medes & Persia

6. Rome, who conquered Greece

7. The Revived Roman Empire, the kingdom of the Antichrist

This is not to suggest that Satan, because of his dominance over these kingdoms, is all-powerful, or has the ultimate authority. Only Almighty God is all-powerful and He has the ultimate authority. In the Tribulation Period however, Satan, the Antichrist, and the False Prophet are given limited authority over a world order that is in rebellion against God.

Satan's description is also a close approximation to that of the Antichrist, who has seven heads, ten horns and ten crowns (Revelation 13:1). *Birds of feather flock together*, as they say. The ten horns in both descriptions link us back to Daniel 7:7 and 7:24, which explains the ten horns as the ten kings who constitute the revived Roman Empire, so they are yet future from a current day perspective. Since the ten horns (as opposed to the heads and crowns) appear in Daniel and Revelation, they are more central and meaningful to a world controlled by Satan and the Antichrist during the Tribulation Period. This will be unfortunate for Israel in particular, and for man in general.

Verse 4 continues with the expulsion of Satan and a third of the angels from heaven, which occurred "in the beginning". Verse 4 also recapped Satan's historical role as he stood ready to devour (destroy) the child as soon as it was born, but verse 5 tells us:

"And she brought forth a man child, who was to rule all nations with a rod of iron: and her child was caught up unto God, and to his throne."

Obviously, Satan did not succeed. Clearly, Satan, no matter what he attempted, or will attempt to do, could not, and will not overcome God's purpose. This verse is an obvious reference to the birth and ascension of Christ, who will establish His kingdom at the end of the Tribulation Period. With the historical background provided, let's move forward to see what happens.

As you recall, Jesus, in confirming Daniel's prophecy, said in Matthew 24:15-16 that when the abomination of desolation happens, those in Judea should flee to the mountains. Don't stop to pick up anything. Grab the kids though, but let the food burn on the stove, leave the clothes in the closet, and forget about running to the ATM. This is when that happens. Revelation 12 tells how Israel's flight will occur in the future. Israel, understanding the abomination is an open act of war against the Jews, breaks camp and high-tails it out of town. The peace treaty signed at the beginning of the seven-year period is now not worth the paper it was printed on. God now steps in in a major way.

Revelation 12:6 tells us:

"And the woman fled into the wilderness, where she hath a place prepared of God, that they should feed her there a thousand two hundred and threescore days."

Revelation 12:14 also provides similar information about Israel's flight:

"And to the woman were given two wings of a great eagle, that she might fly into the wilderness, into her place, where she is nourished for a time, and times, and half a time, from the face of the serpent."

These verses tell us Israel will be provided with food and make a rapid escape to safety. But while on the run, Israel will be cared for by the providence of God. I'm sure you recognize the time period in both verses as three and one-half years, which indicates this occurs in the second half of the Tribulation Period, following the abomination in the temple. God, remembering His covenantal promise to save Israel, provides for the nation to continue through a remnant. Israel does not get off scot-free, however. They have to pay for their sins too, and the price will be high. We'll see just how high when we get to The Second Coming of Christ.

Two other points need to be made with regard to this event:

1. As stated previously, Satan had been kicked out of heavenly places. Remember, this occurred during the blowing of the 5th trumpet in Revelation 9. What those 5th trumpet verses don't tell you is supplemented by this parenthetical chapter. Satan and his posse of angels lost a war with the Archangel Michael and his angels (Revelation 12:7-9) and, as a result, are now limited to earth's confines. That means no more heavenly access! Does it surprise you that Satan still had access? Well, he did. He just couldn't call heaven his home, and he couldn't "spend the night" up there anymore. Remember the story of Job? Satan had access to God (Job 1:6) way back then. Satan was also in the presence of the Lord during the trial of Joshua, the high priest (Zechariah 3:1). Well, those days are over. Not only can he not call heaven his home, he can't even show up there. He's been banned. His freedom has been severely restricted as he becomes earth-bound. He cannot roam around now beyond the bounds of earth.

2. And, as you might imagine, Satan won't be too happy with this restriction. I imagine most of you have experienced this kind of punishment at least once in your lifetime. You act a little crazy and think you're grown for a minute. The girls get a little "too cute" for their own good and talk back to momma. The boys get a little bass in their voice and think they can take on dad. But parents remind you who pays the bills around here, and send you up to your room ... or help you pack your bags so you can then do whatever you want to do. At least that was the deal when I was growing up. God didn't give Satan that option, by the way. He just kicked him out. Satan, in addition to releasing the

demons mentioned in Revelation 9:2-3, gets angry and becomes personally involved in the effort to destroy Israel, as we are told in Revelation 12:12-13:

> *"...Woe to the inhabiters of the earth and of the sea! for the devil is come down unto you, having great wrath, because he knoweth that he hath but a short time. And when the dragon saw that he was cast to earth, he persecuted the woman which brought forth the man child."*

The woman, as identified in verse 1, is Israel. Satan, knowing he's coming to the end of his road, makes it his mission to destroy Israel. Satan can read. He knows of God's promise to protect his chosen ones. He also knows that if he destroys Israel, he defeats the plan of God, which we, as believers, know is impossible. But he's going to try anyway. God, however, intervenes. So, Israel will flee into the wilderness to a place that God has prepared for her. There she will be protected and cared for by God, possibly through other believers. Satan aggressively pursues her, with a flood, probably a reference to an army of his followers (verse 15). But the earth helps the woman. While no one can be certain what "earth" means here, it is symbolic of something that makes getting to the woman (Israel) impossible. Or it could mean Christians help defend the territory. Either way, it is all through God's divine protection. One thing is certain: *Satan will not succeed* (verse 16). In fact, when he is thwarted in his attempts, Satan becomes so enraged he then goes after the remnant of her seed, as we are told in verse 17:

> *"And the dragon was wroth with the woman, and went to make war with the remnant of her seed, which keeps the commandments of God, and have the testimony of Jesus Christ."*

As we saw a little bit ago, the seed of the woman is Christ (go back to Genesis 3:15); hence, the remnants of her seed are Christians. The fact that those persecuted have the testimony of Christ confirms this. So, the saints of that time will be on quite a few enemy hit lists. Christians will be persecuted by Satan, the beast (Revelation 13:7), the False Prophet

(Revelation 13:15), and the False Church (Revelation 17:6). Don't be disturbed about this though. Christians persecuted for doing right on behalf of the kingdom are blessed, and will be rewarded. Jesus said in Matthew 5:11:

> *"Blessed are ye, when men shall revile you, and persecute you, and shall say all manner of evil against you falsely, for my sake."*

The Apostle Paul would say to them (Romans 8:18):

> *"For I reckon that the sufferings of this present time are not worthy to be compared with the glory which shall be revealed in us."*

To that we say, Amen!

The Seven Vial Judgments

Now that we've covered the parenthetical period, let's run the table on the remaining judgments, which signal the imminent return of Christ. The 7th trumpet, which is the last of the three woes, was sounded in Revelation 11:15, but the results are not revealed until Revelation 16. Here's what happens.

1. Revelation 16:2, *the 1st vial* is poured out on the earth, which causes painful sores to appear on those who have taken the mark of the beast. That means a lot of people are going to be miserable and grouchy. The King James Version describes these sores as "noisome" and "grievous", which implies they are prominent, big, and extremely painful. Think of fever blisters on the lip, or pimples ... only these will really hurt, cover the body, and will be much bigger than pimples. You'd think those infected with these sores would ask, "What's up with that?" Those who come to Christ during this time will be spared from this and the following vial judgments that affect people directly.

2. Revelation 16:3, *the 2nd vial* is poured out on the sea. The seas become as the blood of a dead man, which means it is no longer life sustaining. As a consequence, every living thing (aquatic life) within the seas dies. The term "seas" here is meant to include the

oceans of the world. When God created the heavens and the earth, He called the waters "seas" (Genesis 1:10). That means two-thirds of the earth will be filled with dead marine life.

3. Revelation 16:4, *the 3rd vial* is poured out on to the rivers and fountains of water, turning them into blood. This is where drinking water comes from, so man's ability to satisfy thirst is even more negatively impacted.

4. Revelation 16:8, *the 4th vial* is poured out on the sun, which then begins to emit intense heat. It's gonna get really hot ... scorching hot! Men will be scorched, but not repent. Men will blaspheme the name of God. Now that's just stupid. That's like asking the person who's disciplining you to discipline you some more.

5. Revelation 16:10, *the 5th vial* is poured upon the seat of the Antichrist, plunging his kingdom into utter darkness. This will be so traumatic that men will gnaw, or bite at their tongues for pain. Men will continue to blaspheme God because of the pain and sores from the 1st vial, yet they will still not repent! They still haven't learned, have they? They should be begging for mercy.

I admit to being a little curious about this judgment. My first question is how to define the kingdom of the Antichrist? Is it his headquarters, or capital city? Or, is it the whole world? Some scholars believe it is the whole world. However, the word "seat" is translated from the Greek word meaning "throne", which implies something local, as opposed to global. Also, because the battle of Armageddon is still to be fought at this juncture, I find it hard to image the nations of the world mobilizing armies and armaments in such utter darkness. So, I think the kingdom of the Antichrist has to do with his headquarters, or from where he rules and governs. I happen to think his seat or throne is "Babylon", which we will cover under its own section. Also, the Bible does not specify how long the effects of this judgment will last. I presume it will last until the second coming.

6. Revelation 16:12, *the 6th vial* is poured out upon the river Euphrates causing the river to dry up. We're not talking about a little pool of water here. The Euphrates River is approximately 1,740 miles long ... and it dries up. This is key because the dried river bed becomes a pathway to the staging area for the armies of the kings of the east, who many believe to be China and the other oriental nations.

   The kings of the east might think this is fortuitous, but in reality God is setting the stage for their destruction. These kings, upon crossing the dried river bed, will gather together with the kings of the rest of the world in preparation for the Battle of Armageddon. How does this come about? They are incited, or duped, into doing so. Three (evil) spirits, one from Satan, one from the Antichrist, and one from the False Prophet, will go out into the world to gather these forces together specifically for this battle. This is yet further evidence of how susceptible and impotent mankind is when it comes to spiritual warfare. Without Christ, we can easily succumb to the influence of evil spiritual forces (Ephesians 6).

7. Revelation 16:17, *the 7th vial,* is the final judgment. When poured out, this vial results in the strongest earthquake that has ever occurred on the face of the earth. While no doubt this earthquake causes extensive damage throughout the world, Babylon is singled out. This earthquake will be so severe that the great city, Babylon, will be divided into three parts. Some have identified "the great city" (verse 19) as Jerusalem based on the identical description given of her in Revelation 11:8. Revelation 17:18, however, also identifies "the great city" as the Harlot, who is spiritual Babylon. Thus, in the context of this judgment, it is Babylon that is being severed in three, not Jerusalem. Besides, God promised to protect and defend Jerusalem (Zechariah 12 and 14). Babylon is singled out because God had it in for her as Revelation 16:19 tells us:

   "And the great city was divided into three parts, and the cities of the nations fell: and great Babylon

came in remembrance before God, to give unto her the cup of the wine of the fierceness of his wrath."

Oh, and another consequence of the 7th vial will be that some really, really, really big hailstones will fall, measuring a talent in weight. Depending on which source is used to measure this talent (Hebrew, Greek, Egyptian, or other), the lightest weighs approximately 56 pounds! How would you like *that* falling on your head? And men continued to blaspheme God. How unbelievably hard-headed and hard-hearted!

Babylon, literally and figuratively, represents the center of the Antichrist's political, commercial, and religious system. As such, it is given special parenthetical attention in two chapters, Revelation 17 and 18, which we will discuss shortly.

The emptying of the vials pretty much ends the judgments on mankind. When the 7th vial is poured out, a voice from the temple of heaven exclaims, "It is done" (Revelation 16:17). The pouring out of God's wrath on earth is complete, which signals the end of the judgments occurring during the Tribulation Period. All that remains is Christ's Second Coming, which will, simultaneously, end the reign of the Antichrist, who gets kicked to the curb ... *permanently*.

Recap

We've covered a lot of activity so far. Let's summarize the major events that have occurred by focusing on the events in a somewhat chronological order (first half versus second half). Keep in mind that many of the things that occur are simultaneous. For example, the Antichrist and the Two Witnesses are given a full three and a half years to do their thing in the second half of the Tribulation Period, so their activities overlap. The second half activity of Israel is also three and a half years.

Here's what occurs in the first three and a half years. This starts after the Rapture of the Church, and constitutes what Jesus described as the "birth pains":

- The Antichrist covenants with Israel, which allows them to resume their sacrificial practices.

- The 6 seal judgments begin, the first of which introduces the Antichrist as the Antichrist.

- The one-world church, known as Babylon, The Great Whore, sanctioned by the Antichrist, sets up shop. We'll cover more of this in Revelation 17 and 18.

- The 144,000 witnesses begin their campaign to save souls.

- There are global wars, famines, plagues and earthquakes.

- 25% of the world's population perishes, including many saints who are martyred.

The last three and half years include the following:

- The Antichrist suffers a mortal wound, but is healed. Admittedly, this could overlap both periods.

- The Antichrist breaks the covenant with Israel, enters the temple, and demands worship as God. The saints of God are persecuted and martyred.

- The False Prophet plays a more prominent role and becomes the Antichrist's right-hand man and promoter. He will perform signs and wonders that will mislead many people into following the Antichrist. He will also cause many to worship the image of the Antichrist and take the "mark of the beast", or be killed.

- The 7th seal is opened, which ushers in the trumpet judgments followed by the vial judgments in rapid succession. This begins the pouring out of God's wrath during the Great Tribulation.

- God sends His Two Witnesses to Jerusalem. These witnesses are supernaturally empowered to defend themselves against any and all who come against them, and inflict the earth with plaques.

- Satan is cast to earth and restricted. There he releases his demons to torture all of mankind, then turns his sights on Israel. He relentlessly pursues and persecutes Israel and the saints of God.

- An additional 33% of the world's population dies.

What hasn't been fully covered, as yet, within the Tribulation Period, include the following:

- The rule of spiritual Babylon ends, and both it and the physical capital (the center of the Antichrist's empire) are destroyed.
- The Antichrist and his armies attack Israel
- The Second Coming of Christ, which ends the Tribulation Period

Clearly the last three and a half years contain a lot more destructive activity than the first three and a half years. That is why it is called the Great Tribulation period. You do not want to be a part of that! Actually, you don't want to be a part of any of the Tribulation Period, but especially the last part. The good news is that there is still time to avoid it all.

Anyway, before we wrap up, let's break away and look at some good news. You might wonder what the raptured Christians are doing during the time of the seal, trumpet, and vial judgments. We're not just sitting in heaven munching on popcorn and watching what's going on, although it would be the ultimate reality television show. So what are we doing? The answer is ... drum roll, please....

The Judgment Seat of Christ

2 Corinthians 5:10

> *"For we must all appear before the judgment seat of Christ; that every one may receive the things done in his body, according to that he hath done, whether it be good or bad."*

Revelation 22:12

> *"And, behold, I come quickly; and my reward is with me, to give every man according as his work shall be."*

While the inhabitants of earth are going through the dreadful experience of God's wrath, we'll be sitting pretty ... well, kind of. Raptured believers in heaven will be undergoing a judgment of our own before our Lord, Jesus Christ. This judgment is known as "The Judgment Seat of Christ", taken from the above verse. This same term is also found in Romans 14:10, which suggest it was particularly meaningful to Paul. Why? Because, like salvation, this judgment has repercussions beyond this mortal life! It is a judgment of the *works* we have done in our Christian lives which will result in awards given and responsibilities assigned in the Millennial Kingdom of Christ. Everything that a person has done since becoming a Christian will be revealed—good and bad. So, you're being watched ... and recorded! Did you know that? Well, if you didn't, now you do. How does that make you feel? That's why I said "kind of". I can't imagine anyone feeling smug when the bad is replayed.

But maybe this will help you relax just a bit. Like I said, this is a judgment of works, so let's keep this in context. This judgment isn't a moral evaluation, nor is it a sin issue per se. The word interpreted "bad" (*phaulon*) in the above verse means "worthless", so it applies to our works for the Lord, not our standing as Christians. We were purchased with the precious blood of the Lamb (1 Corinthians 6:20). That means we are valuable to Christ. So you should want to be here. And believe me, you'd rather be here than at the other judgment ... the Great White Throne judgment. That is the judgment of the unsaved; those who will be cast into the Lake of Fire and separated from God for all eternity.

Okay, so how does this work? Simply stated, the works we do for the Lord translate into rewards. It's like frequent flyer rewards ... the more we "fly" for the Lord, the more rewards we get. If you "fly" all the time, you'll have a bunch of rewards. If you "fly" infrequently, then you don't get much, if any. And, you can't borrow someone else's miles to get a reward.

Since works precede rewards, let's go over that first. What are works, and how are they measured? The Apostle Paul spoke about works at some length in his writings, so let's look at a few of his statements on this matter.

Paul says in 2 Corinthians 5:9:

> *"Wherefore we labour, that, whether present or absent, we may be accepted of him."*

The basis of our labor, or work, should be with the mind of pleasing the Lord while present in this mortal body. This is first and foremost. Not only that, it is with the knowledge that when we are absent from this body (when the body sleeps), our works would prove to be acceptable to the Lord. He followed this with verse 10 about the Judgment Seat of Christ, thereby linking the two together—works and the Judgment Seat. But before we go any further, let's be clear about this. We are *not* saved by our works (Ephesians 2:8-9, Titus 3:5). Works follow salvation—*not* the other way around. Salvation is only through accepting Jesus Christ. It is not something that can be earned.

In 1 Corinthians, the Apostle Paul writes a lot about works because of issues that brewed in this local church, and boy did they have a lot of issues. If you read 1 Corinthians and make a note of all the issues Paul addressed, you'll understand the challenges that church was going through.

The Apostle Paul addressed the Christians in Corinth about what he called carnal issues, which led to unnecessary drama and division within the Church. Paul even called them "babes in Christ" which was a nice, mature way of telling them they were acting like children. Perhaps being a new or young church contributed to their behavior. Without going into all of their issues, I want to narrow our discussion to 1 Corinthians 3, to cover the topic of this chapter. In addressing some of these divisive issues however, Paul spoke about labors, or works, in an attempt to place the focus where it really belonged ... the growth of the Church. Paul uses two analogies to bring home his point, beginning in 1 Corinthians 3:6-7:

> *"I have planted, Apollos watered; but God gave the increase. So then neither is he that planteth any thing, neither he that watereth, but God that gave the increase."*

This analogy compares our works to farming. One guy planted the seeds, and the next guy watered the ground so the seeds would grow and sprout. They worked separately to achieve a common goal, but it was God who blessed the labor of their hands. It wasn't a question of whose work was more important because no matter what we do, whether we plant the seeds or water the land, we can't make the seeds germinate and grow. It was God who caused the increase. So Paul is essentially saying we should be working toward the same goal—that being the growth, or building of the Church and recognizing it is God who caused the increase. But the work is required so God can bless it.

The second analogy Paul uses is found in 1 Corinthians 3:9:

> *"For we are labourers together with God; ye are God's husbandry, ye are God's building."*

Here, Paul again spoke metaphorically about our works for God, comparing believers to a building, as in a temple for the Lord. On that basis, Paul argues that since we belong to God, our works should be for Him. Our works, then, go toward maintaining and improving this building, for God and His program, not for ourselves and our own programs. At the risk of sounding redundant, our works for the Lord should be for the Lord, and not for anyone or anything else.

For good measure, Paul then added this in 1 Corinthians 3:10-11:

"According to the grace of God which is given unto me, as a wise masterbuilder, I have laid the foundation, and another buildeth thereon. But let every man take heed how he buildeth thereupon. For other foundation can no man lay than that is laid, which is Jesus Christ."

Paul said he laid the foundation for the church in Corinth, meaning he started, or founded this church. But other people did works to improve upon, or build upon, this local church. Paul acknowledged the foundation for building The Church was Jesus Christ who laid **THE** foundation and any work we do should add upon Christ's foundation. Christ is the foundation of our salvation, not Paul or any other person. When Jesus said "I will build my Church" in Matthew 16:18, He was not talking about a physical structure. He was talking about a body of believers, the "called out ones". That too is what Paul was talking about building upon … these called out ones. The works we do, whether individually or collectively, should serve to grow, edify, and strengthen the body of believers … The Church. So we ought to be careful about why we do what we do when it comes to works. If I say or think, "Look at what *I* did", then the foundation cannot be Christ. The tithes and offerings we give should be for the Lord, not to show how much money we can put in the plate. Preachers preach to win souls, not to show off what they know, or gain recognition as smooth sounding orators. Choirs and singers sing to praise God in song, not to show off how high an octave they can hit. We attend church functions and activities to fellowship and learn, not to "hit on" some good-looking person of the opposite sex at the altar or in Bible class. The bottom line is our works should be directed to grow, edify or strengthen the Church! That's all that really matters. Once we understand this truth, it is clear the basis for judging our works is whether they add to the foundation laid by Jesus Christ. So, metaphorically speaking, whether we are a farmer or builder, works matter. That's because we work for the Lord so the Church can increase, grow, or be edified.

Now that we know we work for God, and the works we do should add to the foundation of Christ, the question becomes: How are our works judged? Answer: They go through the furnace.

1 Corinthians 3:12-13 tells us:

> *"Now if any man build upon this foundation gold, silver, precious stones, wood, hay, stubble; Every man's work shall be made manifest: for the day shall declare it, because it shall be revealed by fire; and the fire shall try every man's work of what sort it is."*

First, let's look at how the works are valued. They can be categorized in one of two ways:

1. Valuable, or something precious, like gold, silver, or precious stones, or,

2. Not valuable, or something of no intrinsic value; worthless like wood, hay, or stubble.

Each person's work will be tried by fire, which purifies or burns away that which has no value. If anything remains, it must be valuable. If nothing remains, then there was no value. Valuables, like gold, silver, or precious stones can stand the heat of the fire better than wood, hay or stubble, which is consumed quickly. Obviously, we should want to build something that can take the heat; something of permanence; something long-lasting that hopefully appreciates in value. For example, many pastors have started churches with groups of two, three, five, or ten people that have become churches of hundreds or thousands. Because of their dedication and commitment to the Lord, souls have gotten saved; the Word has been spread. That's permanence; that's value. Some people have started small Bible study groups with two or three people that have become much larger, and Christians have grown and matured spiritually. That's something of value. Anything you do to build upon the foundation, or supports it, or makes it grow, is valuable. You don't have to be a pastor, or minister, or Bible teacher. Paul addressed this when he discussed the gifts we are given.

Romans 12:5-6 says:

> *"So we, being many, are one body in Christ, and every one members one of another. Having then gifts differing according to the grace that is given to us..."*

Ephesians 4:11:

> *"And he gave some, apostles; and some, prophets; and some, evangelists; and some, pastors and teachers."*

By the grace of God, we are all given gifts to work with. Paul himself was a master builder. He started many churches (1 Corinthians 3:10). So use your God-given gift to build upon the foundation that is Jesus Christ. Here's the clincher.

1 Corinthians 3:14-15:

> *"If any man's work abide which he hath built thereupon, he shall receive a reward. If any man's work shall be burned, he shall suffer loss: but he himself shall be saved; yet so as by fire."*

Once the fire has been applied to our works, we will either gain a reward, or rewards, or suffer loss. I hope we all come out on the plus side of the column, but it is possible that some Christians will suffer a complete loss of rewards, but still be saved. That's what the last line of the verse means. It could be that nothing a particular believer did added to the foundation of Jesus Christ—the thief on the cross for example. Of course, he didn't have much time to do anything. There may be those whom the Lord took as soon as they were saved. Somebody was probably praying real hard for that person. And of course, there are carnal Christians, who don't get around to serving the Lord as many others do. They had the time to do something, but didn't. The use of the word "suffer", I believe, implies some emotion attached to the loss of works that will be deemed worthless. I should point out, however, that some scholars interpret "suffer" as a loss or forfeiture of rewards, as opposed to experiencing emotions like sadness or shame. However you choose to interpret what "suffer" is intended to mean, I believe the overwhelming experience will be positive for all Christians during this time.

As was suggested earlier, the result of works includes recognizing the intent behind the works.

1 Corinthians 4:5 tells us:

> *"Therefore judge nothing before the time, until the Lord come, who both will bring to light the hidden things of darkness, and will make manifest the counsels of the hearts: and then shall every man have praise of God."*

God will judge your intent as well as your actual deeds. So, what was done might be valuable in terms of how it was used for Christ, but the intent was not. If that's the case, you lose out. No reward. The reason or motive for doing whatever you did "for the Lord" will come to light. If it was honorable, then it passes the fire test. If it was to get your name on a building or plaque, or for other selfish purposes, then it gets torched.

Having said that, let me also say there is nothing wrong with "going for the gold", so to speak. The fact that we will receive rewards in heaven supports the idea that it is okay to strive to gain them. Just do it for the right reason. Rewards are given for faithful and effective service, for the Lord, while we are on this earth. Striving for them is, in fact, encouraged. Jesus told us to lay up treasures in heaven (Matthew 6:20). So keep laying those bricks on the foundation that is Christ. Paul told us to run the race to win the prize (1 Corinthians 9:24). So run like somebody is chasing you.

What rewards will be given out? For starters, the Bible speaks of five types of crowns. In summary they are:

1. The Crown of Glory—1 Peter 5:4:

    "And when the chief Shepherd shall appear, ye shall receive a crown of glory that fadeth not away."

    This crown is given to pastors and elders of the Church.

2. The Crown of Life—Revelation 2:10:

   "Fear none of those things which thou shalt suffer: behold, the devil shall cast some of you into prison, that ye may be tried; and ye shall have tribulation ten days: be thou faithful unto death, and I will give thee a crown of life."

   This crown goes to believers who endure sufferings and tribulations because of their faith in Christ.

3. The Crown of Righteousness—2 Timothy 4:8:

   "Henceforth there is laid up for me a crown of righteousness, which the Lord, the righteous judge, shall give me at that day: and not to me only, but unto all them also that love his appearing."

   This crown is given to those who faithfully and steadfastly live a righteous life in serving the Lord and to those who look forward to His appearing.

4. The Crown of Rejoicing—1 Thessalonians 2:19:

   "For what is our hope, or joy, or crown of rejoicing? Are not even ye in the presence of our Lord Jesus Christ at his coming?"

   This is often referred to as the soul winner's crown, given to those, like Paul, who wins and cultivates souls for the Lord.

5. The Incorruptible Crown—1 Corinthians 9:24-25:

   "Know ye not that they which run in a race run all, but one receiveth the prize? So run, that ye may obtain. And every man that striveth for the mastery is temperate in all things. Now they do it to obtain a corruptible crown; but we an incorruptible."

   This crown is awarded for living a disciplined Christian life. The analogy Paul uses suggests that as we train or temper our bodies (mental and physical) in preparation for a race, so we train or temper our bodies (spiritual, mental, and physical) to live a consistent life of Christian service.

Does everybody get a crown? I don't think so, but some scholars and students of the Bible do think so. Remember the people whose works were burned up? I tend to think they won't receive a crown. Don't get me wrong; I hope they do. But if they don't, there are alternatives.

Other rewards will be handed out. The basis for this belief is rooted in the parable of the Ten Talents (Matthew 25:14-30). In summary, this parable tells of a man who gives talents (money) to his three servants to invest while he's away. Two of the servants invest wisely and generate a 100% return. The third servant decided to chill and take the day off. He failed to generate a return for his master. Definitely not cool!

The verses I want to point out relate to the awards that were given to the two servants who earned a return on the investment, as found in Matthew 25:21 and 23. The two verses are similar, so we'll just look at verse 21:

> *"His lord said unto him, Well done, thou good and faithful servant: thou hast been faithful over a few things, I will make thee a ruler over many things..."*

While most may say this is a heavenly parable of faithfulness, the reward should not be ignored. The reward is not a crown, but the servant being made a ruler. The Apostle Paul tells us in 1 Corinthians 6:2-3:

> *"Do ye not know that the saints shall judge the world...? Know ye not that we shall judge angels?..."*

When Christ sets up His Millennial Kingdom, we will be busy helping Him run stuff, if you prove to be a good steward like the two servants. 2 Timothy 2:12 says we will reign with Him. Revelation 2:26-27 tells us that he who overcometh (talking about saints) will be given power over the nations, to rule them with a rod of iron.

So, at the Judgment Seat, rewards and responsibilities will be handed out based on what we have done, in His service, while on earth. So if you are a little behind the eight ball, you still have time to start working to accumulate heavenly treasures. Just remember *who* it is you are working for!

While the judgments are being poured out on earth, gifts (rewards) and responsibilities are being handled out in heaven. All in all, this will be a great time of rejoicing!

Is this all we'll be doing in heaven while the judgments take place on earth? Nope! Now it's time to celebrate.

The Marriage of the Lamb

This is more good news ... *for the Church*. It is a celebration of the redeemed of the Lamb. Jesus Christ, the bridegroom, marries His bride, the Church.

To understand this and what follows a little bit better, we need to understand how marriages and weddings took place in Jesus' day. Many marriages were arranged in Old and New Testament times. Joseph and Mary's marriage was arranged. Generally, the way it worked was the parents of a young boy would agree with the parents of a young girl to enter into a marriage contract. This marriage contract would bind the boy and girl to marry when they became of age. The parents of the boy would pay a sum, called a "dowry", also referred to as a "bride price", to the parents of the girl. The payment of a dowry could also involve older children or adults. In the Old Testament, Jacob's willingness to work seven years to marry Rachel is an example of a dowry, or bride price. Jacob had no money, so he "worked it off" with Laban. (Just so you know, this custom is practiced in our day, but not in America. When my daughters were married, I didn't get anything! But then again, their marriages weren't arranged either.)

Anyway, when the children became of age and were ready to marry, the young man was accompanied by his closest male friends to the home of the young woman to whom he was betrothed. He would then take his bride back to his father's house where they would marry. Following the marriage, there would be a wedding feast, also known as the marriage supper. Historically, going back to Old Testament times, the Jewish wedding feast lasted seven days (Genesis 29:27 and Judges 14:12). How does this apply to Christians?

As we covered earlier, before His ascension, Christ instituted a program of "called out ones", known as the Church. These "called out ones" are uniquely His. When we come to a saving knowledge of Christ as Lord, we become members of the Church, which also known as the Bride of Christ, drawing on the analogy of the husband-and-wife relationship found in Ephesians 5. Expanding on the husband-wife analogy, Christians became betrothed (engaged) to Christ when we accepted Him as our Lord and Savior. Those who come to Christ, even in this day and age, are also now betrothed to Him. Christ paid a dowry, his blood, to God the Father, for all things belong to Him. 1 Corinthians 6:20 tells us we were bought with a price. This places the Church, and therefore all Christians, in the engagement period.

Christ, knowing that the kingdom would not be established in His day promised to return for His bride, the Church (John 14:2-3). At some future point in time, Christ will come back for His bride, and take them home to be with Him. We call this particular event the Rapture, which we've also discussed in detail. Consistent with tradition and according to His Word, Jesus will come back with His friends, the holy angels, so we get a big time escort when we are taken up. While we are in heaven the marriage takes place.

Revelation 19:7-8:

> *"Let us be glad and rejoice, and give honour to him: for the marriage of the Lamb is come, and his wife hath made herself ready. And to her was granted that she should be arrayed in fine linen, clean and white: for the fine linen is the righteousness of saints."*

A wedding ceremony takes place, and the bride (the Church) will be looking good too ... decked out in fine clean white linen of righteousness. After the wedding ceremony, then comes the marriage supper of the Lamb.

Revelation 19:9 tells us:

> *"And he saith unto me, Write, Blessed are they which are called unto the marriage supper of the Lamb..."*

Bible scholars and students have debated whether the marriage supper takes place in heaven or on earth. I won't debate this point, but I tend to believe the marriage supper will take place in heaven—in "my Father's house" as Jesus would say, since that was the tradition in His time. Wedding feasts, however, can go on for a long time. Typically, it is seven days, but it's not unheard of that some last for weeks, depending on the wealth of the groom or his parents. In that vein, some believe the Marriage Supper will go on for the entire Millennial Period. Imagine that ... a 1,000-year party. Who would object to that?

Those who believe that the Marriage Supper will occur on earth also believe that it will not occur until after the first resurrection (Revelation 20:4-5). The first resurrection is when the physical bodies of Old Testament saints, and those who came to Christ during the Tribulation Period, are resurrected and rejoined with the spirit. If the Marriage Supper occurred at this time, then the marriage supper would have, as invited guests, these resurrected saints, which would be nice. Alternatively, the Marriage Supper could begin in heaven, and continue on earth. Let's not quibble where it's going to be held ... just enjoy the celebration.

The point is that we (the Church, the Bride of Christ) will marry the Bridegroom (Jesus Christ) and celebrate the wedding with a feast, known as the Marriage Supper of the Lamb. Please come and have a seat at the table!

Whether it takes place in heaven or on earth, the unsaved are not invited to this party. They're going to miss a great time!

The Bigger They Are...

Meanwhile, back on earth, the judgments (seals, trumpets, and vials) have ended, and Christ is prepared to return and set up His millennial rule. You probably expect Revelation to cover that next, but it doesn't. Neither chapters 17 nor 18 address Christ's return. Instead, another big parenthetical flashback is offered. This particular flashback reveals God's judgment on big, bad Babylon, and all that it entails. The timeline related to this flashback is a little tricky because it covers two separate judgments against Babylon. That's why two chapters are dedicated to its coverage. Timewise, both judgments are executed in the second half of the Tribulation Period, but the first one occurs closer to the beginning, the last one occurs toward the end. So although we are just getting this information, the reality is Babylon, the seat of the Antichrist, has gone down.

These two chapters (17 and 18) are dedicated to revealing the *nature and judgment* of Babylon. That means we are reading about what was done, why it was done, and the judgment of God on both. We're also talking about an accumulation of past activities, going back to the beginning of the Tribulation Period, when the one-world church became established by the Antichrist. Judgments are passed based on what *was* done, not on what *will be* done. And that's why Babylon was judged, for the things it had done.

The name Babylon has roots going back before the Tower of Babel. Remember, Babel was founded by Nimrod, one of the sons of Cush, who was the son of Ham, who was the son of Noah (Genesis 10). Babel was where the people tried to build a tower to reach the heavens in defiance of God's command to spread out and multiply. I guess they thought they were going to show God who's boss. Little did they know! Somewhere along the line, Babel became Babylon, and continued in its defiance of

God. As we now know, God used Babylon to discipline Judah, and then punished Babylon for its evil. Babylon was also the first of the Gentile powers revealed to Daniel, as mentioned in Daniel 2.

As you will see, "Babylon" represents a literal place, which may or may not be named Babylon. Its name is really not that important. What is important is what it represented during the Tribulation Period, and that was the center of gross spiritual idolatry and wickedness on one side, and the center of political and economic power (corruption) on the other side. These characterizations are in keeping with Babylon's history throughout the ages, and are now continued through its ruler, the Antichrist, during the Tribulation Period.

Naturally, there are several different interpretations of Babylon—what it is, where it is or isn't, and what it represents. Based on these two chapters, I believe Babylon to be a literal place, particularly in light of the earthquake and the reference to the "great city" mentioned in the seventh vial judgment. I do not take the position, however, that what you are about to read is absolute and all others interpretations are wrong. This is just one interpretive opinion. No matter which interpretation you subscribe to, the end is still the end. That's the important thing. And how Babylon came to an end is revealed in these two chapters.

Flip a Coin

Babylon is the focus of both chapters (17:5, 18:2, and 18:21), so there is no dispute that it is the subject matter. But it is mentioned in different contexts. Chapter 17 focuses on spiritual matters; chapter 18 focuses on material and political matters. Both are supported by the Antichrist and represent two distinct sides of the same coin, so to speak. Just like any coin used in the United States, each side has a different image or impression than the other side. One side, however, is not worth more or less than the other. It doesn't matter which side is face up when presented to a vendor or bank. A penny is a penny, and a dime is a dime. So it is with Babylon. No matter which side or aspect you're looking at, it is still Babylon, and worthy of destruction because of her acts.

In chapter 17, one of the angels of the seven vials showed John the judgment on what he described as "The Great Whore" ("Prostitute" or "Harlot" in some versions) in verse 1. She is described this way because she leads men away from Almighty God and into false worship and idolatry. Sounds a little bit like what Jeroboam did to the Northern Kingdom, doesn't it? Such is the nature of this Harlot, or religious system. The use of the title "The Great Whore" also reminds me of the Old Testament story where God commanded His prophet Hosea to marry a prostitute to demonstrate Israel's idolatry and infidelity, so this title of "Harlot" has a historical and comparative basis spiritually. From these two stories, you should get a sense for how much God really hates it when people are led astray, particularly by its leaders. Look at her title. It is clearly a title of condemnation. Just as Jeroboam's name will always be associated with the fall and captivity of the Northern Kingdom, The Great Whore will always be associated with worldwide gross immorality and idolatry during the Tribulation Period.

While Revelation 17 gives a formal title to the Harlot (verse 5), chapter 18 does not provide any such title because it doesn't need one. This is an extension of the whole, or what has already been described—the flip side of the same coin. In fact, side B just adds to the résumé. Spiritual Babylon is mentioned first, I suspect, because spiritual matters matter more when judgment is meted out. This harlot is in direct violation to the first of God's Ten Commandments ... she demands worship.

John explains what the angel showed him in Revelation 17:3-5:

> *"...I saw a woman sit upon a scarlet coloured beast, full of names of blasphemy, having seven heads and ten horns. And the woman was arrayed in purple and scarlet colour, and decked with gold and precious stones and pearls, having a golden cup in her hand full of abominations and filthiness of her fornication: And upon her forehead was a name written, MYSTERY, BABYLON THE GREAT, THE MOTHER OF HARLOTS AND ABOMINATIONS OF THE EARTH."*

Look at the terms used to describe this religious system ... "full of blasphemy", "full of abominations", filthiness of her fornications", "mystery", "mother of harlots". Not exactly what I'd call great character traits. Although "decked out" in full dress mode to look regal and enticing, this is representative of gross iniquity and wickedness. It is seduction at its best. It is obvious that her dress and adornments reflect a strategy or methodology deployed to entice man into buying what she's selling. The golden cup full of abominations and her fornications are evidence of that, and suggest that her strategy is effective. There is nothing righteous or redeeming about what she represents! And for a while, she gets her way. The kings and men of the earth are seduced by the Harlot (verse 2) and follow her into gross idolatry. So her reach is clearly world-wide. And to make matters worse, spiritual Babylon also will be responsible for the deaths of the saints of God as found in Revelation 17:6:

> *"And I saw the woman drunken with the blood of the saints, and with the blood of the martyrs of Jesus..."*

No doubt these saints will refuse to renounce their faith in Jesus Christ, and for that they will be put to death.

It is important to note the source of this woman's authority, which is also a key to understanding the nature of Babylon. She sits upon the beast, the Antichrist, who was described as having seven heads and ten horns in Revelation 13. Guess who else had seven heads and ten horns? The seven heads and ten also clearly identify this woman with Satan, minus the crowns, as found in Revelation 12:3. Drawing worship to her and away from God is all she does, just as it is for Satan and the Antichrist.

To be clear, this is a religious system, not a person, so the descriptions aren't literal, but the point is that the trappings, i.e., her dress mode, are comparable to that which looks good to the eyes. It's the lust of the eyes working overtime. In this case, mankind will be drawn away from God into what looks good. Here, what looks good is the one-world religious system. But John sees it for what it is—an abomination that seduces the kings and men of the earth; a false god that seduces many into fornication (worship of idols), and martyrs the saints. But no matter how it looks in the eyes of man, the point is to see it from God's point of view. Just as

Daniel saw beasts in his dream, John looks at this religious system from God's point of view, and sees a harlot.

The angel offers John some insight on what he is seeing and what will happen. Despite the fact that most of the preceding verses in this chapter centers on the woman, the angel begins his explanation with the beast in Revelation 17:8:

> *"The beast that thou sawest was, and is not; and shall ascend out of the bottomless pit, and go into perdition..."*

I don't think the angel starts with the beast by accident or randomly. The angel makes a point about the beast first, not the woman. In his comments, the angel makes it clear ... the beast is doomed! He will go into perdition (eternal punishment). That it is described as a scarlet-colored beast in verse 3 might be significant in the sense that it symbolizes the color of something that has been blood soaked or stained with the blood of the saints, but I've found no consensus on its interpretation. However, the fact that many saints will be murdered by the beast does add some support to that interpretation. It seems to me to know this beast is from Satan really is enough for this lesson. We discussed the bottomless pit (or abyss) in connection with the fifth trumpet and identified the star that fell as Satan. So the pit and those who come out of it are of Satan. And this Harlot, or one-world religion, who sits upon the scarlet-colored beast, is of Satan as well.

The Harlot will embark on a worldwide campaign of persecution to eliminate any belief, religion, or program which conflicts with, or is in opposition to, her ambition. And because she is supported by the beast, she will be somewhat successful in her quest. She will not, however, eliminate all the saints. God does have some say in the matter. But because the Antichrist will provide her with a tremendous amount of support, this woman will be riding high. Aside from the Antichrist, she will probably be as influential as any other personality, or entity, on the scene during the first half of the Tribulation Period. Her position in the world hierarchy is clear, as Revelation 17:18 points out:

> *"And the woman which thou sawest is that great city, which reigneth over the kings of the earth."*

Even the kings of the earth will fall under her ... for a short time, at least. Up to this point, because she is supported by the Antichrist, she will have carte blanche over the world, at least with respect to religious matters, in all she wants to do. Now, all of that is about to end.

Here's her problem. We know the abomination of desolation will happen at the mid-point of the Tribulation Period. At that point, the Antichrist enters the temple and demands to be worshiped as God. This act will put him at odds with spiritual Babylon. You've got the Antichrist now demanding to be worshipped, and the Harlot still seeking to be worshipped. There's an old adage that says "too many cooks spoil the broth". That certainly applies here. We can't have two cooks in the same kitchen, can we? Both of them can't be in charge. That would never work. Guess who loses? Rhetorical question, I know. So how does her end come about? Here's how.

The ten horns (kings) begin to have a problem with this woman. The Bible doesn't provide a reason, and we cannot glean one from the information given. Maybe the financial demands of this system will be too much, or perhaps she demands too much attention from the kings. Maybe she's a "high maintenance" kind of gal. Not many people like that. Maybe she thinks she's "all that and then some". Most people don't deal very well with that either. Maybe it's the kings. Maybe it's a macho thing on their part. We don't know the root cause. But we do know the kings are dedicated to serve the Antichrist, not the Harlot, as Revelation 17:13 tells us:

> *"These have one mind, and shall give their power and strength unto the beast."*

Unified in purpose and mind, the ten kings will give their power and authority to the beast, not the Harlot. With the Antichrist pronouncing himself as god, and the kings giving their full support behind him, the kings deal with the Harlot ... directly and brutally. To borrow from the movie *The Godfather*, they won't even make her an offer she can refuse. No negotiation, no reasoning. It's a classic "leave the gun, take the cannoli" scenario ... and they take her out, as we discover in verse 16:

> *"And the ten horns which thou sawest upon the beast, these shall hate the whore, and shall make her desolate and naked, and shall eat her flesh, and burn her with fire."*

Sounds brutal, doesn't it? Well, what the kings don't realize is they are puppets on a string. God will use them to accomplish His will, just as He has used evil men to punish wickedness in times past. Remember, God used Nebuchadnezzar's Babylon to punish Israel for their disobedience and idolatry. Here, God will use the kings of the earth to accomplish a similar purpose. Revelation 17:17 tells us how God will use the kings.

> *"For God hath put in their hearts to fulfil his will, and to agree, and give their kingdom unto the beast, until the words of God shall be fulfilled."*

Now how cool is that? God will use Satan's own tools to defeat the enemies of the saints and accomplish His will. This takes care of spiritual Babylon. This occurs sometime after the mid-point of the Tribulation Period, following the abomination of desolation. But physical Babylon, the center of the Antichrist's political and economic rule, remains, which brings me back to an earlier point. Spiritual Babylon and physical Babylon are two sides of the same coin. So let's flip to the other side of the coin to see the physical judgment.

John sees yet another angel come down from heaven in Revelation 18:1, and this angel makes a great pronouncement in verses 2-3:

> *"And he cried mightily with a strong voice, saying, Babylon the great is fallen, is fallen, and is become the habitation of devils, and the hold of every foul spirit, and a cage of every unclean and hateful bird. For all nations have drunk of the wine of the wrath of her fornication, and the kings of the earth have committed fornication with her, and the merchants of the earth are waxed rich through the abundance of her delicacies."*

This angel triumphantly proclaims the fall of physical Babylon, following the seventh vial, and describes its final condition. This is a confirmation that time wise, this judgment had been completed! The seventh vial in Revelation 16:17 took care of physical Babylon, the seat of the Antichrist's domain. Its final condition, "the habitation of devils, "foul spirits" and "every unclean and hateful bird", should be a reminder to you of earth's condition when Satan and his angels were banished to it prior to Genesis chapter 1.

Notice that the angel's charges against physical Babylon in Revelation 18:2-3 are both spiritual and economic in nature. There are common references to drinking wine and fornication in both chapters. In my view, these verses, along with Revelation 18:21-24, link chapters 17 and 18 together, spiritual Babylon and physical Babylon.

The wares of physical Babylon also were described in valuable and attractive terms: gold, silver, precious stones. Look at Revelation 18:12-13:

> *"The merchandise of gold, and silver, and precious stones, and of pearls, and fine linen, and purple, and silk, and scarlet, and all thyine wood, and all manner vessels of ivory, and all manner vessels of most precious wood, and of brass, and iron, and marble, And cinnamon, and odours, and ointments, and frankincense, and wine, and oil, and fine flour, and wheat, and beasts, and sheep, and horses, and chariots, and slaves, and souls of men."*

Here's another good lesson for us all. We must never allow the appearance or pursuit of wealth to draw us away from Almighty God. As young adults, you should know by now that everything that looks good isn't; everything that smells good isn't; and everything the world says is worth having, isn't worth having. The path to the accumulation of wealth and material things is alluring, wide, and destructive, and can cost you your eternal soul if you do not firmly plant yourself in the arms of God. Do not allow these things to draw you away. While there is nothing wrong with wealth in and of itself, Jesus Himself said it is hard for a rich man to enter into the kingdom of heaven (Matthew 19:24). He compared it to a camel going through the eye of a needle! Do not allow yourself to get caught up in the pursuit of earthly treasures to the detriment of your spiritual growth. Don't make it hard on yourself by pursuing wealth.

Gotta Go!

Here's another cool part. Before God did His final number on Babylon with the seventh vial, He issued a warning (Revelation 18:4):

> *"And I heard another voice from heaven, saying, Come out of her, my people, that ye be not partakers of her sins, and that ye receive not of her plagues."*

From all that we can tell, Babylon was a terrible place. Not too surprising since it is the kingdom of the Antichrist. It housed the Great Whore until the Antichrist had no need for her anymore. It was responsible for the slaughter of many saints of God. It misled many of the unsaved to their doom. It lured many others by the glamor of wealth. As such, you might wonder why God's people would be there. However, this isn't a judgment on why they are there or even if they should be there. There is no condemnation mentioned about the saints being in such a place in verse 4 or anywhere else in chapter 18. What you should recognize is God continued to be gracious and continued to demonstrate His love by calling out His redeemed, the saints, from this place before its destruction. This is another demonstration that believers are not subject to God's wrath, as we have covered. Consistent with that, God called them out of there! Babylon, however, will suffer the full extent of His wrath, which is recorded in Revelation 18:8:

> *"Therefore shall her plagues come in one day, death and mourning, and famine; and she shall be utterly burned with fire; for strong is the Lord God who judgeth her."*

The judgment will come quickly ... in one day. Here today, gone tomorrow. This will be the total and complete destruction of Babylon.

Now, many people will have a problem with this, although not for the reason you might think if you're anywhere close to being sane. The kings of the earth (verse 9), the merchants who buy and sell the merchandise (verse 15), and the shipmasters who transport the merchandise from point A to point Z (verse 17) all have a conniption over this. And it won't be because of the people who died in Babylon from this destruction, or the billions of people that have died up to this point in the Tribulation Period. It also won't be because of the plagues and famines that have ravaged people and places all over the earth, or because the natural elements (seas, rivers, plant life, and ocean life) have been decimated. No, none of that stuff will bother them. They will mourn the destruction of physical Babylon because it will mean they cannot accumulate more wealth (verses 11 and 19). They exhibit no sympathy or compassion for those who suffered and died. All that mattered to them was the wealth. If you read all of chapter 18, you'll find that the kings, merchants, and shipmasters "shall bewail her and lament for her" (verse 9), "shall weep and mourn over her" (verse 11), "cast dust on their heads, and cried, weeping and wailing" (verse 19). My goodness! Can you believe that? All this drama for being deprived of the opportunity to accumulate more wealth? Unbelievable! That is warped thinking. But what this does is demonstrate the mindset of people who value wealth above all else. It's safe to say they missed the point. Jesus said in Matthew 16:26:

> *"For what is a man profited, if he shall gain the whole world, and lose his own soul? or what shall a man give in exchange for his soul?"*

These people act the fool over the loss of material gain, but ignored the greater issues. The ignored the truth. They ignored the judgments of Almighty God, and blasphemed His name in the process. They sacrificed their own souls for wealth. But while they're lamenting "woe is me", singing the blues, and crying a river, heaven is rejoicing. Revelation 18:20 tells us:

> *"Rejoice over her, thou heaven, and ye holy apostles and prophets; for God hath avenged you on her."*

Here God partially fulfilled His promise to the martyred saints mentioned in fifth seal (Revelation 6:10-11). That's a good start, but there's more to come on that score. The better news is the destruction of

Babylon. As Revelation 18:21 puts it, Babylon "shall be found no more at all"! Good riddance!

The sins of spiritual and physical Babylon are summarized in Revelation 18:23-24:

> *"And the light of a candle shall shine no more at all for thee; and the voice of the bridegroom and of the bride shall be heard no more at all in thee: for by thy sorceries were all nations deceived. And in her was found the blood of the prophets, and of saints, and of all that were slain upon the earth."*

Babylon is closed for business permanently. Not so much as a light bulb will come on, or candle will be lit. But, this really shows not only how seductive the enemy can be, but how impotent man is when subjected to the enemy's deceptions. Apart from God, mankind is vulnerable. The unsaved has no natural defense to protect themselves from these spiritual assaults, thus making it easier for the enemy to deceive all the nations, in this case, through sorcery. The word "sorceries" comes from the Greek word "pharmakeia", commonly interpreted as the use of magical spells. Sorcery was expressly forbidden in the Old Testament (Deuteronomy 18:10-12), but it is through this practice the nations were led astray. Babylon committed acts of murder against the prophets, saints, and others. Those acts resulted in the judgment and destruction of Babylon, and effectively put an end to its history, and rule on earth.

The Second Coming of Christ

This is **THE** major event that concludes God's redemptive program. This is when Jesus Christ physically returns to earth to set up His kingdom. The wrath of God poured out during the Tribulation Period has ceased, and Babylon has been judged, sentenced, and executed. Approximately 50% of the world's population has died, and the Times of the Gentiles is coming to an end. There's still some clean-up work to be done though. The good news is millions of people have been saved, largely through the efforts of the 144,000 and the two witnesses. Christ's second coming will put an end to the domination of the Antichrist and False Prophet, the kings of the earth will become paupers, and Satan gets lassoed. There's a new King coming to town, and He will begin to set things in order before He sets foot on the ground. This will be some really exciting stuff!

Let me make this clear. I'm certainly not objecting to His coming back. In fact, I anxiously await His return because I'll be coming back with Him. Are you wondering why Christ comes back now? Sure, you can say it's because the judgments have ended, but there's a better answer; one we've already been told. Those of you who have been paying attention probably know the answer. But here's the biggest clue.

In Matthew 24:22, Jesus said:

> *"And except those days should be shortened, there should no flesh be saved: but for the elect's sake those days shall be shortened."*

Remember now? The above verse is how Jesus responded to His disciples when asked about the end of the world. The Tribulation Period ends to save the elect, who are defined as the Jews and those who come to

Christ during this period. All of mankind would perish if the consequences of the judgments went uninterrupted. Left alone, the events still in play would lead to the destruction of the Jews first, and then undoubtedly lead to the end of the saints as well. It is those events that are interrupted. Let's see how this flows.

The second coming of Christ follows closely the Antichrist's obsession on the destruction of the Jews, so let's look at those circumstances in a little more detail.

The Opening Act

Here's the recap of what has already occurred that directly affects the Jews. Don't forget, most of the major events occur in the last half of the Tribulation Period.

- The Great Tribulation starts with the Antichrist's breaking of the treaty and demanding all worship Him. The Jews know they can't and won't do that, and are now in deep trouble. So many will leave town and head for the mountains where they will be protected by God (Revelation 12:6). We don't know how many leave, but since there is a battle to come in Jerusalem, we know they don't all skip town. Regardless of how many leave or don't leave, wherever they are they will be hunted, pursued, and persecuted.

- Satan was kicked out of heavenly places in the fifth trumpet judgment, and having lost the war with Michael and his angels is now earth-bound. His activities limited to the confines of earth, Satan throw a hissy fit and then goes after the Jews who fled, but through the divine intervention of God, fails in his attempts to destroy them.

- The sounding of the 6th trumpet judgment in Revelation 9:14-16 announces the release of four angels (demons) bound in the river Euphrates. And just so you know, the Euphrates river is one of the boundaries God set for the land of Israel (Genesis 15:18), so I don't think for a second it was an accident these angels were bound there. I believe these demons were bound there to be used by God as part of His final plan to discipline Israel, and bring them into repentance. These demons control a massive army of two hundred million horsemen, who when unleashed, will kill one-third of the remaining population. There is also a nexus between this army and the judgment of the 6th vial, so let's go there.

- The 6th vial is poured out in Revelation 16:12. Two things happen here. The first is the river Euphrates dries up to prepare the way for the kings (plural) of the east. This means the Euphrates is dried up to pave the way for, and help mobilize, eastern nations who will cross this river headed toward Israel. So clearly a major military campaign is brewing. There are some who believe the 200,000,000 army is from the kings of the east, which is plausible. The population of the Asian nations, which include China and India, total 4.3 billion, as previously mentioned. Supporting an army of 200,000,000 would be no problem for them. The second result of this vial is the gathering of the kings of the world to do battle. The kings of the world are influenced by evil spirits coming out of Satan, the Antichrist, and the False Prophet in preparation for this battle (Revelation 16:13-14). This verse also tells us "the kings of the earth and of the whole world" will gather to do battle. That, then, has to include the two hundred million, or a portion thereof. So here we have a gathering of the armies of the world and a dried-up pathway to get the kings of the east to the same place. There, they "set up shop". Where's there?

- Revelation 16:16 gives us the name of the place where they will gather to do battle—Armageddon. Armageddon is translated from the Hebrew words meaning "Mount" (har) of "Megiddo". This place is located in Israel, in the Valley of Esdraelon, aka the Valley of Jezreel. Care to guess where they're headed?

- Jerusalem! And in doing so, they will fulfill prophecy. The Antichrist believes he is about to take over a piece of real estate he doesn't own, but desperately wants, which is Israel. And from the Antichrist's perspective, the takeover is going to look pretty good too, for a while anyway. But here's his problem, as prophesied in Zechariah 14:2:

> *"For I will gather all nations against Jerusalem to battle; and the city shall be taken..."*

Here, God says that *He* is bringing the nations of the earth *to Jerusalem* to do battle and that Jerusalem will be taken. Forget about the intent of the evil spirits from Satan, the Antichrist and the False Prophet. They planned to one thing, but God will trump them. What's really going on here is our omniscient God is using the plans of the enemy as part of His plan to discipline and redeem Israel, bring them to repentance, and destroy these invading armies at the same time. It's really pretty cool if you think about it. You might say the unholy trinity got *played*. This is much like when God used the kings of the earth to take care of the Harlot in Revelation 17:17. Only here, God warns Jerusalem that it will come under siege by the nations. If you read on in Zechariah 14, you will find the enemy (the armies of the Antichrist) will do tremendous damage in Jerusalem, going so far as to take half of the people captive. Israel will come under the control of the Antichrist's military troops, and will clearly be in dire straits

So the scene is set. Some of Israel is on the run, but protected by God. The rest stay put. Israel has been invaded and the remaining armies of the Antichrist are perched nearby, ready to pounce and finish the job. However, a lot of what is about to happen is not in Revelation. The end of it all is, but not the intermediate steps which directly lead to the end. For that, we have to go to the book of Zechariah, so let's go there to see what these intermediate steps are.

The Second Act

To appreciate what's about to happen and the scope of God's miraculous deliverance, we must understand the odds against Israel. Think about this. Israel is a tiny country with a *total* population of approximately 7,822,000 people according to the Central Intelligence Agency *World Factbook*. There will probably be far fewer than that following the Antichrist's "I am god" speech. Some will leave, but many will stay. They will be grossly outnumbered. Let's take a look at their suspected competition. China's pool of *eligible manpower* for military service is over 385,800,000 men (18-49 years old) compared to Israel's 1,518,000. Iran has 20,149,000; Iraq has 6,591,000; Egypt has 18,061,000; Syria has 5,056,000; and Turkey has 17,665,000. Many scholars believe Russia will be one of the invading countries. They have a pool of 34,766,000. Some of these armies, and more, will be pledged to the Antichrist. Needless to say, Israel will be hopelessly outnumbered by the Antichrist's armies.

Also, let me make a quick point about Zechariah 14. This chapter is a rehash of earlier events recorded in Zechariah, but culminates in the Second Coming of Christ, which is the point of chapter 14. So, going back a couple of chapters, let see what's been rehashed and how it leads to Israel's restoration and the second coming of Christ.

At this point in the prophetic future, some of the armies of the Antichrist are in Jerusalem (Zechariah 14:2). Terrible destruction and brutality to men and women will have taken place. The invaders are on the verge of victory. The Antichrist will no doubt assume he is well on the way to winning this battle. But that's okay. Let him think what he wants to think because victory will elude him. That's because of God's supernatural intervention! Jerusalem will not and cannot be destroyed. God has done this deliverance thing before—on multiple occasions. When all seems lost, God steps in and delivers. I've already mentioned the story of Gideon. The deliverance of Israel from Egypt is another, as is the Hebrew boys from the fiery furnace. The Apostle Peter was delivered from Herod's imprisonment. There are many more such examples throughout the Bible.

But now God now gets personally and directly involved in the deliverance of Jerusalem from the Antichrist. If you read Zechariah 12, you'll find the prepositional phrase "in that day" repeated over and over and over. I count six times in the King James Version of the Bible. This phrase, as used in Zechariah, is in reference to the day of deliverance. It is the day the Lord delivers Jerusalem from the Antichrist's invasion. In short, "in that day" God supernaturally steps in. Zechariah 12:2 provides the setting:

> *"Behold, I will make Jerusalem a cup of trembling unto all the people round about, when they shall be in siege both against Judah and against Jerusalem."*

In Zechariah 12:2, God uses a metaphor ("cup of trembling") to tell His people that although Jerusalem and the surrounding cities will be invaded (in siege), the tide will turn "in that day". In fact, Jerusalem will be the cause of trembling among the Antichrist's forces. Have you ever watched a person who was really nervous try to pick up a glass of water, or hold cup of coffee to drink? The hands shake so badly the contents spill out. The pitch of the voice shoots up a couple of octaves and the eyes get wide and bug out a bit. That's what it's going to be like for the invaders. Why? Because they've bitten off more than they could chew. They're no longer fighting against the inhabitants of Jerusalem. Now they are fighting against the Lord God … and I believe they will recognize that. They will know something fishy is going on here, evidenced by their trembling. I really wouldn't want to be in their shoes.

With regard to Jerusalem, here are some of the things God will do to defend them "in that day":

Zechariah 12:4 tells us:

> *"In that day, saith the Lord, I will smite every horse with astonishment, and his rider with madness: and I will open mine eyes upon the house of Judah, and will smite every horse of the people with blindness."*

God is starting His ground war against the horses and riders. They won't know which way to turn. The horses will act crazy and the riders will go crazy. If it is actual horses John sees in his vision, as opposed to a symbolic representation, then we see what will happen according to the verse. They will be like a deer in headlights! If the horses represent conveyance vehicles, like tanks or other ground vehicles, then I imagine instrumentations won't work, and the drivers will still go crazy. That'll be some sight to see. Can't you just picture them bumping into one another? It'll be like the *Dumb and Dumber* on steroids.

Zechariah 12:6:

> *"In that day will I make the governors of Judah like an hearth of fire among the wood, and like a torch of fire in a sheaf; and they shall devour all*

the people round about, on the right hand and on the left..."

The military leaders (governors) will be made indestructible, like a hearth in a fireplace which cannot be consumed by fire, or like a fire torch among sheaves (a bundle of dried plants) which means the sheaves are at the mercy of the fire torch. The military leadership will be made strong by God and unable to be defeated, leaving no doubt who wins the remaining battles.

Zechariah 12:8:

"In that day shall the Lord defend the inhabitants of Jerusalem; and he that is feeble among them at that day shall be as David..."

The governors will have what amounts to military supermen fighting with them. The feeblest of them will fight like David, and that's really saying something. David was a mighty warrior of Israel. He killed bears, lions, and Goliath (1 Samuel 17), so he wasn't what I'd call a wimp. David's bravery was never questioned. For Israel, that means there will be no cowards or 100 pound weaklings. The combination of strong military leadership and David-like warriors on all sides means Israel will have an army, supernaturally empowered by God, which cannot be beaten and they will turn the tide against the armies of the Antichrist.

Zechariah 12:9:

"And it shall come to pass in that day, that I will seek to destroy all the nations that come against Jerusalem."

God affirms His intent to destroy all those who come against Jerusalem. With the armies of the Antichrist now made jittery by God, compared to the armies of Israel, now supernaturally empowered by God, the outcome will not be in doubt. God ordained this outcome to demonstrate His sovereignty and deliver on His promise to Israel. The result is not in doubt. God is omnipotent ... He gets His way.

Here's the good news to come—no doubt the best news. Israel will come to recognize Jesus Christ as the Messiah.

Zechariah 12:10:

> *"And I will pour upon the house of David, and upon the inhabitants of Jerusalem, the spirit of grace and of supplications: and they shall look upon me whom they have pierced, and they shall mourn for him, as one mourneth for his only son, and shall be in bitterness for him, as one that is in bitterness for his firstborn."*

I believe this is when all of Israel, and mankind, will see Christ appear in the heavens (Matthew 24:30, Revelation 1:7, Revelation 19:11). God's Spirit will be poured out upon Israel, and when they see Christ in the heavens, they will recognize Him for who He is. This will be more than a simple "my bad" apology from Israel. Israel will recognize God's deliverance of the nation from the armies of the Antichrist, see Christ in the heavens, and will weep, mourn, and repent for rejecting Him as the Messiah. Their response will be comparable to parents who weep over the death of a first-born child. This is a deep sadness, gut-wrenching, or something heart-breaking. This is when the partial blindness on the part of Israel ends. They will come to a state of full recognition and repentance.

Finally, let's look at Zechariah 13:8-9:

> *"And it shall come to pass, that in all the land, saith the Lord, two parts therein shall be cut off and die; but the third shall be left therein. And I will bring the third part through the fire, and will refine them as silver is refined, and will try them as gold is tried: they shall call on my name, and I will hear them: I will say, It is my people: and they shall say, The Lord is my God."*

As a consequence of Israel's disobedience, two-thirds of the nation perishes, but it is not destroyed. If you remember, the world will suffer a 50% casualty rate. Not Israel. They will suffer more. But, God spares the nation through His deliverance of a one-third remnant. This will fulfill God's promise for the nation to continue under the everlasting covenant God made with Abram.

These events are going to be really bad news for the Antichrist and his forces. Having now been overthrown in Jerusalem, the only thing they can do is await the death blow, which Christ delivers on His return concurrent with Israel's recognition, so let's go there.

The Final Curtain

The stage for the Battle of Armageddon is set. The course of the battle in Jerusalem has been reversed. The armies of the Antichrist in Jerusalem are fighting it out ... and losing. What remains of Antichrist's combat soldiers, tanks, missiles, and pea-shooters are camped out for their final assault in the Valley of Jezreel. No doubt there are naval resources nearby.

But allow me to throw in a bit of a curve ball. Despite what we've read concerning the goings-on in Jerusalem, and the staging of the armies at Armageddon ... despite all appearances, this fight really isn't against Israel. How do we know this? Jumping ahead just a little bit, Revelation 19:19 tells us:

> "And I saw the beast, and the kings of the earth, and their armies, gathered together to make war against him that sat on the horse, and against his army."

The rider on the horse is Jesus Christ! So says the description given of the rider in Revelation 19:11-13. So in reality, this means the Antichrist, the kings, and their armies are in a spiritual battle. They are gathered together to make war against him who sat on the horse and his armies. Consequently, if the Antichrist and his armies came to make war against Christ, then the true battle, although directed against Israel, can't be about Israel. Israel is a sub-plot, or a means to an end. This is not an uncommon tactic of the enemy. Satan will often attack a target that is meaningful to you. This "war" should take you back to what was presented much earlier ... we are involved in spiritual warfare (Ephesians 6:12). It is merely played out on this physical plane called earth.

But wait a minute. There's something else. We've already said the physical cannot overcome the spiritual, so what's with all of this weaponry? It can't harm a spiritual opponent. So what's up with that? Well, what's up is the goal and strategy hasn't changed. The invasion of Jerusalem is still a means to an end ... the end being to defeat God by destroying Israel, whom God has covenanted to last forever. That's what Satan was trying to do in Revelation 12, but failed. The Antichrist now takes up the cause in an attempt to do the same thing. Only now he has an overpowering military force, relative to Israel anyway, to work with. There is no other reason for the Antichrist to gather "the kings of the earth and of the whole world" (Revelation 16:14) to Armageddon. It is their final attempt to defeat God by overwhelming and destroying Israel. But, God moved in to take control in Jerusalem, and now Jesus arrives on the scene to wrap things up. Again, this coincides with the defeat of Antichrist's armies in Jerusalem. John tells us what he sees in Revelation 19:11-14:

> *"And I saw heaven opened, and behold a white horse; and he that sat upon him was called Faithful and True, and in righteousness he doth judge and make war. His eyes were as a flame of fire, and on his head were many crowns; and he had a name written, that no man knew, but he himself. And he was clothed with a vesture dipped in blood: and his name is called The Word of God. And the armies which were in heaven followed him upon white horses, clothed in fine linen, white and clean."*

The world at large has witnessed many spectacular events in the prior seven years, but it is about to witness something that will elicit absolute praise from those who are at peace with God, and absolute terror in the hearts of those who are at war against God. Mankind will be on one side or the other. This will not be a ho-hum event. It will be an awesome sight! Jesus told His disciples that it's gonna be dark on that day—the sun and the moon will not give off light, which certainly will add to the drama. Stars will fall, and the power of the heavens will be shaken. Then the climax ...

The heavens part open, and Jesus arrives on the scene ... and He is not alone. Everybody, and I mean everybody, will see Him. If people freaked out when they saw the two witnesses get up after being dead for three-and-a-half days and ride a cloud up to heaven, then I imagine they will be absolutely terrified when they see Christ, in the air, no doubt with millions of saints *and angels* hovering over them! Remember how king Belshazzar's knees knocked against each other when he saw the fingers writing on the wall (Daniel 5:6)? That will pale in comparison to what happens next!

Christ comes in all His glory, bringing with Him a heavenly army. Jesus mentions coming in glory a few times in the New Testament. Look at Matthew 16:27, Matthew 24:30-31, and Matthew 25:31. Each set of verses attest to this event. Each set of verses also mentions the angels. Further, Matthew 24:30 tells us He is coming in *power and great glory*. This tells me that this isn't a mere appearance in the sky. Jesus isn't coming just to pose for a picture. He is coming not only in power, but with great glory ... large and in charge; magnificent and magnified. For the armies of the Antichrist, just the appearance of Christ in the clouds alone will, I believe, evoke terror and awe, but seeing Him with the angels will multiply that terror and awe by orders of magnitude. Daniel saw an angel in one of his visions, and he trembled (Daniel 10:11) even though he loved God, and was loved by God. Still, he trembled. And angels were nothing new to him. Even though the angel told Daniel not to fear (Daniel 10:12), he struggled to regain some composure. Imagine how this army will feel when millions of angels appear with Christ in the clouds. It will be an overpowering sight!

This event will be filled with God's greatness, and be a testimony to His power of deliverance. Here is one of the great things the angels will do, as found in Mark 13:26-27:

> *"And then shall they see the Son of man coming in the clouds with great power and glory. And then shall he send his angels, and shall gather together his elect from the four winds, from the uttermost part of the earth to the uttermost part of heaven."*

The elect will be gathered by the angels to be with the Lord! Matthew 24:31 tells the same story. Imagine what that's going to be like. Each and every believer, Jew and Gentile, no matter where they may be, will be picked up and escorted to be with the Lord. Talk about a joy ride! There are different interpretations on when this particular event occurs, meaning it may happen during Christ's return, or after His return. But no matter when it may be, it will be unlike any ride these believers will ever experience.

Getting back to Revelation 19, Jesus is known by many names, but verse 11 tells us the names Faithful and True express His rule as Judge over all the earth. He will faithfully carry out God's will for man to rule on earth (Genesis 1:28), as was originally intended. The name "True" reflects the character of His reign of truth and justice. The will be no ambiguity regarding who is in charge and what He means when He speaks. No need to worry about political correctness or the offensive political posturing so prevalent nowadays so as to not offend the masses. Jesus, the Son of God and the Son of man, will rule as a man. The fire in His eyes symbolizes His coming in righteous anger to make war against those who would destroy Israel and persecute His saints. I know I wouldn't want to be on the receiving end of His anger, especially with all those angels as backup. But He is coming against the nations that serve the Antichrist, and to judge sin. Jesus is coming to make things right. His clothing (vesture) dipped in blood is the fulfillment of prophecy found in Isaiah 63:1-6, which foretold the slaughter of His enemies. His crowns (plural) declare His Kingship over all others who would dare call themselves king. These crowns are royal diadems, indicating absolute sovereignty and rule, unlike the crowns we receive for doing good works. This means the "kings of the earth" will be deposed and disposed. They don't stand a chance. So the return of Christ will satisfy multiple purposes, the primary one being to establish God's everlasting kingdom.

This will not be a sneak attack. It has been prophesied for centuries. I suspect any Bible-believing person still alive during the Tribulation Period will know the countdown. Even Satan knew the countdown, which is why he knew he had but a little time left according to Revelation 12. John saw a prelude to this early on in Revelation 1:7:

> *"Behold, he cometh with clouds; and every eye shall see him, and they also which pierced him: and all kindreds of the earth shall wail because of him. Even so, Amen."*

As awesome a sight to behold as this most certainly will be, it won't be much of a fight, as Revelation 19:15 makes clear:

> *"And out of his mouth goeth a sharp sword, that with it he should smite the nations: and he shall rule them with a rod of iron..."*

The sharp sword is another metaphor used to symbolically demonstrate the power of God's Word. It is sharp because it is powerful! Nothing can withstand it, and nothing can defeat it! And this is how Christ will defeat His enemies ... by just speaking the Word. Talk about power from on high! There will be no need for drones, missiles, or nuclear weapons from above. Christ will just speak the Word, whatever that word or words will be, and it will all be over. No negotiations, no summits, no peace talks, no truce, no deals ... no way, no how. The time for talk is past! The enemies of the Lord will be destroyed by His coming and His spoken Word. But before He speaks, Christ takes care of the Antichrist and the False Prophet first.

Revelation 19:20 tells us:

> *"And the beast was taken, and with him the false prophet that wrought miracles before him, with which he deceived them that had received the mark of the beast, and them that worshipped his image. These both were cast alive into a lake of fire burning with brimstone."*

The Antichrist and False Prophet are tossed alive into the Lake of Fire. These guys, who thought they had it going on, and had the nerve to think they should be worshipped, skipped hell altogether and went straight to the Lake of Fire. That takes care of the leaders ... now for the rest of them.

Revelation 19:21 says of them:

> *"And the remnant were slain with the sword of him that sat upon the horse, which sword proceedeth out of his mouth: and all the fowls were filled with their flesh."*

Christ then speaks the Word, and the remnant becomes bird food. The remnant is what's left of the armies of the Antichrist. The results of Christ's spoken Word are not in dispute, or subject to any other interpretation. I can't wait to hear what word or words are spoken, and see the power of His Word on His enemies. The result of the spoken Word will clearly demonstrate His great power and the remnant will be utterly destroyed.

Revelation 19:17-18 tells us the birds of the air were summoned in advance of this slaughter, to feast on the remains. This is the fulfillment of the prophecy in Revelation 14:17-20 that speaks about a second harvest. This second harvest is a prophetic revelation on the judgment of the armies of the Antichrist at Armageddon. The Valley of Jezreel, where this slaughter will take place, is a huge plain in Israel of approximately 236 square miles. Revelation 14:20 tells us there will be so much blood that it will rise up to the horses' bridles for 1,600 furlongs, which is about 200 square miles. That's a lot of space for dead people, horses, and blood ... and a lot of food for the birds. I do believe the number (1,600) John provides is literal, so the coverage area of blood is immense. I don't know whether the blood up to the horses' bridles is real or symbolic, but whether real or symbolic, it is prophetic of a complete and totally one-sided victory. It's a shutout victory—like winning a basketball game 100-0. It's a total victory for Christ and a total loss for the enemy. And all He had to do was speak the Word!

With the Antichrist, False Prophet, and their armies taken care of, all eyes turn to Satan. He's not going to enjoy the spotlight. Here's what happens to him:

Revelation 20:1-3 tells us:

> *"And I saw an angel come down from heaven, having the key to the bottomless pit and a great chain in his hand. And he laid hold on the dragon, that old serpent, which is the Devil, and Satan, and bound him a thousand years, And cast him into the bottomless pit, and shut him up, and set a seal upon him, that he should deceive the nations no more, till the thousand years should be fulfilled: and after that he must be loosed a little season."*

Satan will be knocked down, tied up and thrown back into the bottomless pit for 1,000 years. After the 1,000 years, he will be released for a very short time. We'll cover this when we discuss Unfinished Business. This prison sentence runs concurrent with the Millennium Period, so he won't be around to tempt mankind during that time.

Mankind is now free from Satan for a short while, and the Antichrist and False Prophet are history. The elect are spared from the ravages of the judgments, and Israel has been delivered and preserved. God promised a one-third remnant, and Jesus delivers on that promise when He speaks the Word and the remaining forces of the Antichrist are destroyed ... all of them. Further, this affirms the physical cannot overcome the spiritual! All that weaponry the Antichrist had at his disposal couldn't make any real difference. Christ just speaks the Word and the physical is destroyed. The spiritual has power over the physical, *not* the other way around. This demonstrates the need to be spiritually strong. It helps us overcome the physical temptations and challenges that we face. Maybe now you'll believe me.

With the Antichrist and False Prophet thrown in the Lake of Fire, the armies now bird food, and Satan bound and imprisoned, there are two things that occur before the Millennial Kingdom begins. There will be a resurrection of the righteous (the first resurrection) and the separation of the "sheep and the goats".

The First Resurrection

Revelation 20:4 says:

> *"And I saw thrones, and they sat upon them, and judgment was given unto them: and I saw the souls of them that were beheaded for the witness of Jesus, and for the word of God, and which had not worshipped the beast, neither his image, neither had received his mark upon their foreheads, or in their hands; and they lived and reigned with Christ a thousand years."*

In his vision, John sees thrones (plural) and martyred saints who came out of the Tribulation Period. Christ is now on earth, as we have read in the previous section, and as the King of Kings sits on *His* throne. He promised His disciples, however, that they would sit on thrones judging the 12 tribes of Israel (Matthew 19:28 and Luke 22:29-30), so I'm inclined to believe that is what the first set of thrones in the above verses represents.

John also tells us these martyred saints will live and reign with Christ for 1,000 years. That means there is a resurrection, which is a rejoining of the body with its departed soul. The body is now raised incorruptible, just as the raptured body was changed from corruptible to incorruptible (1 Corinthians 15:52). John calls this the first resurrection (Revelation 20:5).

John records a blessing and an ominous note in Revelation 20:6:

> *"Blessed and holy is he that hath part in the first resurrection: on such the second death hath no power..."*

Those who have a part of the first resurrection are called blessed and holy because they will be with Christ as He sits on His throne as King over all the earth during His millennial reign. This is the time we believe all the Old Testament saints will also be resurrected. There are several verses that attest to this resurrection, such as Isaiah 26:19 and Daniel 12:1-3. But my favorite is Job 19:25-26:

> *"For I know that my redeemer liveth, and that he shall stand at the latter day upon the earth: And though after my skin worms destroy this body, yet in my flesh I will see God."*

Job knew the end, and that's what he looked forward to—seeing his Redeemer in his resurrected body. We'll get to meet all the notable Old Testament saints such as Job, Abraham, Moses, Noah, Rahab, Joshua, David, Isaiah, and Daniel. Obviously this is not intended to be a complete list, so don't get too excited or anxious because I didn't list one of your favorites. This resurrection will include all of the Old Testament saints who have exercised faith and believed in God. This will be a time of great fellowship. We get a chance to talk to the Old Testament saints ... our forefathers, as it were. Imagine hearing the stories of their experiences! This is one part of the Millennium I really look forward to experiencing.

Getting back on point, the first part of Revelation 20:5 refers to the second resurrection, but verse 6 goes so far as to call it the second death. The remaining dead will be resurrected and judged after the 1,000 years are up. That is known as the Great White Throne judgment, which we will address shortly. That will be the final judgment of the unsaved.

The Separation of the Sheep and the Goats

Some people will survive the Tribulation Period and be ready to enter the Millennial Period. As we saw earlier, at least 50% of the world's population will die as a result of the judgments. Conversely, 50% will live. Those who survive will now be judged by Jesus Christ. And what is this judgment? It is the judgment that determines who stays and who goes. That is, who remains with Christ in the Millennial Kingdom and who gets sent packing to you know where. Here's how that happens.

In Matthew 25:31-46, Jesus told a parable about those who will enter the Millennial Kingdom and those who will not. This is known as the parable of the sheep and the goats. You should read this parable in its entirety before going any further, but some of the more important verses are included below.

Matthew 25:31 gives us the timeframe:

> *"When the Son of Man shall come in his glory, and all the holy angels with him, then shall he sit upon the throne of his glory."*

This verse refers to Christ's second coming, which we just read about in Revelation 19. When He comes and have defeated those who fought against Him, He will be seated on His throne, in judgment, before all the nations, meaning people of the *Gentile* nations (not Israel) who survived the Tribulation Period. At this judgment, a separation of people takes place, as indicated in the verse below (Matthew 25:32-33):

> *"And before him shall be gathered all the nations: and he shall separate them one from another, as a shepherd divideth his sheep from the goats. And he shall set the sheep on his right hand, but the goats on his left."*

Christ the King does the separating and then pronounces blessings to those on His right, the sheep.

Matthew 25:34:

> *"Then shall the King say unto them on his right hand, Come, ye blessed of my Father, inherit the kingdom prepared for you from the foundation of the world."*

Christ also pronounces judgment to those on his left, the goats.

Matthew 25:41:

> *"Then shall he say also unto them on the left hand, Depart from me, ye cursed, into everlasting fire, prepared for the devil and his angels…"*

Jesus doesn't separate the two groups based on the "eeny meeny miny moe" method. The basis of the separation is explained in the passages that follow after the one side is ushered in to the Kingdom, found in Matthew 25:35-36, and the other side is sent packing, found in Matthew 25:42-43. Here it is, abbreviated and paraphrased.

The basis of their blessing (ushered in) or curse (sent packing) is their treatment of those whom Christ calls "the least of His brethren" during the Tribulation Period. What is meant by "brethren" is yet another term that scholars debate. Some interpret it as the righteous, some as the poor, some as Christians, some as neighbors, and others still as the Jews. I lean toward interpreting it as the Jews for reasons I will explain shortly, but first things first.

How do we know that Christ is referring to the treatment afforded during the Tribulation Period? Because Matthew 25:31 told us! The primary indication is the timing. Christ comes in His glory with His holy angels to sit on His throne *after* the Tribulation Period. We just covered this very thing under the chapter titled The Final Curtain. Christ is now fulfilling Revelation 19:11, which tells us He came to "judge and make war". Well, the war is over. It's time to judge. Matthew 25:32 tells us the nations are gathered before Him, and it's not to hear Him tell jokes, as the subsequent verses make clear. Remember, everyone who entered the Tribulation Period was unsaved. Christians were raptured out of here prior to that. Those who died during the Tribulation Period were judged when they died. The only judgment that remains falls to those who are still alive.

Going back to the parable, it specifically identifies three groups of people central to understanding the lesson:

- The sheep
- The goats
- The least of His brethren

During the Tribulation Period, one group will give aid to the distressed of another group. They rendered these services to those who were hungry, gave water to those who were thirsty, sheltered the homeless when they had no place to stay, clothed those who had no clothes, took care of the sick, and visited those who were in prison (Matthew 25:35-36). The group who rendered service are the sheep ... and they did these things in the worst of times. They are the first group mentioned above.

Alternatively, there will be those who did not render service to the distressed group; they did not do the things the sheep had done. They did not provide food, or clothing, or shelter, etc. (Matthew 25:42-43). They are the second group mentioned above. These people are the goats.

The third group is "the least of His brethren". They clearly lacked food, shelter, and clothing, medical care, and were imprisoned. This is the group that received benevolent services from the sheep, the first group. However, the goats kicked them to the curb.

Both the sheep and the goats will basically ask the same question: "When did we do, or not do these things?" beginning in verses 37 and 44, respectively. The answer is during the Tribulation Period, which immediately precede this judgment and separation.

Let's examine the question, "who are 'the least of His brethren'?" The term "brethren" is not uniformly interpreted. Based on what happens during the Tribulation Period, we know both Jews and Christians go through unprecedented and direct persecution by Satan and the Antichrist. Satan and the forces of the Antichrist were out to destroy the Jews, particularly in the last three and one-half years of the Tribulation Period. Christians are martyred by the millions. And only those who *do not* have the mark of the beast, Christians, will be willing to aid the Jews. How do we know they were Christians? We know because out of the nations only Christians enter the Millennium Kingdom with Christ. They must be the sheep. They are the first group mentioned. That's the main point of the parable ... who enters the Millennium Kingdom. The unrighteous, the goats, do not enter the Millennium Kingdom. In my view, "brethren" implies a family or kinship relationship, not a neighborly or "all men are brothers" relationship. Since Jesus is of Jewish descent, the term "least of my brothers" apply. Christ is related to the Jews in that manner, although they do not have the kind of relationship to Him that Christians have. Having said that, will a Christian help another Christian in need during that time? Absolutely! As previously mentioned, some interpret the "brethren" as Christians since they too will go through persecution. While I don't agree, I'm okay with this interpretation. I understand why someone might interpret "brethren" that way. Christians helping other Christians and Jews during that time (and now) is the right thing to do. Those with the mark of the beast certainly won't be willing to aid the Jews. Christ already told us in Matthew 24:12 that the hearts of the unredeemed will "wax cold" and iniquity will abound. These people will have no interest in helping anyone, particularly the Jews.

Let me say one last thing about the Jews, as it applies here. This goes back to, and is rooted in, God's promise to Abram in Genesis 12:3. God said He will bless those who bless Israel and curse those that curse Israel. There can be no better example of that application than what happens during the Tribulation Period. The beneficiaries of this blessing are the sheep ... they blessed Israel, and as a reward, get to enter into Christ's Millennium Kingdom. Again, not by their works, i.e., helping Israel, but because their works reflect a conversion to Christ. The inheritors of the curse are the goats ... they get to wish they could enter the Kingdom, but will end up in hell because of how they treated the Jews, i.e., they cursed Israel during the Tribulation Period. Their treatment of the Jews reflects their unredeemed and unrepentant status before God. The sheep deliver during the worst of times—the Tribulation Period, and are blessed with entry into the Millennium Kingdom.

Helping out people in the here and now is a good thing to do. It is not, however, the point of this parable. But this isn't an escape clause for how we are to treat others today. We are still to do good things now, as the sheep will do in that day. In fact, it is required. Micah 6:8 tells us:

"...and what doth the Lord require of thee, but to do justly, and to love mercy, and to walk humbly with thy God?"

Jesus put it another way in Mark 12:31:

"...Thou shalt love thy neighbor as thyself. There is none other commandment greater than these."

Along with the Christian Gentiles who enter the Kingdom, Jews will be living in the Millennial Kingdom as well. Remember, a remnant of Jews will have repented, accepted Christ as the Messiah, and secured their place in the kingdom. While two-thirds will perish during the Tribulation Period, one-third will be saved (Zechariah 13:8-9). All those who do will enter the kingdom and preserve the nation.

After these things, Christ begins His Millennial Reign. And it will be a wonderful blessing. Let's look at some of the goings on during Christ's 1,000-year earthly reign.

The Millennial Reign of Jesus Christ

Isaiah 11:9:

> "...for the earth shall be full of the knowledge of the Lord, as the waters cover the sea."

This introduces a time when there will be worldwide knowledge of the Lord among every living thing (see also Jeremiah 31:34 and Habakkuk 2:14). This will be a wonderful, prosperous, peaceful time, beginning when Christ takes His first step on earth. And it's no wonder. The world will be ruled by Christ and will be inhabited by Christians, those in incorruptible bodies and those in corruptible bodies.

Jesus Christ will reign and rule on earth from Jerusalem as we are told in Isaiah 2:2-3:

> *"And it shall come to pass in the last days, that the mountain of the Lord's house shall be established in the top of the mountains, and shall be exalted above the hills; and all nations shall flow unto it. And many people shall go and say, Come ye, and let us go up to the mountain of the Lord, to the house of the God of Jacob; and he will teach us of his ways, and we will walk in his paths: for out of Zion shall go forth the law, and the word of the Lord from Jerusalem."*

The nations will come to Jerusalem to hear His words and learn His ways. Mountains are symbolic of kingdoms or governments, as we have stated previously. Here, Christ's kingdom is at the top of the mountains, which indicate that all other kingdoms are subservient to his. As we saw earlier in 1 Corinthians 6:2 and Revelation 5:10, the saints will rule with Christ. So Christians will be the vehicle through which Christ manages the affairs of the world during the Millennium. Some will be rulers over cities or towns and the like. Remember the parable of the talents? Others may be administrators or serve in other capacities as the Lord dictates. No doubt these assignments will be among those handed out as rewards at the Judgment Seat of Christ.

Christ will rule with a "rod of iron", so don't think you can party like it's 1999 and get away with it. Things will not go back to normal, that is, as in pre-Tribulation days, like nothing ever happened. Christ will rule as God intended man to rule. What does that mean? In the Garden of Eden, God ruled. The nation of Israel was to be God governed. The Millennium Kingdom, then, will be a theocratic government, led and ruled by the man, Christ Jesus. Under His rule, mankind will prosper and benefit greatly … the way God always intended. Since only Christians and the remnant of Jews who come to Christ will enter the Millennium, I believe there will be non-stop joyful celebrations. Who knows … what if the Marriage Supper continues? Imagine the fun and fellowship!

Everyone who survives the Tribulation Period will still be in their natural bodies, and many will have children who will live very long lives, as you'll see in a moment. During this time, there will be no outside or ungodly influence on man's heart to cause him to sin. Satan is bound and imprisoned and cannot influence man's behavior. Governments, which I believe will still exist, will not be the political, self-serving side shows they are today. No Democrats, no Republicans, no Independents, no Tea Partyers, no Communists, no Socialists, or any other political affiliations. Can you say "Praise the Lord"? People won't have to worry about political partisanship, abuse of power, misrepresentation, term limits, corruption, tax bias, special interest preferences, negative campaign ads, or any of the other trappings of human political systems that plague society. All will be ruled by Christ through those He places over them. Yes, from man's point of view, it is a dictatorship, but it is a *righteous* dictatorship, a perfect dictatorship, for it will be based on a theocracy, or God-governed society. Christ will rule justly.

The New Beginning

In a world physically ravaged by the seal, trumpet, and vial judgments, Zechariah 14:4 tells us that Christ will return on the Mount of Olives (Acts 1:11-12), which will split in two when His feet touches the ground (Zechariah 14:4). Now that's power! Acts 1:11-12 also prophesies His return on the Mount of Olives. Great things begin to happen immediately.

Zechariah 14:8 tells us:

> *"And it shall be in that day, that living waters shall go out from Jerusalem; half of them toward the former sea, and half of them toward the hinder sea; in summer and in winter shall it be."*

Living waters, which means life giving and sustaining waters, not rain water or salt water, will come out of Jerusalem toward the Dead Sea (former or east sea) and the Mediterranean Sea (hinder or west sea), which means both of these seas will be revitalized to sustain life. If you remember, the trumpet and vial judgments killed all life within the seas. Of particular note is the revitalization of the Dead Sea. Its high salt content prohibits sustaining life, but the living water will now allow life to flourish.

Ezekiel 47:8 reports:

> *"...These waters issue out toward the east country, and go down into the desert, and go into the sea: which being brought forth into the sea, the waters shall be healed."*

Ezekiel saw something similar to Zechariah 14:8, only his perspective was from the temple. Living waters, from the temple threshold, flow into the seas and rivers (verse 9), which will be healed. Marine life will thrive (verse 9), and fish will once again flourish and be in abundance.

Ezekiel 47:12 says:

> *"And by the river upon the bank thereof, on this side and on that side, shall grow all trees for meat, whose leaf shall not fade, neither shall the fruit thereof be consumed: it shall bring forth new fruit*

according to his months, because their waters they issued out of the sanctuary: and the fruit thereof shall be for meat, and the leaf thereof for medicine."

The living waters flowing from the temple (verse 1) will heal all the waters. As a result, trees will grow and yield fruit in abundance. Their leaves will be good for medicine.

Ezekiel 34:25:

"And I will make with them a covenant of peace, and will cause the evil beasts to cease out of the land: and they shall dwell safely in the wilderness, and sleep in the woods."

Isaiah 11:6:

"The wolf also shall dwell with the lamb, and the leopard shall lie down with the kid; and the calf and the young lion and the fatling together; and a little child shall lead them..."

This means all the wild animals that were let loose under the fourth seal to kill man will be tamed. God will cause the beasts to cease their attack on man and be removed from the land. And not only that, they will not attack one another. There will be no predator or prey. The animals will live in harmony. The wild animals will settle for straw (verse 7) as food. Children will be able to play with the animals and not get hurt (verse 8-9). You will no longer have to worry about pit bulls running around the streets in your neighborhood, and the "running of the bulls" of Pamplona, Spain, will be a thing of the past. Come to think of it, matadors and animal trainers may have to find new occupations.

Isaiah 27:6 tells us:

"...Israel shall blossom and bud, and fill the face of the world with fruit."

There will be no more food shortages ... no more world hunger. Crops will grow in abundance to satisfy man's nourishment (Isaiah 35:1-2; Ezekiel 47:12).

Here's a big one.

Isaiah 65:20:

> "There shall be no more thence an infant of days, nor an old man that hath not filled his days: for the child shall die an hundred years old; but the sinner being an hundred years old shall be accursed."

What this means is human beings will have extended life spans. This applies to those who survive the Tribulation Period, and enter the Millennium as sheep. Many of these people will have children. Those born into this period will be considered children at 100 years old, an indication of how long lifespans will be extended.

Further, those who die at 100 years old will be considered cursed. What this also means is there will be some sin and rebellion, which is hard for me to imagine, but is nonetheless true. God always gives human beings free will. Some will exercise it poorly, even in an ideal environment like the Millennial Kingdom. However, death will come to those who sin and rebel against the authority of Jesus Christ, who, let me remind you, will rule with a "rod of iron". So, don't mess with Him ... and don't try to play Him!

Here's another interesting point. There will be a fascinating mix of people walking around at this time. In the Millennium, there will be those with glorified bodies, and those with natural bodies. Obviously only those who come back with Christ will have glorified bodies. All others who survive the Tribulation Period and enter the Millennial Period will have natural bodies. While the Millennial Period is characterized by healing, those in glorified bodies will not be affected by that which can affect natural bodies. External influences or circumstances like heat, cold, and illness, will not affect glorified bodies. The natural world cannot affect glorified bodies. Yaaa!!! The Apostle Paul gives a wonderful explanation on the differences between natural bodies and glorified bodies in 1 Corinthians 15:39-44. In short, we who are in glorified bodies will have bodies just like Christ, according to 1 John 3:2 and Philippians 3:21.

But here's an interesting question. Will the inhabitants of the world know the difference between those in glorified bodies compared to those in natural bodies? Will you be able to tell, visually, who has what body? The Bible does not describe how glorified bodies will look. The only clues given are found in certain verses. Revelation 19:14 says we are clothed in white linen upon our return, so maybe that will be our "dress code". Revelation 3 talks about wearing white garments, so perhaps white will be the order of the day. White is the color for victory and holiness, so perhaps those in glorified bodies will wear white all the time to demonstrate victory and holiness throughout the entire Millennial Period.

There will be definite differences, however, other than how the natural world affects glorified bodies. The question is how do they manifest themselves? Look at the some of the things Christ did in His physical body, after His resurrection. For instance, He still ate food which, granted, is pretty normal for someone in a natural body. But it's nice to know those in glorified bodies can do the same. That being said, I think our diet will be limited to fish (Ezekiel 47:10), fruit and vegetables (Ezekiel 47:12). I'll miss my Philly cheesesteaks, but I'll learn to do without them. How about this for amazing? In Luke 24:31, we're told that Jesus disappeared in their midst. By that I mean He didn't sneak out the back door. Gives new meaning to hide-n-seek, huh? In John 20:19, He either walked through a closed door, or rematerialized in a closed room. Beam me up, Scottie! I'll take either-or. In Acts 1:9, we're told that the risen Jesus had nature (a cloud) provide Him with personal limousine service, which suits me just fine. Flying in airplanes was never my preferred mode of travel. However, the point of His grand ascension in Acts 1 was to tell the disciples that Jesus would return the same way He left, so maybe the cloud was a one shot deal. When Christ returns, it is with clouds. Still, I'm hoping!

That those in glorified bodies will be able to do such things is admittedly speculative, but you have to admit, that's some pretty cool stuff. While we will be "just like Him", I'm not certain we'll be able to do all of the things Jesus did. He is, after all, the Son of God! You have to admit, though, it is fun to think about ... if you're a Christian. The point of this is to relay that our new, glorified bodies will be like Christ's resurrected body.

Here's another pretty cool benefit.

Isaiah 35:5-6 says:

> *"Then the eyes of the blind shall be opened, and the ears of the deaf shall be unstopped. Then shall the lame man leap as an hart, and the tongue of the dumb sing…"*

Those entering the Millennium with physical infirmaries will be healed. This passage specifically mentions the blind, the lame, and those who are mute. They will be healed. I think if you suffer from other physical ailments such as arthritis, bad hips, bad knees, allergies, corns and bunions, etc., you will be healed as well. You guys who are bald or going bald, well, I don't know about getting new hair. Sorry … but keep hope alive!

Isaiah 65:24:

> *"And it shall come to pass, that before they call, I will answer; and while they are yet speaking, I will hear."*

This is sweet, and one of my favorites. Every time I read this, I get so excited. Imagine this: God hearing, knowing, and responding to our prayers before we finish speaking! This is the kind of intimacy Christians should long to have. We will get to understand, just a bit, how Daniel must have felt (Daniel 9:21). Our God is a great God indeed!

There are many more verses that address the things that will happen during the Millennium that I have not mentioned here. Isaiah 65 also mentions building homes and planting crops. Considering the devastation that will occur during the Tribulation Period, it's no surprise that a huge rebuilding program would commence (Isaiah 65:21). There will also be the reinstitution of the Feast of Tabernacles (Zechariah 14:16-19). This Feast will require all the nations to visit Jerusalem once a year to worship the Lord. Those nations that do not abide will be cursed with no rain and/or plagues.

The Millennium will be a wonder to us all, especially coming on the heels of what transpired during the Tribulation Period. Christ will be living among us, and ruling. The seas and rivers will be healed, aquatic life will flourish, people will live long, healthy, and rejuvenated lives, and plenty of babies will be born by those in natural bodies to essentially repopulate the earth. There will be plenty of food and very little death—all under the rule of a righteous judge. It will be a peaceful, pleasant time.

Unfinished Business

On the heels of the Millennial Period, only two things remain to be done before eternity is ushered in.

1. Satan will be released from the bottomless pit
2. The Great White Throne Judgment will take place

Let's discuss these briefly.

Satan's Last Stand

During the 1,000-year reign of Christ on earth, Satan will be imprisoned in the bottomless pit. Through the Millennium Period then, mankind will be freed from his evil influence, which leads to temptation, which leads to sin. At the end of the 1,000 years, he will be released. After all this time, why ruin a good thing? Here's why.

As we read earlier, during the Millennium Period, man (this includes you too, ladies) will have an extremely long life span, perhaps similar to that which man of the early Old Testament days had, particularly before the Flood. Those guys lived very long lives to populate the earth. Adam lived 930 years (Genesis 5:5), and Noah lived 950 years (Genesis 9:29). Have you ever heard the expression "old as Methuselah"? Well, he was a real person who lived before the Flood, and died at the age of 969 years old (Genesis 5:27). He has the honor of having lived the longest life. The extended life spans during the Millennium will accomplish the same thing. The earth will be repopulated. That means millions, if not billions, of people will be born by those still in natural bodies.

Mortal man, though now blessed with a long life span, will still have a sinful nature. Of course, without the external influence of Satan, any person who sins during the Millennium will sin only because it is in his or her heart to do so. Man won't be able to blame Satan for any sin committed. But, despite the knowledge of the Lord, which will be in all who live, despite the righteous theocratic leadership of Christ, despite the blessing of long life and health, despite the abundance of food and protection from the beasts of the earth, many people will not like to be ruled by Christ. Many people will still not be content. Obviously they will not accept Christ in their hearts. These people will decide they want something else. Apparently they're smart enough to know not to buck the system lest they face death. But they want to be self-governing, as opposed to being ruled by Christ. The release of Satan from the bottomless pit will give them an opportunity to show their true colors.

Revelation 20:7-9 says:

> *"And when the thousand years are expired, Satan shall be loosed out of his prison, And shall go out to deceive the nations which are in the four quarters of the earth, Gog and Magog, to gather them together to battle: the number of whom is as the sand of the sea. And they went up on the breadth of the earth, and compassed the camp of the saints about, and the beloved city…"*

Satan will do what he does best … deceive. In this case, he will deceive those people who want to do their own thing. He will gather these malcontents together and make an attempt to dethrone Jesus, the King of Kings, in Jerusalem. Really? Yes, really. We have no idea how many people will embark on this foolish coup, but it must be millions at least … "as the sands of the sea" by comparison. They will encircle the camp of the saints, which is Jerusalem, the Holy City. Man, are they in for a surprise!

Remember one of the "last words" Christ spoke on the cross in Matthew 27:46? Jesus said, "My God, my God, why have you forsaken me?" Well, this won't be that! There will be no need.

Revelation 20:9:

> *"...and fire came down from God out of heaven, and devoured them."*

God will respond immediately with fire and destroy them. I think the fact that there is no mention of anything closely related to a battle means there will be no battle. Christ is ruling to fulfill God's will for man and to fulfill Scripture ... and God will not allow Satan another chance. The world will finally be purged of those who are unrighteous and unwilling to accept the will of Almighty God and His Son, Jesus Christ. Notice that Satan, an eternal being, is not destroyed by the fire. Those he led were destroyed, which is the typical result for those who are foolish enough to follow him.

What happens to Satan? Revelation 20:10 tells us:

> *"And the devil that deceived them was cast into the lake of fire and brimstone, where the beast and the false prophet are, and shall be tormented day and night for ever and ever."*

The fall and final judgment of Satan is quite remarkable if you really think about it. Before his fall, he was above all the angels. But that wasn't enough. He wanted more ... his pride and his greed got to him. Consider what he had versus where he ended up. This once anointed cherub, who was created in perfect beauty and wisdom, will suffer the consequences of his pride, his murders, his deception, and his lies for all eternity. His sins and his challenge to the sovereignty of Almighty God will result in the eternal damnation of this perfectly created being who dared to challenge God's authority, and dared to suggest he was on par with Almighty God. He wanted all others to worship him, and managed to convince one-third of all the angels to follow him. He entered the heart of Judas to betray Christ the Lord, and walked about over the ages, seeking whom he may devour. The list of sins and evil acts he committed goes on and on and on.

To this present day, Satan moves about just looking for ways to mess things up for everybody, not just Christians. He is still at war against God and those whom He loves. I'm sure he's messed up at least one or two of your days, and mine as well. But, praise be to God! After this, mankind will never, ever have to worry about Him anymore.

And for those who refused the truth and rejected God's Son, Jesus Christ, it is now time for their judgment.

The Great White Throne Judgment

In Revelation 20:11-15, John tells us of a judgment that will take place immediately after Satan is cast into the Lake of Fire. This judgment is first referenced in Revelation 20:5, and is called the second death in verse 6. It is the final judgment of the *unsaved*—those who died not knowing or acknowledging Jesus Christ as Savior. The fact that people are here, at this judgment, confirms that they died without Christ and, up to this point, have been tormented in hell. If you've truly accepted Jesus Christ as your savior, as the only one who can redeem you from the penalty of your sins (at least two, right?), you won't be judged here. Christians are judged at the Judgment Seat of Christ, and that judgment is a judgment of works, for which we get rewards, not punishment for the sins we have committed as Christians. This judgment, however, is for the dead—the unsaved of all ages past.

This judgment is commonly called the Great White Throne Judgment, because of the description given in Revelation 20:11:

> *"And I saw a great white throne, and him that sat on it, from whose face the earth and the heaven fled away; and there was found no place for them."*

This will be a terrifying time for those present, beginning with the cataclysmic destruction and removal of the earth and heaven (the sky in this case) from the presence of God. As the final vestiges of sin are eliminated from the universe, these people will be judged *before* the new heaven and new earth comes to replace the old.

2 Peter 3:7, 10, and 12 mentions the pending destruction of this present earth, and the timeframe of these verses corresponds to this day of judgment. Verses 7 and 10 read:

> *"But the heavens and the earth, which are now, by the same word are kept in store, reserved unto fire against the day of judgment and perdition of ungodly men."*

> *"But the day of the Lord will come as a thief in the night; in the which the heavens shall pass away with great noise, and the elements shall melt with fervent heat, the earth also and the works that are therein shall be burned up."*

Clearly God planned the destruction of the earth as indicated in verse 7 of this chapter. The earth has been reserved until the day of judgment. Verse 10 provides further description of the cataclysmic act itself. There will be lots of noise, lots of heat, and lots of burning. Fire is used to represent judgment and purification. So this is the purging of sin within the natural, physical confines of this polluted world we know today. The final purging will be the people who are sentenced at this judgment.

The Bible does not mention where the Great White Throne Judgment takes place. It's probably not in heaven considering the sin nature of those being judged, which leaves what we know as outer space, or perhaps some other spiritual plane such as Hell. Wherever this judgment takes place, I doubt people will argue about where they *are* as much as where they'll be *going*. The other unanswered question is where are the saints who will inherit the new earth during the destruction of the present heavens and earth? Perhaps we will be in the New Jerusalem, which we will get to in a moment.

John describes the participants of this judgment in Revelation 20:12:

> *"And I saw the dead, small and great, stand before God..."*

All those who have died outside the faith and without Christ since the dawn of time will be standing before Almighty God. This will not be a comfortable time, to put it mildly. Have you ever stood before a judge or someone else who had your fate in his hands, and both of you knew of your guilt? Here, these people will stand before God! Not just a judge, He is THE JUDGE ... ALMIGHTY GOD seated on His throne! The thought of standing before Almighty God, in condemnation and judgment, has to be terrifying.

I once used what you might call "incorrect language" in a fit of anger to a teacher. I was in the 8th or 9th grade. I was a little guy; a little bit over 5 feet tall. He was 6 feet 7 inches. Stupid, I know. I was scared to death. What's worse is this happened during a time when teachers were authorized to use paddles as a means of discipline, and I had seen this teacher, on occasion, apply this trade. He was really good at it, and when he applied it, it was brutal. I knew in my heart I deserved it, and almost cried at the thought of what was about to happen to me. But he let me off the hook because I was generally a well-behaved, decent student. Maybe he felt a little responsible too. He really did start the verbal exchange. But my point here is that as a relatively tiny student standing before this giant of a teacher, I knew I was guilty, and he had me dead to rights. The punishment, if he chose to inflict it, would be very painful and very embarrassing. Everybody there was just standing around waiting to see what he would do. I was terrified, but he let me go without the deserved penalty. That won't happen here at this judgment. Everyone here gets their just due.

Status in life won't matter ... whether great in terms of stature, wealth, prestige, power, social class, military rank, a seat in government, chief executive officer of a Fortune 500 company, A+ student, or the proverbial *big fish in a little pond*. And the reverse is true as well. None of that will matter. The only criterion that matters at all is whether the person accepted Christ as savior. These people at the Great White Throne Judgment did not. If you haven't and you don't, you will be here! In life, these people have told God, "I don't need you" or "I don't believe in you" or "I don't believe in your Word". But here, they will. The Bible tells us in Romans 14:11:

> "For it is written, As I live, saith the Lord, every knee shall bow to me, and every tongue shall confess to God."

The Apostle Paul was quoting from Isaiah 45:23, where God swears by Himself, because there is no authority higher than His own, that every knee will bow and every tongue will swear in the righteousness of the

Word that comes out of His mouth. I believe everyone here will confess their guilt because they know they had opportunity.

Romans 2:4-6 tells us:

> *"Or despisest thou the riches of his goodness and forbearance and longsuffering; not knowing that the goodness of God leadeth thee to repentance? But after thy hardness and impenitent heart treasurest up unto thyself wrath against the day of wrath and revelation of the righteous judgment of God; Who will render to every man according to his deeds;"*

The Apostle Paul said that God's goodness, or kindness, was purposed to lead us to repentance. It was not because we deserved it, felt justified, entitled, or simply believed "it's about time I got mine". It was to recognize that all good things came from God, and repent in acknowledgment of His goodness! God demonstrated not only His goodness, but His forbearance. He allowed you time to "get yourself together" and not strike you down immediately, just as He patiently dealt with Israel. God "put up with it" and continued to forbear. God had been patient. He waited and waited. But, continued hard-headedness (hardness and impenitent heart) and non-repentance only led to one thing ... the storing up of wrath against the day of judgment. Now it's too late! It was the ultimate "I told you so!" It is judgement day for those who rejected God's goodness, His forbearance, and His patience. It goes without saying that they rejected His Son, Jesus Christ, and did not repent. Now their deeds come into play.

Just as the recorded works of the righteous were used to determine the rewards given at the Judgment Seat of Christ, so shall the recorded deeds of the unrighteous be used to determine their level of punishment, as Revelation 20:12 makes clear:

> *"...and the books were opened: and another book was opened, which is the book of life: and the dead were judged out of those things which were written in the books, according to their works."*

Notice two things here. The first is *what is done in this life is being recorded* ... in several books no less. And when it's time to stand before Almighty God, these books will be opened and read. Now I don't know who in heaven is recording the things we're doing, but I'm pretty certain these scribes do a perfect job because they serve a perfect God who sees all. God's will in heaven is accomplished, so no beat is missed. Further, and more importantly, God is omniscient and has a better memory than we do. He knows all, so don't count on heaven missing a beat when it comes to recording those events. We may wish some things were forgotten or not recorded, but it will be too late for that. Every sin, every intention of the heart, will be brought before God and judged.

The second thing is *the degree of punishment for each person at this judgment will be determined by what that person did in life on earth* ... "according to their works" as the verse puts it. That means the degree of punishment will not be the same for each person. This verse tells us that everyone here will be judged according to the things written in the books. There is no "he said, she said" testimony. The basis for punishment will be what was done. With the exception of the Book of Life, the other books are not named. One of these books could be the Bible, or rather, what we know or have been taught from the Bible. In other words, you can't say you didn't know if you sat in church every Sunday, or every other Sunday, or once a month, or even once in a blue moon when you were growing up. James 4:17 puts it this way:

> *"Therefore to him that knoweth to do good, and doeth it not, to him it is sin."*

Perhaps many people at this judgment will have grown up in the Church, and know more of what is required than some others. The fact that they're here means they not only rejected God and His Son, but also rejected the Word that was preached to them. As a consequence, their punishment will be greater. To support this, let's look at what Jesus had to say in Matthew 11:20-24:

> *"Then he began to upbraid the cities wherein most of his mighty works were done, because they repented not: Woe unto you Chorazin! Woe unto thee,*

> *Bethsaida! for if the mighty works, which were done in you, had been done in Tyre and Sidon, they would have repented long ago in sackcloth and ashes. But I say unto you, It shall be more tolerable for Tyre and Sidon at the day of judgment, than for you. And thou, Capernaum, which art exalted unto heaven, shalt be brought down to hell: for if the mighty works, which have been done in thee, had been done in Sodom, it would have remained until this day. But I say unto you, That it shall be more tolerable for the land of Sodom in the day of judgment, than for thee."*

What does this mean? It means that the cities of Chorazin, Bethsaida, and Capernaum (Jewish cities) were shown "mighty works", meaning they received more light of the Gospel than Tyre, Sidon, and Sodom (Gentile cities). Since the Jewish cities received more light of the Gospel, they will receive greater punishment because they rejected "more light", or greater revelation than the Gentile cities. Christ said that if Tyre, Sidon, and Sodom had been shown the mighty works that were done in Chorazin, Bethsaida, and Capernaum, they would have repented. The same principle applies to those who received more light, but rejected the light they are given. They will receive the greater punishment than those who received less light. Simply put: They should have known better because of the light they were given and exposed to during their lifetime. The application applies to those who grew up in the Church, but rejected the light of the Gospel. Those who rejected the light will experience greater punishment because they rejected the light they were given.

Even so, in addition to rejecting the light they were given, those who do evil will be punished based on the evil deeds they did. Jeremiah 17:10 paints a picture of how they will be recompensed for their works:

> *"I the Lord search the heart, I try the reins, even to give every man according to his ways, and according to the fruit of his doings."*

I can only imagine people such as Hitler and his henchmen, Nero, Caligula, Stalin, Idi Amin, and many others who shared a penchant for extreme brutality will experience worse punishment than people who, though unsaved, were basically nice or decent people. Unfortunately, being nice and decent is not the basis for skipping this judgment.

Before the unsaved are finally judged, a resurrection takes place as we find in Revelation 20:13:

> *"And the sea gave up the dead which were in it; and death and hell delivered up the dead which were in them: and they were judged every man according to their works."*

No matter where a dead body's final physical resting place is—be it land or sea, buried or cremated, the physical body will be resurrected and rejoined with that person's spirit (from hell, for this judgment), as the above verse attests. Need I remind you that hell is not a fun place, so no one here has been is enjoying the ride thus far. Hell is a place of torment, as the story of the rich man in Luke16: 22-23 affirms.

After each person here has been judged, then comes the final act. Revelation 20:14-15 tells us:

> *"And death and hell were cast into the lake of fire. This is the second death. And whosoever was not found written in the book of life was cast into the lake of fire."*

It is in the Lake of Fire that each person experiences the degree of punishment decreed at the Great White Throne judgment. After this, there will be no more sin, judgments, punishments, or hell.

After the Great White Throne judgment, we get to the end of human history. Christ, His work now finished, turns the kingdom back over to God as the Apostle Paul masterfully summarized in 1 Corinthians 15:24-28:

> *"Then cometh the end, when he shall have delivered up the kingdom to God, even the Father; when he shall have put down all rule and all authority and power. For he must reign, till he hath put all enemies under his feet. The last enemy that shall*

be destroyed is death. For he hath put all things under his feet. But when he saith all things are put under him, it is manifest that he is excepted, which did put all things under him. And when all things shall be subdued unto him, then shall the Son also himself be subject unto him that put all things under him, that God may be all in all."

Jesus Christ, having finished His redemptive work, having put down all earthly rule, and having conquered death by His resurrection, then turns in the keys to the kingdom to God the Father. In His final act, Christ subjects Himself to God so that God will be all and in all. In other words, as we are one in Christ, and Christ is one in God through the Trinity, we are all in all—one big happy family. You don't want to be left out of this great occasion. So get a head start. Work the will of Christ in your life just as Christ, in the flesh, worked the will of God in His.

It's Not Too Late

As we learned in Revelation 20:15, the final destination of the unbeliever is not hell, but the Lake of Fire. It is not God's will that any should perish and suffer in torment for eternity. That's why He sent His Son to redeem mankind. Many people don't believe a loving God will do this. What they don't understand is God is holy, a God of justice, and that His holiness and justice demand a payment for sin. It has been that way since the beginning of man! Nothing, in that regard, has changed. God provided the sacrifice in the Garden, and He provides the only way now, the only provision, through which His holiness and justice can be satisfied—that way being through His only begotten Son (John 3:16).

You can try to blame someone else for your being at the Great White Throne Judgment. Blame Reverend Wrong all you want. Maybe you're right … maybe he didn't do all he was supposed to do. Maybe he talked about money all the time from the pulpit, then got into his top of the line Mercedes Benz wearing a custom made silk suit and drove home to his mansion off the lake. Maybe he hoarded church money instead of helping out some of the poor people in the church. Because he did those things, you decided you can't be a Christian if that's what it's like to be a Christian. The problem with that conclusion is Reverend Wrong is not the standard. The Bible, God's Word, tells us what we must do to avoid being at the Great White Throne judgment! No one there will be able to blame anybody else for being there. Recently, I heard some guys complain vociferously about what "this church over here" did, or what "that church over there" didn't do to help somebody along the way. Then the complaints focused on Reverend Wrong and all the messed up things he was doing and saying ... and then I tell them. Neither "this church" nor "that church", nor Reverend Wrong is the standard. The Bible is the standard ... for "this church" and "that church" and for Reverend Wrong! God will judge them for what they did or didn't do. And God will judge you for what you did and what you didn't do! Then I asked the question, "Are you doing what the Bible teaches?" The complaints stopped after the stuttering, so I guess I made my point.

If you are not saved but embrace the message of the gospel of Jesus Christ, salvation is yours for the asking. One of my favorite verses relating to salvation is found in Romans 10:9-10 (yes, I know it's a repeat verse, but I really like it):

> *"That if thou shalt confess with thy mouth the Lord Jesus, and shalt believe in thine heart that God hath raised him from the dead, thou shalt be saved. For with the heart man believeth unto righteousness; and with the mouth confession is made unto salvation."*

If you truly believe this in your heart and confess the risen Lord Jesus, you are saved. It's really not complicated, but it does require a true belief. It is an act of faith in God, and the belief that what He says is true.

God's program of redemption is completed after Jesus turns in the keys of the kingdom, but His blessing continues. To all Christians, old and young, recent and old heads, God has more wonders planned for us. As the expression goes: *it only gets better from here!*

Out With the Old, In With the New

1 Corinthians 2:9:

> *"But as it is written, Eye hath not seen, nor ear heard, neither have entered into the heart of man, the things which God hath prepared for them that love him."*

Whatever shall we do in eternity? Will it be like the Millennium, which will resemble the closest thing to a utopia that man will ever know up to this point? Other than providing a pretty good description of our new home in Revelation 21 and 22, the Bible doesn't provide a specific answer to what it is we will do. Sure, we know there will be a whole lot of praising and fellowship going on, and I look forward to it. But some things cannot be known until we experience them. For example, a Christian knows what it's like to be saved from the penalty of sin, but the unsaved have no clue. Hopefully they see the change in us, but they can't understand it until they become saved. I've always wanted to visit France since taking French lessons as a 6th grader. I fantasied over it again and again. But until I actually went there, I could only imagine how great it would be. A similar, but more everyday example is the Philly Cheesesteak or soft pretzel. You will never know the taste of a great Philly Cheesesteak or a warm Philly soft pretzel with mustard until you've had one. I can talk about how great they are until the cows come home, but you can't know what it's like until you've had one. So it is with eternity. We can guess, but we won't know until we get there. But knowing the goodness of God and of all He creates, I believe we're going to have a great time of worship and fellowship with God, Jesus, each other, and all of God's creation. Perhaps that may not help the curious of mind, but have faith! In the meantime, here's a little something that might help you look forward to this experience.

The Apostle Paul had a wonderful heavenly experience that he talked about in 2 Corinthians 12. In verses 2-4, he tells of this experience.

"I knew a man in Christ above fourteen years ago, (whether in the body I cannot tell; or whether out of the body I cannot tell: God knoweth) such an one caught up to the third heaven. And I knew such a man, (whether in the body, or out of the body, I cannot tell: God knoweth;) How that he was caught up into paradise, and heard unspeakable words, which it is not lawful for a man to utter."

In these verses, Paul was speaking of himself; how he was "caught up" and taken to the third heaven, the dwelling place of the throne of God, where Christ is presently. This is where the angels surround the throne and praise God 24/7, as mentioned earlier. For perspective, the first heaven is the sky above the earth, and the second heaven is what we call outer space. The term "caught up" used in this verse is the same term used to describe the Rapture, so Paul got a bit of a preview of what that's going to be like.

Paul wrote 1 Corinthians sometime around 55 A.D., and he wrote 2 Corinthians shortly thereafter, around 56-57 A.D. So, although Paul mentions his heavenly trip in 2 Corinthians, he experienced it 14 years earlier ... *before* he wrote 1 Corinthians 2:9. So when he wrote 1 Corinthians 2:9, the verse that starts this chapter, he knew what he was talking about. Paul knew the things God prepared for those who love Him. Because of his experience, Paul had knowledge of things that were so wonderful and so magnificent they could not be expressed in words. Further, even if he had the words to express, he was not permitted to reveal what he saw (2 Corinthians 12:4). He was under a gag order, as the legal profession would say. In fact, because Paul was given an abundance of revelations, including this latest experience, he was given a thorn in the flesh—to keep him humble and earthly-minded (2 Corinthians 12:7). Likewise, since Paul was humbled because of it, I think we too would be humbled; otherwise we'd be so heavenly-minded that we would be no earthly good.

In my humble opinion and based on Paul's experience, I believe one of the reasons we are not given much information about eternity is because God knows we cannot understand or absorb the thought of it, at least while in our present mortal form. Let's look at 1 Corinthians 13 to augment this position.

In this well-known scripture passage, Paul talks about the preeminence of love and how it should be an essential characteristic of every believer. As a very young man, I remember a speaker preaching on this passage. So great was the sermon, we playfully called him the "love man" afterward. But he made His point. Apart from the giving of His Son, love is preeminent among God's gifts to man. But the Apostle Paul also provided some interesting information on the temporary nature of things, which is often overlooked.

In 1 Corinthians 13:8-9 he writes:

> *"Charity never faileth: but whether there be prophecies, they shall fail; whether there be tongues, they shall cease; whether there be knowledge, it shall vanish away. For we know in part, and prophesy in part."*

What this means is spiritual gifts like prophecies, tongues, and knowledge serve a temporary purpose, but they will end. There will be no use for them in eternity. In eternity, prophecies about the kingdom, knowledge about the kingdom, speaking in tongues, and other spiritual gifts won't matter because the kingdom would have come and been handed back over to God the Father. Love (charity), on the other hand continues ... it is permanent ... it will never end ... it is always in the present tense. Thus, it never fails. Why? Because God is love (1 John 4:8), and He exists eternally. It is God's love that sustains all that is good and it will continue to sustain throughout eternity. But let's focus back on the temporary. In addition to being temporary, these gifts are in part, meaning not complete. In short, we don't have complete knowledge of all things. We are limited in what we can know.

Paul then tacks on this verse found in 1 Corinthians 13:10:

> *"But when that which is perfect is come, then that which is in part shall be done away."*

There is no consensus on what Paul meant by "perfect" in this verse, which seemed a little odd to me. There are lots of opinions out there on this one. Here is mine.

One of the principles of Bible interpretation is words should be interpreted as they are normally used, and also should be interpreted within the context of the passage. It seems to me that "perfect" as used here is just that—something that is ideal, absolute in truth, without flaw. Then the question is what is "that which is perfect"? Let's look at the chapter to put the question in perspective.

Broadly speaking, the focus of the entire chapter is love ... its pre-eminence and permanent nature. It is contrasted to the temporary nature of spiritual gifts. Since Paul was talking about the permanent (love) and temporary (tongues, knowledge and prophecy) nature of things, "that which is perfect" cannot be temporary ... it has to be permanent—that's what the last part of the verse is saying. The temporary, "that which is in part", shall be done away with when "that which is perfect" is come. What's the conclusion? "That which is perfect", then, has to refer to eternity or the eternal state. Sin, obviously, cannot be part of "that which is perfect". This present earth and heavens are also temporary ... they will be destroyed according to 2 Peter 3. So, within the context of this chapter, I believe "that which is perfect" is a state, or condition, which exists only in eternity with God and Christ. It is a permanent state of holy perfection.

Paul concludes his point by connecting "that which is perfect", the eternal state (eternity), to what we know now. 1 Corinthians 13:12 says:

> *"For now we see through a glass, darkly; but then face to face: now I know in part; but then shall I know even as also I am known."*

I know there are people out there that have 20-20 vision. There are some people whose vision is even better than that. Paul was telling everybody, however, that no matter what your ophthalmologist, optometrist, or grandma says, you see things darkly—that is, *not clearly*. Because we are corruptible, we are not able to see as God sees. But then, when that which is perfect is come, i.e., eternity, when God is "all in all", then we will see, know, and understand in full. The temporary and "in part" will be replaced by the permanent and full. We will know, understand, and experience God at a level we cannot know or understand today. You will see me and know me fully, even as I will see you and know you fully ... with perfect vision ... with perfect knowledge. Only then we will be able to grasp eternity and absorb the thought of it. In eternity, 1 Corinthians 2:9 will make perfect sense.

So we will not, *cannot,* know what we will do in eternity or even understand what it will be like, until that which is perfect has come. Then we will see clearly. But we should know, based on what Paul said in 1 Corinthians 2:9, and what he experienced in 2 Corinthians 12, it will be beyond wonderful!

The Grand Finale

The Millennium Period is over, the Great White Throne Judgment is a memory, and the old heaven and earth are no more. Sin has been purged from the physical universe. So what happens now?

It gets even better! Perfection ... eternity is ushered in! The Bible provides a brief glimpse of our new home and surroundings. God, preparing man for an eternity of fellowship with Him, takes it up a notch, as revealed in Revelation 21-22.

Revelation 21:1:

> *"And I saw a new heaven and new earth: for the first heaven and the first earth were passed away; and there was no more sea. And I John saw the holy city, new Jerusalem, coming down from God out of heaven, prepared as a bride adorned for her husband."*

John witnesses something spectacular! With sin now purged from creation, John sees a new, not renovated, heaven and earth. I would love to know more about what John saw, but he only commented on the fact that there is no more sea, so we'll have to make do with that. In the here and now, the seas cover approximately two-thirds of the earth as we now know it, so its elimination is truly noteworthy. Since there was no sea, that would mean there would be a lot more land and living space. But wait ... there's more.

John also sees the new holy city, Jerusalem, our new home, coming down from God, meaning something not made with human hands as in the times past. Descriptively, this city will be beyond awesome. Get a load of this! *The New Jerusalem will measure approximately 1,500 miles in length, width, and height* (Revelation 21:16; you'll have to do some math to verify this)! To get a grip on how big the new holy city is, the United States of America measures approximately 3,300 miles from Maine to California. The new holy city of Jerusalem will be approximately just less than half of that. That is immense! New York City, the Big Apple, will be the Little Appleseed compared to this thing. A city of that height would extend into the bounds of the earth's exosphere, which is the uppermost area of earth's atmosphere (it extends up approximately 6,200 miles). What a view from the top that would be!

There are other unique aspects of this city you might be interested in knowing. One is its shape. There is no consensus on the shape of the holy city. Some believe it will be cubed; others believe it will be a pyramid. Further, some, excluding me, believe that the holy city will be suspended in mid-air. I don't get how some arrived at that interpretation, but neither the shape (cube or pyramid) nor the location (mid-air or land based) of New Jerusalem is of real importance. Honestly, I'm still trying to wrap my mind around its size and height. But we are told what is important in verse Revelation 21:3:

> *"And I heard a great voice out of heaven saying, Behold, the tabernacle of God is with men, and he will dwell with them, and they shall be his people, and God himself shall be with them, and be their God."*

God (the manifested glory of His presence) and the Lamb will dwell with His people in New Jerusalem, which is a departure from Old Testament times. In the Old Testament, God's presence was in the temple, but in the eternal state there will be no need for a temple because God and the Lamb will live among the people in New Jerusalem. We will have a direct, intimate relationship with God and Christ in New Jerusalem.

Let me add that New Jerusalem, no matter how big it is, can hold God. All that is God could not "dwell" in New Jerusalem. Solomon stated as much upon dedication of the first temple in 1 Kings 8:27:

> *"But will God indeed dwell on the earth? behold, the heaven and heaven of heavens cannot contain thee: how much less this house that I have builded?"*

So what we're talking about is God's manifested presence being permanently resident among His people in New Jerusalem, and not the embodiment of God Himself. Of course there may be some who disagree with this based on Revelation 22:4, which states:

> *"And they shall see his face; and his name shall be in their foreheads."*

Scholars and Bible students are not all in agreement about how to accurately interpret this verse. Some see "his face" as Christ; others interpret it as God, which could be problematic. Can mortal man see God and live? Of course not! God told Moses in Exodus 33:20 that no man can see His face and live, even though verse 11 of the same chapter tells us that God spoke to Moses face to face. Obviously, verse 11 meant something else. God had a personal conversation with Moses, and did not have a literal "face-to-face" conversation. Also, quite a few verses support the fact that no man has ever seen God at any time (see John 1:18; 5:37; and 1 John 4:12, for example). Therefore, we understand that no mortal man, in the flesh, can see God.

The rub comes in when we talk about man in his resurrected, glorified state. Can that man see God face to face? Some say yes, others say no. I believe, or more accurately hope, the answer is yes, but again, this is something we'll find out in the by-and-by, as our old folks used to say. The greater and more important point, to me, is we will experience a closeness and intimacy with Almighty God that we never could on this present earth. How close? The analogy is so close that God shall wipe away all tears from our eyes (Revelation 21:4).

Anyway, back to New Jerusalem. This was so stunning that John repeated the vision of it coming down from God out of heaven in Revelation 21:10, only here he begins to provide a more detailed description about New Jerusalem.

Apart from its immense size, its physical beauty will be stunning. Let's examine its physical features.

- The city will be made of *pure gold* and look like clear glass (21:18).
- The wall of the city is built upon 12 foundations. Each foundation is named after one of the 12 apostles (21:14).
- Each of the *12 foundations will be adorned with different precious metals* (21:19), one unique stone (a precious metal) for each foundation.
- There will be *12 gates*, three on each side. Each gate is named after one of the 12 sons of Israel (21:12). The gates will remain open 24/7 (verse 21:25).
- Each gate will be *manned by an angel* (21:12).
- Each gate will be *made of one pearl* (21:21).

Revelation chapters 21 and 22 also offer some tidbits of the inside of New Jerusalem as well.

- *Within the city will be the throne of God and the Lamb* (22:1). How'd you like to get a view of that?
- There will be no temple. God and Christ, the Lamb, are the temple (21:22).
- The *glory of God and the Lamb will light the city* (21:23).
- There will be *no more nights* (21:25). There will never be a need for sunlight or moonlight.
- A *river of living waters will flow from the throne of God and the Lamb* (22:1). No more thirst!
- Apparently there will be streets, since Revelation 22:2 mentions "in the midst of the street of it". I believe this, as well as the fact that there's a river, further supports the belief that New Jerusalem will be on earth as opposed to suspended in mid-air.
- The *tree of life* (22:2) will be there. It will yield her fruit, and the leaves will be for the healing of the nations.

And this will be our home! Can't wait!

We should all, by faith, look forward to this time. And, more importantly, we should live our lives as though we look forward to this time. To say it will be exciting is an understatement. We can't possibly imagine what this time will be like, as 1 Corinthians 2:9 tells us.

Did you notice John made no mention of personal experiences, just like Paul? John merely relayed his observations and descriptions of physical structures and the landscape. Also, this makes it clear our eternity is set on the new earth, and not in heaven.

Neither Revelation, nor any other book of the Bible, to my knowledge, answers all the questions that might arise concerning the new earth, Jerusalem, or eternity. While I have my personal beliefs on what this time will be like based on my study and interpretation of the Bible, I also understand and accept that God reveals to us only what He wants us to know. What God doesn't reveal only means that we must accept, by faith, that what is not revealed is also a part of God's purpose. So, if you don't understand all of it after prayer and thoughtful consideration, leave it alone and stop spinning your wheels. Don't blow a gasket. Don't feel forced to come up with an answer. The process of divine revelation was and is revealed *over time*. Some things are best understood through the lens of experience. The saints of the Old Testament didn't have all the books of the Bible as we have today, so it's safe to say we have more information concerning God's intentions, plans, blessings, etc., than they did. They did have faith however, just as we must to believe God is true to His Word, and in what His Word, the Bible, tells us. In eternity, we will know the fullness of God's plans and all these questions will be answered. Frankly, I think we'll be so happy enjoying our intimacy with God, Christ, and each other in eternity we may no longer care about the answers to the questions, or the questions for that matter.

Between now and then, have faith, get in and stay in the Word! Live your life expecting the return of our Lord tomorrow.

Revelation 22:21

> **"The grace of our Lord Jesus Christ be with you all. Amen"**

Let There Be Light

Here's just a little bit about me and how this book came to be written.

I'm just a Sunday school teacher. I really don't think of myself as a writer. But I do love God's Word, and I love that He brought it light for me, and for you. It is reported to be the bestselling book of all time, and I can understand why that is. It tells the great story of God's redemptive plan, salvation through His Son, Jesus Christ, and covers many other very important topics.

When I was in elementary school in Philadelphia, PA, in the early 1960s (and, no, dinosaurs did not roam the earth at the time), we started out each day with the teachers reading from the Bible. I remember vividly our teacher reading from the Psalms, and there were certain verses I always adored hearing. Among those verses recited were the following, found in Psalms 8:3-7, written by David:

> *"When I consider thy heavens, the work of thy fingers, the moon and the stars, which thou hast ordained; What is man, that thou art mindful of him? and the son of man, that thou visitest him? For thou hast made him a little lower than the angels, and hast crowned him with glory and honor. Thou madest him to have dominion over the works of thy hands; thou hast put all things under his feet: All sheep and oxen, yea, and the beast of the field; The fowl of the air, and the fish of the sea, and whatsoever passeth through the paths of the seas."*

Although the U.S. Supreme Court forced an end to reading the Bible in public schools I was already hooked, and still read these verses from time to time. For some reason, these verses fascinated me. Even as an elementary school student, I marveled at God thinking of man this way. In all of God's mighty works, He thought enough of man to place His creation under man's care and dominance. It amazed me then, and it amazes me still!

Why do I mention this experience? Because it sparked my interest in the Bible, and it let me know, even as a child, God had something in mind when He created man. God didn't do it "just because". As a young man or woman, deep down inside, many of you have the same thoughts. In my case and at that time, although I was aware of and believed in angels, I had no real understanding of man's relationship to these beings. I just knew they were more powerful than me, and I wasn't going to do anything, knowingly, to mess with them. It was not until much later in life when, as a Christian, I became more interested in studying God's Word. I wanted to understand what it really meant, and how to put it all together.

I was saved by grace at the age of 19 largely through God's use of Rev. Lawrence Walker, a great man with a kind heart. He has a passion for teaching the Word of God to young people. Through his godly patience (and oh, did he need it), he taught the Word of God to me and many others in a neighborhood church in North Philadelphia beginning in the early 1970s. All of what he taught came together for me at a Bible fellowship retreat held at Word of Life (WOL) Bible Institute in upstate New York. WOL held weekend snow camps where we would play basketball, ride snowmobiles, play games, eat plentifully, and hear the Word of God after each meal. We had a great time! Imagine that ... having a great time and having the Word preached at the same time!

During one of these sermons, the minister preached that we must be as righteous as God to enter heaven. Upon hearing that, I remember thinking to myself "if that's the case, then I'm doomed". I was truly shaken at the thought of it. Then the minister went on to explain that God can only see us as righteous through His Son, Jesus Christ, whom God sees when He looks at us, if we are saved. Then it all clicked—that I was in my sin, separated from God, and realized that if I died right then and there I would be eternally apart from Him. I acknowledged my sin, prayed for the Lord to receive me, and forgive me my sins. That was a big "Praise the Lord" moment for me!

One of the many very important lessons Rev. Walker taught remained in my heart and soul to this day, and has proven to be very valuable. That lesson was "know what thus saith the Lord". He would endlessly repeat: "Take your Bible with you when you go to church", otherwise you'll never know if the speaker is reading The Word or his own word. To this day, I always carry my Bible to church … just to be sure. That is a suggestion to you that I strongly endorse! There are still some Reverend Wrongs out there.

This particular book started out as a lesson plan designed to provide our Sunday school class of high school students with answers to questions they were asking about the end times. We'd give an answer and they would ask more questions. It seemed like after every answer someone would say "yeah, but what about …?", or "why that?" I was happy about that though. It showed a genuine interest in learning the "what's" and "why's" about the Bible. I found that I wanted to provide as much information as I could and be as accurate as I could be. Personal interest played a big part as well. Not knowing a lot, but wanting to know more, I studied and studied and studied. Still, I won't say I have all the answers, but I do know a lot more than when I responded to the first question asked. More importantly, learning more about God's redemptive plan has helped my walk with the Lord. Many times during study and research, I would just stop to praise and thank God for revealing His Word to all of us, and increasing our understanding.

Because of the questions asked in our Sunday school classes, and my concern about the spiritual growth of our young people, I felt led to write about certain Bible principles. I consider these to be the basics as I like to call them, that every Christian student, high school and college, must know to "shore-up" and protect themselves against the spiritual warfare raging around us. These basics also help to protect us against the rapidly declining value system of the world. I firmly believe that knowing God's redemptive plan helps us live the Christian life. It makes us stronger in the Word, which then is reflected in the life we lead.

Beyond that, who or what I am is not really important in the grand scheme of things. I imagine there's millions of Sunday school teachers out there just like me. The prophets and New Testament authors God used to put forth His Word are the important writers. Trust me, I'm not trying to compare myself to them. I marvel at their sacrifice and willingness to being used by God to write the Bible. Most of those guys went through a lot of very difficult times and ordeals. The most interesting thing about me is I'm definitely too introverted, or quiet, for some people, as I've been told over and over again. But I'm over that at my age. I'm saved ... I like that about me. I believe in Jesus Christ as my Savior, and trust Him as my Lord. So as the young people say nowadays, "I got mine", and I'm grateful God gave it to me. What is important is God's plan for *your* salvation ... each and every one of you, whoever you are, wherever you may be. Next to that, a study to understand what the Bible teaches is important because it provides a foundation for understanding what God has ordained. And, it will help you grow in grace and in strength. My prayer is that this book will help you understand God's desire to fellowship with you through salvation offered through His Son, Christ Jesus.

May the Lord richly bless you!

I want to acknowledge the authors of the various sources and reading materials I used to write this book. These sources provided me with inspiration, thoughts, interpretive options, and issues to consider.

References

The Holy Bible (*The Thompson Chain Reference Bible*), Fourth Improved Edition; Copyright 1964

The Bible Knowledge Commentary, Old Testament and New Testament. An Exposition of the Scriptures by the Dallas Seminary Faculty

BattleinChrist.com, "*Understanding the End Times Signs: The Day of Christ vs. The Day of the Lord*"

Biblehub.com

Bible.org

Biblestudy.org

Biblestudytools.com

Discoverevelation.com

Gotquestions.org, S. Michael Houdmann

The Great Doctrines of the Bible, William Evans

Prophecy: God's Eternal Drama Prophecy Series (DVDs), Dr. Tony Evans, Senior Pastor, Oak Cliff Bible Fellowship

The Purpose Driven Life, Dr. Rick Warren

The Times of the Gentiles, John F. Walvoord

Understanding the Parenthetical Periods of the Book of Revelation, Netbiblestudy.com